Carl give this to you
dad.

Greg

Spread
Trading

Founded in 1807, John Wiley & Sons is the oldest independent publishing company in the United States. With offices in North America, Europe, Australia, and Asia, Wiley is globally committed to developing and marketing print and electronic products and services for our customers' professional and personal knowledge and understanding.

The Wiley Trading series features books by traders who have survived the market's ever changing temperament and have prospered—some by reinventing systems, others by getting back to basics. Whether a novice trader, professional, or somewhere in-between, these books will provide the advice and strategies needed to prosper today and well into the future.

For a list of available titles, visit our web site at www.WileyFinance.com.

Spread Trading

An Introduction to Trading Options in Nine Simple Steps

GREG JENSEN

WILEY

John Wiley & Sons, Inc.

To my friends and colleagues at Spread Trade Systems

Published by John Wiley & Sons, Inc., Hoboken, New Jersey.
Published simultaneously in Canada.

For general information on our other products and services or for technical support, please contact our Customer Care Department within the United States at (800) 762-2974, outside the United States at (317) 572-3993 or fax (317) 572-4002.

Wiley also publishes its books in a variety of electronic formats. Some content that appears in print may not be available in electronic books. For more information about Wiley products, visit our web site at www.wiley.com.

Library of Congress Cataloging-in-Publication Data:

Jensen, Greg, 1973-
  Spread trading : an introduction to trading options
in nine simple steps / Greg Jensen.
      p. cm.
  Includes index.
  ISBN 978-0-470-44368-2 (cloth)
  1. Stock options.   2. Options (Finance)   I. Title.
  HG6042.J46 2009
  332.63'2283–dc22

                                    2008052151

Printed in the United States of America

10 9 8 7 6 5 4 3 2 1

Contents

Acknowledgments

They told me I have to do this acknowledgments page. It's for thanking people "without whom this book could not have been written." ("Without whom"? Who talks like that?) Apparently, I'm supposed to thank a bunch of people who aren't even the author.

Like my colleagues at Spread Trade Systems. Yeah, right. The only things I ever heard from them about this book were, "No, you can't file a personal injury claim for writer's cramp." For this they deserve thanks?

I'm also (at least judging by other books) supposed to thank my wife for something like "endless support and patience." But other than to threaten me every once in awhile, Heather didn't lift a finger. I didn't talk to her much about the book anyway because I'm in trouble with her. She says I never listen to what she says (or something like that—I don't remember). So, sorry Heather; no thanks for you.

There's also a rumor going around about a guy named Duane Boyce, who supposedly helped me out by doing little jobs like making the book something that could actually be read. Some people seem to think he deserves some "credit." And Mrs. Kimberly White—who seemed like such a nice, amusing girl until we started talking about acknowledgments—I know she helped rewrite some parts, but, hey, she already got her thanks: she actually *gets paid* for what she does as an editor. It's either acknowledgments or money, people.

Okay, so I stole jokes from Dave Barry, James Gordon (a law professor, no less), Joe Glenn, and George Durrant. But that's their fault. If they didn't want people to steal their jokes they never should have *told* them.

I do thank my golfing buddy, however, who helped me write this book by helping me shoot in the 70s. (He says if it ever gets hotter than that, I shouldn't go out at all.) That gave me lots of time to write last summer. He of all people deserves the credit for this book. Thanks, Stu!

G.J.

About the Author

G reg Jensen is cofounder of Spread Trade Systems, an industry leader in investment education. A Registered Investment Advisor, Jensen earned his degree in business management, with an emphasis in finance, from Utah State University. Over the last decade, he has helped thousands learn how to prosper in the stock market through spread trading.

Introduction

If you're brand new to the stock market, good. That's why I've written this book—specifically to help you. I want to show you how to achieve phenomenal results in the stock market *safely*. I will assume you know nothing, and then walk you step-by-step all the way up to the best way of making money in the market known to man or beast.

What I'm talking about is "spread trading," and it's a form of "option trading." If you're not new to the stock market, but just new to these trades, that's great, too. You'll just go faster; you'll run rather than walk.

So I'm assuming you have no training or experience in trading options and that you don't really know what it is (in fact, if you *have* heard of it you've probably heard (1) that it's advanced, and (2) that it's risky), and you're probably a little skeptical that any book can teach a communications major how to do it.

Probably most books couldn't. Most books about the stock market are written by professional traders or college professors who've completely forgotten what it was like *not to know anything*. Trying to learn option trading from most experts is like trying to learn the tax code from an accountant: she'll toss around big words that you've never heard of, while you nod your head periodically and hope you're nodding in the right places. And if you ever actually muster up enough courage to ask what a particular term means, she'll explain it to you using other terms you don't understand. Eventually, you slink away and decide to devote your brainpower to something it can handle more easily, like eating pudding or watching *Survivor* XMVII: Some Island Somewhere. And you feel like you must be a real idiot if that accountant (who, you notice, was wearing mismatched socks) could understand all that and you couldn't.

Well, that's why I've written this book. I *haven't* forgotten what it's like not to know anything, what it's like to start from scratch. I want to give you the basics of making money in the stock market, and I want to do it in a way that anyone can understand. (In other words, I'm going to explain everything very slowly to you, because that's how my wife always explains things to me.) It's the ultimate beginner's guide to trading options.

So the good news is that you really can learn to trade options. In fact, I've made learning it so easy that I think my cocker spaniel could understand it. And *that* means that you really can learn to make money without fear. What you've heard about options being risky is true only of people who trade options *wrong*. (They're people who want to succeed in the worst way ... and mangling options was the worst way they could think of.) Done right, it's the safest and best way to make money that I know of. It's what I just mentioned: *spread trading*. In spread trading we make money *while reducing risk*. We can achieve phenomenal results and yet not be ruled by fear or greed all along the way. Instead of worrying all the time, we can actually sleep at night. Imagine.

The bad news is, you do have to read all 334 pages of this book to get started. That's a lot of pages, I understand. Before you commit, you probably have some questions. I've tried to anticipate them.

QUESTIONS YOU MIGHT HAVE ON YOUR MIND

Question 1: Why spread trading and not just regular investing? If trading options like this is so advanced, and investing is simpler, shouldn't I just do that?

Well, investing *is* simpler to explain, no doubt about it. Nobody needs to write a book to tell you to buy stocks when prices are low and sell them when they go high (although many have . . .). If I were writing such a book, I would call it "Buy Stocks Low and Sell Them High" and all the pages would be empty. But seriously, there actually are a lot of different ways to buy low and sell high, and you should know about them if you're going to chicken out on reading this book. But you should also know that the reason there a lot of different ways to buy stocks low and sell them high is that ... *it's hard to do*, and therefore extremely risky.

If you want to invest long-term, for example, there's only one way to know which companies will be strong for the next 20 years: travel forward in time and see which companies are still around. But if you stay put on the space-time continuum, past performance is the only thing you have to go on, and it's not a sure thing. Better than putting your money in a savings account, maybe, but you could lose your nest egg if the unexpected happens. (Ever hear of Enron? Or Bear Stearns? Or Washington Mutual? Or Lehman Brothers?) And even if you diversify your holdings, economic changes can occur that cause the *whole market* to dive. (Ever hear of 2008? 2009?)

I hate to say it, but the quickest way to end up with a million dollars in this strategy is to start out with two million.

However, if you want to invest and trade your stocks on a short-term basis, everything depends on timing—buying and selling at the right *time*. Because you face risk constantly, you have to know what's going on constantly. Literally. As I heard one such investor say, "If you can't watch stocks all day long, you shouldn't be in the market at all."

I guess I'm out, then, because ... sorry ... I actually like to do other things with my day. I have a sign over my desk that says it all: EAT. SLEEP. FISH. That's it. How could I do that if I did nothing but watch the market—ALL DAY LONG? I believe I make better returns than the adviser who said that, and I do more with my day to boot. I like that combination.

The problem, then, is not with the formula: buy low and sell high. That formula applies in all sorts of places, including in trading options. The problem is in thinking that simply buying and selling stocks is the best way to be in the market in the first place. It isn't.

So I admit it takes preparation to be able to trade options effectively—to spread trade. But learning to do it is more than worth it. I don't know about you, but I'd like to be able to make money *no matter what the market does*. And that's the case with spread trading. Whether the market is up, down, sideways, or inside out, you can make money. It takes a few chapters to see how it works, but you'll get there.

Question 2: Why do it on my own? Isn't it safer and more productive to use a fund manager?

If you trade options the way I'm going to show you, you can do better than the professionals can because you can make money no matter what the market does, and your fund manager can't.

The problem is that professional managers have to do what we talked about in Question 1: they try to *time* the market—diversify their holdings and then buy and sell here and there at the right time. Now it's true that there are some financial geniuses out there, but there are others who just got lucky a few times—and how can you tell which is which? Not only that, but even when professional managers do get the timing right, they control too many shares to be very nimble with them; their investments and trades are so large that they're kind of ... well, *clunky*. Even worse, over time they rarely outperform the market by much—if they outperform it at all—because they *are* the market. They're that big. When the market dives, they dive. And your money dives right along with them.

Here's what I predict: once you learn to spread trade, your fund manager will want to invest *with you*.

Question 3: Come on. If spread trading is that easy, wouldn't everybody be doing it?

Hey, I didn't say it was *easy*. It's definitely harder than falling off a horse. But it doesn't take a genius or a particular kind of background or education to be able to understand the methods we'll be talking about in this book.

Now I know that everybody has different strengths and weaknesses. We're all different. Some people are intelligent; some are good looking. You're probably more intelligent than I am, but I'm probably better looking than you. But neither is required to succeed at spread trading. (Also, even if I am better looking than you, that doesn't mean I have it all. You should see my upper body. I once went to a gym to lift weights, but the laughter made it difficult to concentrate.)

Believe it or not, it *is* possible to figure out all those charts and understand all that lingo without multiple PhDs and the work ethic of a nerdy ant. You just need to be able to read English (one page at a time in the proper order), write words and numbers (spelling does *not* count), add, subtract, multiply, and divide. That's it. That guy who struts around like a super genius because he made tons of money trading options? Yep. Everything he does requires about a fourth-grade education. The difference between you and him (besides personality, I hope) is that someone at some point taught *him* how to do it.

That's what you need. Someone who's willing to take you step by step and explain what's going on. Slooooooooooowly. Someone who won't get impatient just because you don't have a particularly mathematical mind. Someone who doesn't think you ought to get an accounting degree first. Someone like a guardian angel, or a fairy godmother, or, just maybe . . . me.

So, again, if you're brand new to the stock market, that's good. You're the reason I've written this book. And if you're just new to trading options, that's good, too. You'll just be able to go faster. Rest assured: by going slow, I'm not being condescending. (*Condescending* means talking down to people.) I'm just trying to help.

ALL YOU NEED TO KNOW ABOUT THE STOCK MARKET BEFORE YOU READ THIS BOOK

So it's more than okay if you don't know anything about the stock market. You're the main person I'm writing to. And I can tell you everything you really need to know about the market in 10 bullet points. But make sure you read this, because the rest of the book assumes that you get these basics. Okay? Here goes:

- A small company usually begins when the owner gets a loan from a bank or money from investors (from an investment capital company or from his mom), which pays for the stuff he needs to get started. When he turns a profit, the bank or investors or family members get their money back, with interest. When a company starts to get big and successful, it needs a bunch more money—millions of dollars—to continue growing. Mom usually doesn't have that kind of money. So the company will raise that money by *selling* pieces of ownership in the company. So people can actually pay money to literally own a certain (itty-bitty) percentage of the company. This little piece of ownership is a "share," and we call the company a "stock." If you buy a piece of ownership in a company, you are buying a share of stock. (See? I told you I would go slow.)
- The stock market is just what it sounds like: a market. A place where people get together to buy and sell, but instead of fresh produce, sausages, and old watches, they're buying and selling shares of stock.
- And like everything else good and fun, the stock market is mostly controlled by the big guys. I call them Big Investor Guys, or BIGs for short. These are institutional investors—those professional money managers who are so confusing to talk to—who manage huge amounts of other people's money, and who together can buy and sell 5, 20, or even 50 *million* shares every day on a single stock. You and I might buy and sell 100 shares, or maybe even 5,000, but nothing like the volume of the BIGs. We don't have an impact on the market and its prices at all.
- Many companies are owned largely, if not almost entirely, by these institutional investors. There are a lot of BIGs, and they really are big.
- So let's say you bought a share of stock in a company called *For Purposes of Illustration, Inc.* when it was new and relatively tiny. The BIGs are looking at financial information, profit reports, earnings estimates, trends in the economy, and so on, all day long. (This is what makes them so dry and humorless.) If a bunch of them look and see that *For Purposes of Illustration, Inc.* is growing and making lots of money—and if they conclude that it will continue to grow and make lots of money—they all want in. And like anything else, if a lot of people want in, and there's a limited supply, those who already own shares have their pick of who they want to sell to—so they naturally sell to whomever offers the most money. That is, the price of the stock goes up. Now it's worth more than you paid for it. And if you sell your stock while all this is happening, you will make money.

- Because the market is driven by people with huge amounts of money guessing how successful companies will be in the future, all of those things the BIGs look at are extremely important. Like quarterly earnings reports. These are the reports that tell the BIGs if companies are living up to the BIGs' expectations of them. And it's an ugly thing if they're not. Nothing puts the BIGs in a selling mood faster than a disappointing earnings report. Individual investors can make a good guess about what the BIGs (and therefore the market) will do by looking at things like earnings reports and other financial data. Or they can lose a lot by missing some important information. So investors need to know about the economy and the stocks they have invested in, or they can lose their bananas.

- Now even apart from quarterly earnings, let's say a bunch of BIGs look at all their trends, reports, economic indicators, Ouija boards, and so on, and begin to think that *For Purposes of Illustration, Inc.* is going to slow down in growth or even start losing profits. Well, they don't want to be holding on to millions of its shares then. They put them up for sale, and if nobody else wants those shares either, they have to lower their asking price. That is, the price of the stock goes down. Depending on where you bought, if you try to sell your stock in this trend, you will probably lose money.

- As time goes by, the BIGs see that the price of *For Purposes of Illustration, Inc.* is getting nice and low. They see something in some report, or at the bottom of a teacup, that makes them think the company will recover. Then that stock looks like a real bargain. The BIGs start to buy it up, and now that more people are willing to buy it, the price goes up again. You get the idea. The trick is knowing when a stock price will go up and when it will go down, so you know when to buy and when to sell. (And, of course, you can't for sure. Don't you listen? But you can make informed guesses.)

- What most investors, and the BIGs, are all aiming for is to: (1) buy a stock at a low price, (2) hold on to it while the price is going up, (3) sell before the price goes back down, (4) take the profits, and (5) do it again.

- Obviously, just like Scrabble, people who get really into the market do all sorts of other complicated and nuanced things. But you don't have to know all that to be able to play successfully. Just Buy Low and Sell High. The End.

Okay, so that's the big picture. And about that second-to-last bullet point: that's what everyone *else* is trying to do. It's not what we're going to do. We're going to learn about trading options, and then we're going to learn how to trade options in a particular way: we're going to learn how to spread trade.

So that second-to-last bullet point? We're going to do something better than that. Something more flexible. Something more *profitable*. And we're going to do it in nine simple steps. All I'm going to do is tell you a story of two guys figuring out how to trade options with each other. You'll learn as they learn. More than dry formulas, you'll actually pick up the sense—the intuition—of trading options. Then, when these two guys are ready for help from experts (starting in Chapter 19), they'll learn even more. A lot more. But they—and you—will still learn in a way that is simple, methodical, and intuitive. And in short steps. With frequent reviews. See, these guys are a lot like you, and they learn the way we all learn: in small, logical, bite-size pieces, with frequent opportunity to lock in what we're learning.

Come along and see.

Understanding the Long and Short of "Call" Options in the Market

CHAPTER 1

Lon and Shorty

L on was tall, prematurely graying, a creative thinker with interesting hobbies and intelligent children, and he was starting to feel like a real dope.

He was trying to secure his family's financial future, looking for this investment and that, the way a good father and forward-thinking man should, but he was starting to doubt his intelligence. Lon had started playing the stock market.

Well, of course, first he'd had to convince his wife he wouldn't lose everything they had on wild chances. That took some doing. Lon liked to think of himself as a pretty smart guy, but Cass had taken a pretty dim view of his creative enthusiasms ever since they took that trip to China without using a tour guide and spent the better part of a week trying to find a bathroom. And then there was that time he'd bought a time-share in London . . . *Nebraska.* He could never win an argument once she mentioned that.

But invest they must if they wanted to retire well, and Cass knew it as well as he did. They wanted to travel; spoil grandchildren; wear big, high-priced hats—Retire with a capital R. No 401(k) was going to do that for them. And even she knew he wasn't as big a dope as Bruce.

Bruce was the reason Lon and his wife didn't use a fund manager or financial adviser of their own. Bruce was Lon's fat, loudmouthed brother-in-law, and the biggest oaf on the planet. Lon's sister would start a family crisis if they used any *other* money manager, so he had to handle his investments himself. For a while he'd asked Bruce for stock tips just so he could do the exact opposite. That strategy was pretty satisfying on a personal level, but it didn't last long. Even Bruce, who last year had accidentally set his boat on fire before he'd insured it, could make the right guesses often enough to stay ahead of the market. Barely.

So Lon was feeling a little dumb. He, too, performed about as well as the market as a whole, which meant that all his thorough studying, clear thinking, and careful diversifying put him in league with his oafish brother-in-law. Stocks sometimes rose, sometimes fell, and no matter how careful or sure he was, sometimes they surprised him and cost him money. Surely, *surely*, there was a way for an intelligent person to do better than simply hope his luck balanced out.

And without all the stress! *What if this happens, or that?* he would ceaselessly ask himself. Before he started investing he used to spend his free time chatting with his wife or dreaming up contraptions to make with his son; now he was spending half his free time checking financial reports and the rest of it worrying about what he would find the next time he checked.

Tonight, Lon was in his study, thinking about his most recent investment, and fiddling dejectedly with the model spaceship he'd made with his son last summer. He had just bought 100 shares of Plum stock (PLUM) at $40 per share, and, based on his study of the company, he believed the stock price would grow to $55 per share over the next six months. That would be a nearly 38 percent increase, and meant his investment would then be worth $5,500. That kind of increase would be terrific—if it happened.

What would really be best, Lon mused, would be if he could travel through time—go six months into the future. Then he'd know if the price really had grown to $55. And—even better—if he could bring, say, a coupon that promised he could buy Plum for only $40. Then he could buy for $40 and sell for $55 on the very same day, and make $15 almost instantly.

Time travel was pure science fiction, of course. But he couldn't help wondering. *Wouldn't it be great if there were a way I could buy 100 additional Plum shares in six months and still buy them at today's price of $40, rather than the $55 I think they will be selling at by then?*

Lost in thought, Lon swiveled back and forth in his hand-me-down and worn-out office chair. At work, he often completed projects that had started out as no more than an interesting but impossible idea. Maybe there was a way to actually make that happen. Maybe he could make some sort of deal with someone . . . but who? And what *kind* of deal?

Lon's imagination failed him. Anyway, it was late. He turned to cable news for a financial update and went to bed. "How's the money, honey?" Cass asked him drowsily when he leaned over to kiss her.

"Just call me Bruce," he replied. She chuckled and returned to sleep.

Sleep came to Lon eventually, too. But not rest.

*   *   *

Fifteen miles away, on the opposite side of Wichita, Shorty sat at the maple desk in his cramped bedroom, poring over the day's mail. He was a small but muscular man, a steady, clear-thinking accountant in the same firm that employed Lon. Shorty was one of those friends Lon had been talking to about investing. Little known to Lon, their most recent conversation had really gotten Shorty thinking. Surely there must be some way to make money in the stock market that was more certain than just hoping for the best.

Shorty rather enjoyed following the market; its ins and outs and near-unpredictability fascinated him. Sharon, his wife of four years, teased him that he would check financial news even if he didn't invest. But he never risked very much or bought too much of any one stock; he'd worked diligently for his money and didn't like the thought of losing it all on a gamble. Still, he'd had one stretch where every stock he bought immediately went down. In disgust, he'd decided that the best way to make money would be to go around the country, demonstrating his track record to CEOs, and threatening to buy their stock if they didn't pay him a sizeable fee. Extortion? Sure. But what was a person to do?

Still, he knew that investing was his only real chance at the future he envisioned. He dreamed of retiring to someplace warm, maybe by the ocean. He fantasized sitting on a porch with Sharon, worry free, sipping cold soft drinks even in the winter ... maybe writing a nice book. If he wanted that to happen, he simply had to plan ahead. And he was too well-informed to be satisfied with his 401(k). Playing the stock market was the only way he knew to secure that blissfully quiet dream.

Finishing the mail, Shorty turned his attention to his stock picks. He, too, had just purchased 100 shares of Plum at $40 per share. He believed that the price of Plum would grow over the next 18 months, but he had just gotten some news that made him think it might actually go down in the near term—maybe as low as $25 per share, or even lower.

Shorty pondered the situation. He was probably going to lose money on those shares, but he wouldn't sell them because he was pretty sure the price would go back up and above the $40 he had spent. But he wished there was some way he could turn the situation to his advantage in the short term. That was the problem with the stock market. You couldn't know for sure what it was going to do, and now he would have to sit on his $40 shares while the price dropped. Of course he could always sell Plum now and buy again later when the price was lower, but that just required more guesswork, and after all, he wasn't *that* sure that the price was going to drop.

Shorty sighed. What he wanted was a sure thing. Some way to make sure he could make money, or at least not lose money, no matter what happened to the market. *Oh well*, he thought. *Nothing to do about it. That's just not how it works.*

When he finally climbed into bed at 11:30, Sharon asked about his investments. He had to confess he thought his most recent investment would take a hit. "But I'm pretty confident it'll go back up again."

"Then I'm sure it will," she soothed. Sharon was an encouraging, supportive wife, and a pretty good liar.

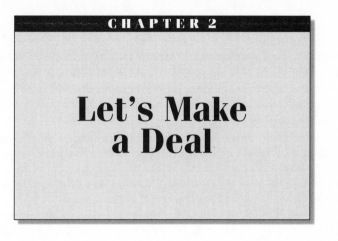

CHAPTER 2

Let's Make a Deal

L on and Shorty had first met three years earlier while playing on the same company softball team. They (and, just as important, their wives) had hit it off immediately. They went to games together, and often met for lunch. Today, Shorty was saving a spot for Lon in the company cafeteria. He had the market on his mind and wanted to talk about it.

"Hi, Shorty," Lon greeted.

"Hi, Lon. How's the market been treatin' you?" Shorty smiled. He was not one to beat around the bush.

"About the same as always. Some good, some bad, I guess. You know how it goes."

"Yeah, I do." Shorty was hoping Lon might have some creative ideas about how to handle the issue of his Plum stock. He was surprised to find out that Lon had also bought 100 shares of the same stock, though really, recent news reports on the company had put Plum on a lot of people's minds. He was also surprised to find that they, two clever (though novice) investors, had different short-term expectations for the stock. He'd thought his conclusions were obvious.

Lon, as they talked, couldn't shake his thoughts from the night before. He'd been thinking about this very stock, but his expectations were just the opposite of Shorty's. Surely this situation had the makings of a deal.

He began formulating a possibility in the back of his mind. *I can't travel through time, but I'm expecting the stock to rise in the next six months, and Shorty is expecting it to fall. What if I could get him to give me a coupon to let me, any time in the next six months, buy his shares for* *the $40 they cost right now? He might do that, since he expects the stock to be worth less than $40. But he certainly wouldn't do that for nothing, because if the stock goes up like I think it will, he'd lose his chance to sell his shares for more. But what if I offered him, say, $5 per share right now for that coupon for the chance to buy them for $40 later? That way he'd be getting something out of the deal even if the price does go up. Paying him would cut into my profit a little bit, because I will have paid him $500, but if the price does go up to $55, I could still sell my shares and make a $10 profit. It would be almost as good as time travel. We could just enter a deal of our own—on the side, just between the two of us—that would be good for both of us. I could pay him now for a coupon to call out his shares for $40 in the next six months.*

On a whim, Lon decided to offer this deal to Shorty—what did he have to lose? He told him about his train of thought from the night before.

"Why don't we make a deal?" he said finally, unable to hide the excitement in his voice. "Like a kind of time-travel coupon. Look, what if I paid you $5 per share right now on your 100 shares of Plum stock. That's $500. And in return, you would give me a coupon that says I have the right to call you up and buy those 100 shares from you any time in the next six months for $40 each. What do you think?"

Shorty was intrigued. He knew it was a good idea to talk to Lon; he always had a unique perspective on things, even if he was a bit "out there" sometimes. Time travel, for heaven's sake. But actually it sounded like a clever idea, and it just might be good for him. . . .

I have good reason to believe the stock might go down in the next while, he thought. If I make this trade with Lon, I'll put $500 into my account immediately. If the stock goes up, say, to $45 or $50, or even $55, then Lon will no doubt use his coupon to buy my shares and I'll have to sell them to him for $40. I'll miss out on making all that profit, but I'll still have the $5 per share he's already paid me for the coupon in the first place—so I've still made something. Moreover, if the stock goes down, say, to $25, like I think it will, then I come out way ahead: in that case Lon won't exercise his right to call out my shares because he only has the right to buy them at $40—and he won't do that if they're only worth $25 (why would he want to pay me $40 when he could pay $25 for them on the open market?). So I'll get to keep my shares, plus the $500 he's already paid me. I can even use that $500 to buy more shares of Plum stock, and now at a lower price! I end up owning more shares than I had before, at a lower price, and Lon paid for it all! This might be exactly what I've been looking for. In this situation, I may not make a huge profit, but I will definitely, for sure, make $500 no matter what.

"There are just two things I don't like about this deal," Shorty said. "First, I don't like the word *coupon*. It sounds like you're buying groceries from me. Can't we just say you get to call me out, or call out my shares, or call *away* my shares?"

"Well, we have to have some word for the contract we're entering into."

Shorty raised an eyebrow. "Let's just call it a *call*," he said, finally, "since the deal you're buying is the right to call out my shares."

Lon shrugged his acquiescence. It was the first time (but it wouldn't be the last) that he would find making deals with Shorty involved using extremely boring vocabulary.

"The second thing is our friendship. It seems likely to me that you'll be out $500 from this deal. Should friends make deals with each other when one of them could lose out?"

Lon obviously hadn't thought about it. "That's a good question," he said, and paused. "But look," he began, obviously thinking aloud, "we're both likely to come out ahead on this kind of deal. I'm willing to take a chance, and $500 is not too much to pay for what I think I'll gain. And if I do gain it, we're both ahead: I'm ahead because the stock price has risen, and you're ahead because you've got $500 you didn't have before. The only possible downside is that I might be wrong, in which case I'm out the $500. But that's okay with me. I've lost a lot more than that before. From my point of view, this is still a really good investment. It's the only chance I have to take advantage of what I think will happen in the near future. And besides, it was my idea, so I certainly can't blame you if it doesn't work out for me."

"Okay, let's do it," agreed Shorty. "I'll take $5 per share right now and give you the right to call out my shares any time in the next six months and pay me $40 for them."

"Done," said Lon.

"But . . ." Shorty hesitated.

"But what?"

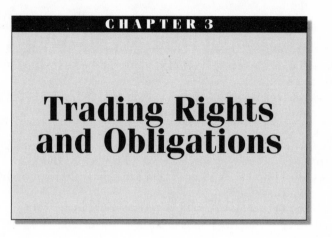

CHAPTER 3

Trading Rights and Obligations

"**B**ut if we're going to do this," Shorty finally continued, "we have to write it all out. If we have different memories about this later, we'll probably hate each other, and Sharon would never forgive me."

"Amen," Lon replied, with true religious feeling. He had never forgotten the time he loaned Bruce his edger for "the weekend." Bruce had claimed to remember a deal for "every weekend," and Lon hadn't seen his edger since. Cass had eventually bought him a new one, with a card that read, "Now you have two edgers!" Lon saw the humor, but he hadn't laughed much.

Lon pulled out a pen and paper and began. "I'll put my part of the deal like this":

By paying Shorty $5 per share I have agreed to the following conditions:

- I have the *right* to call out and *buy* 100 of Shorty's shares for $40 if I want to.
- I have the right to do this any time in the next six months.
- I have the right *not* to call out Shorty's shares if I don't want to. I have paid for the *option* to be able to buy his shares at $40 in the next six months, but I don't have to. I can just let this possibility, this option, expire in six months.

"And here's my part of the deal," said Shorty.

By accepting $5 per share, I have agreed to the following conditions:

- I have the *obligation* to *sell* Lon my shares at $40 if he calls them out.
- I have the obligation to do this any time in the next six months if Lon calls them out.
- I have one right. I sold Lon this option for $500, and I get to keep that whether he ends up calling out my shares or not.

"I think this is really going to work," Shorty remarked, as he finished. "It's actually a very clever way to take advantage of the market. I'm not selling you shares of stock directly. I'm selling you the *right* to buy shares at a particular price, later."

"And I'm not buying shares now, just the right to buy them at a particular price later, if I want to." Lon was pleased. He had that flush of happiness he always felt when one of his ideas worked. But, like many creative people, he didn't have quite the head for detail that Shorty had. He wanted to hold on to this idea, because he had an inkling it could come in handy again.

"It's a solid plan," Shorty was saying as he dug into his lunch. "I sell you rights, so now I have obligations to you, but you pay me for them. It's a fair trade that we're both happy with."

"Not quite," Lon broke in with a laugh, "since you won't let me use the words that help me remember what's going on here!" He turned to the next page in his notebook. "So if you won't let me talk how I want to, I'm going to have to make myself a little review to make sure it stays clear in my mind."

REVIEW

"I have _____ a certain dollar amount to enter this trade. By doing so, I now have the right to _____ for $40 if I want to. I also have the right to do this _____.
I also have the right _____ if I don't want to; I can let my option _____. If I do, I _____ the amount I paid to Shorty.

  "Shorty, for his part, has _____ a certain dollar amount from me to enter this trade. By taking my money, he now has the obligation to _____ for $40 if _____. Shorty has to do this if I exercise my option any time in _____. If I never exercise my option, Shorty still gets to _____ I have paid him."

"You know, . . ." Shorty began, thinking deeply.

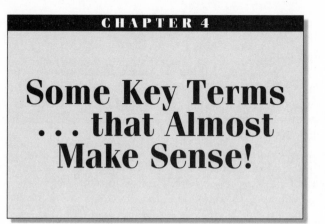

CHAPTER 4

Some Key Terms ... that Almost Make Sense!

"This would probably be simpler if we used some other key terms, like we did with *call*. We've got a bunch of long sentences in there."

"Okay, you're right," Lon agreed. "Let's start with what I'm buying: 'the right to buy if I want to.' That phrase needs a word."

"Easy. You're paying for the *option* of buying at $40. Let's just call it an *option*."

"Well, I was thinking it's kind of like a grocery coupon. . . ."

Shorty started to object, but Lon laughed. "Just kidding. We can use *option*. But can we use the word *strike* for the price? I mean the price we agreed that I can pay for your shares? I was just thinking that in baseball a strike is bad for the batter and good for the pitcher, just like—if the market price goes up—the $40 price is good for me but bad for you. And, of course, the reverse is true if the market price goes down."

Shorty snorted. "I'm not sure I like sports analogies any more than grocery analogies. Lucky for you, there's a better reason to use the word *strike*. After all, we *struck* a deal for $40, so we can call it a *strike price* if you want to."

"So we have a call, an option ... and look, since I have the option to call out your shares, can we combine them to create another term? Let's just say it's a *call option*. If I want to do this again, I can just say: Shorty, I want to buy a call option."

"Absolutely. And let's just call this whole thing a *contract*. An *option contract*. That's obvious."

"How about *bargain?* No ... *handshake* is better."

"But there's one more set of terms I think we should add," Shorty went on.

"A *blood oath?*"

Shorty ignored him. "I think we ought to talk about being *long* and *short* in the stock. The stock market talks like that. And it's kind of handy. Being short means you're selling, and being long means you're buying."

Lon gestured frustration with his panini (he loved these famous New York Italian sandwiches, even when they were made in Kansas). "That's not only boring; it makes no sense at all."

"Well, it kind of makes sense," said Shorty. "A long time ago people in the market (at least some people in the market) began the practice of agreeing to sell stock to someone before they even owned it. The idea was to set up a deal to sell a stock at a certain price within some time period down the road, expecting the stock to drop lower than that in the meantime. Then, when the stock did drop below that price, they would buy it and then turn around and complete the original deal to sell at the higher price—pocketing the difference as profit. Notice that everything about this was built around *selling*, selling a stock that one didn't even own—that one was 'short' in. Not only that, but this way of operating obviously put these people in a deficit position with their brokers, requiring them to borrow stock from their brokers in the short term: as I said, they were entering deals to sell stock that they didn't even own yet. Long story short—(Lon groaned)—that kind of deal was called shorting, and people just started referring to selling as 'being short.' "

"Only you would know this."

"And on the other hand," Shorty went on, "people would normally buy stock intending to keep it for a 'long' time. So they started talking about buying stock as being 'long in the stock,' and selling as being short."

Lon answered: "Actually, geeky as that was, I think the terms could really come in handy. We're using 'call' to talk about our deal, but we're doing different things in it. We could say that the deal from my end is a 'long call' because I'm *buying* the option."

"Right, and from my end it's a 'short call' because I'm *selling* it."

Both men sat silent for a moment, Shorty chewing and Lon smiling at his notebook pages. Lon was thinking that this had turned out to be more fun than he'd expected. It was almost like making up a new language. It ranked up there with the summer he'd learned basic Klingon. Shorty, however, was thinking that the problem with making up all these technical terms was that it would be a pain in the neck to explain the terminology to someone else if he ever wanted to make this kind of deal again. He'd have to keep a copy of Lon's notes.

Oh well, Shorty thought, *might as well go all the way.* "One more thing," he said. "The $5 per share you pay me ... let's call that a *debit*. That's the proper accounting term."

"Like a debit card," Lon nodded. "Painfully boring and obvious, but we'll do it your way. And I guess we'll call it a *credit* for you, since you got the money."

Shorty smiled. "Now you're thinking like an accountant. Excellent!"

"None of *that* kind of talk. I'll get sick. Let me just summarize all this new lingo of ours: I'm buying, so I'm long. What I'm buying is the right to buy your shares for $40 each, anytime in the next six months. I'm making a long call. You are selling to me the right to buy your shares for $40 in the next six months. You are making a short call. I'm paying money, so it's a debit trade for me. You're getting paid, so it's a credit trade for you. The whole thing together is a contract, an option contract." Lon looked over his notes. "I think everything's covered."

"Except what do we call the date, the six-months-from-now date that this ends on?"

Lon shrugged. "Do we need a special term for everything? Let's just say 'this is the date the contract ends or expires or dies' or whatever."

"*Expires* is the right word," Shorty said decisively. "So that makes this date the 'expiration date.' Good."

Again, Lon shrugged his acquiescence, though he personally would have preferred a more interesting term. "I guess 'death date' is out?" he asked.

"Yes," answered Shorty, raising a single eyebrow again. " 'Death date' is out."

"All right then. Our option contract has an 'expiration date' of six months from now."

"Okay; makes perfect sense. But let's stop there. We've got a lot to keep track of, so let's summarize this whole thing in some kind of table. Here's a start." (See Figure 4.1.)

FIGURE 4.1　Trading Rights and Obligations

"I think that's all," Shorty said. "And here's a review to make sure we keep it all straight."

REVIEW

"Lon has bought from me an _____ of a certain type. Because he has the right to _____ or _____ at $40, this kind of option is called a _____. The $40 amount we agreed to is called the _____. Since Lon is buying this option, we say that he is _____. Since I am selling this option, we say that I am _____. Thus, from my end, this is a _____, and from Lon's end it is a _____. The $5 Lon is paying me is for him a _____ and for me a _____. So we might say I am doing a _____ trade and he is doing a _____ trade. The whole trade might be called an option _____, and the date it ends is called the _____."

"You know," observed Shorty, after finishing the review, "when you think about it, we could have agreed to a different amount than $40. That's where we struck a deal—it was our strike price—but it didn't have to be. You could have offered a strike price of $45 or $50, or any other amount for that matter. Know what I mean?"

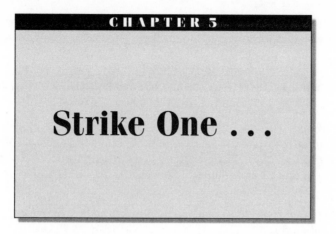

CHAPTER 5

Strike One . . .

"That's right," agreed Lon. "Let's think about it for a minute. Let's say I had offered to make a deal at, say, $30 or $35. Since the stock was trading at $40, those strike prices would have been worth money immediately: I would have been buying the right to buy stock at prices *already* lower than the market price. Think about it. If I bought at those prices, and then turned around and sold on the market, I would be profitable *automatically*."

"Yeah, those strike prices already have monetary value for you; they're 'in the money' right from the start."

"So let's do this," urged Lon. "Since Plum stock is currently trading at $40, let's create a list of possible strike prices around that number and see how we would think about them." He wrote the following dollar amounts on a page:

Strike Price
$25
30
35
40
45
50
55

"Of course, I could have put these numbers in the opposite order," Lon observed, "starting with the high numbers and going down. But, actually, it makes sense to me to have the *first* number we read be the low number. Then as we read the other numbers they get progressively higher. Make sense?"

"Actually, I would have done it the other way," responded Shorty. "Still, if I think of this list in terms of the first number being the lowest, I can make sense of it. I'll try to remember that that's how it works."

> *It couldn't be any simpler: buy low and sell high.*

"But notice something else," said Shorty. "*Every* strike price under $40 is good for you immediately. They're all worth money right out of the gate. If the stock is trading at $40 and you can buy the right to buy it at $35 or $30, or even $25, then, in that respect, they're *automatically* profitable. As I said, they're all 'in the money,' so to speak, from the start. So why don't we just call all of these strike prices *in the money* (or ITM, for short)—strike prices that are worth money to you immediately?"

Lon thought about this for a minute, trying to get clear on the principle. *The basic idea of any buy/sell operation is to try to buy low and sell high. That's what the stock market is all about. I try to buy stocks at a low price, have them go up in value, and then sell them at the higher price. That's how I make a profit. Well, it looks like that's how these strike prices work. If I could pick the right strike price—one that's low enough—then, if the stock goes up, I have put myself in a position to later BUY the stock at this LOW STRIKE PRICE and then turn around and SELL the same stock at the HIGHER MARKET PRICE. I've managed to BUY LOW AND SELL HIGH. Shorty is suggesting that we call any strike price that would put me in this "buy low/sell high" position—any strike price that is lower than the market price—an "in-the-money" strike price. It's because those strike prices have monetary value for me immediately. But why should we name these strike prices based on what's good for ME? Why not name them based on what's good for Shorty?*

"The problem is, those strike prices aren't necessarily the good ones for you," answered Lon. "I think you might like the higher numbers—the ones appearing lower on the list. Then you're making a deal where you could automatically *sell* shares at a higher price than they're selling for right now."

"Yeah, but since you're the one shelling out the money to make the deal, I suggest we name these in terms of what's 'in the money' for you. We have to start somewhere, so why not do it this way?" asked Shorty. "It doesn't bother me."

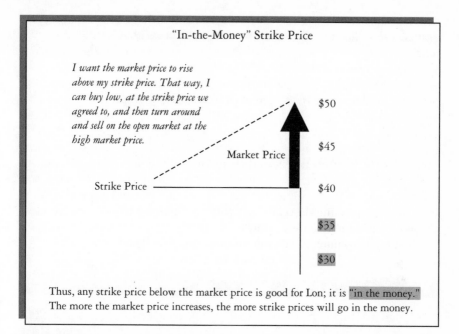

FIGURE 5.1 "In-the-Money" Strike Prices

"All right, fair enough. Any strike price that's lower than the market price is *in the money* because it has actual, tangible monetary value for me. So with a long call, here's what I want." (See Figure 5.1.)

"So all I have to remember is that I will be buying at the strike price, and I want to *buy low*—and that means I want the stock price to move above it. That's how the strike price stays low: by the market price moving higher."

"So in the case we're talking about," he continued, "where the strike is at $40, I guess we would say that the higher strike prices—the ones at $45 and above and that appear later on the list—are currently *out of the money* (or OTM) for me. They're not worth anything to me right away because they're actually higher than the current market price: if I bought shares at those prices, and then sold them on the market, I would automatically *lose* money. Again, I'm hoping to buy low."

"Okay, that makes sense," said Shorty. "*Out-of-the-money* strike prices are higher than the current stock price. But then what would we call the strike price where we actually made our deal? Forty dollars isn't *in* the money for you, and it's not *out* of the money, either. It's right *at* the money."

"Why not call it that, then? *At the money* (or ATM). What's wrong with that?" questioned Lon.

"Nothing, I guess. In fact, I like it. But, actually, that may not happen all that often: having a stock price and strike price that are identical. So maybe we should have a category called *near the money* (or NTM). That will capture close cases."

"So here we are," continued Shorty. "We're going to name these strike prices in terms of what they mean for you, since you're the one who's *long*—the one who's shelling out money for the deal, and buying. Any strike price that's lower than the current stock price is *in the money*, because it has an actual, tangible monetary value to you immediately. Any strike price that's higher than the current market price is *out of the money*, because it doesn't have any actual monetary value for you at this point; in fact, if you bought at any of those prices, you would *lose* money. And any strike price that's the same as the current stock price is simply *at the money* (or *near the money* if it's close)—it's neutral."

"Okay, so let me create a review of these ideas," said Lon.

REVIEW

"The chart of strike prices is based on the idea of the _____ strike price appearing _____ on the list. So as we read more strike prices, down the list, the strike prices get _____. Now, we've decided to name strike prices in terms of what is good for the person in the _____ position. Strike prices that are below the market price of the stock are called _____. This is because they are worth _____ to me immediately. If I agree to a strike price that is below the market price, I can already _____ low and sell _____, and that's what I am trying to do. In general, I want a deal that sets me up so that, sometime in the next six months, I can buy _____ and _____ high. So an 'in-the-money' strike price is one that is _____ than the market price of the stock. By this same logic a strike price that is higher than the market price is _____, and a strike price that is the same as the market price is _____."

"All this makes sense," said Shorty, "but let's think about this some more."

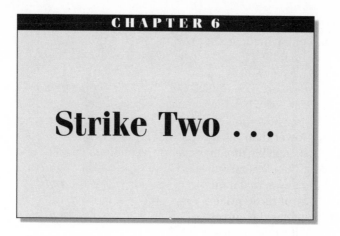

CHAPTER 6

Strike Two ...

"See, you offered me $5 per share to make our contract at the money. But what would you have offered me if you had wanted to make the deal at a strike price *in* the money—say, at $35 or $30?"

"Well, let's look at the picture of our situation again, somewhat simplified." (See Figure 6.1.)

"The lower the price I can buy shares for, the better it is for me," continued Lon, thinking it through. "If the stock goes to $55 like I think it will, then I'm better off if I can get the shares for $35 than for $40. That's $5 more in profits. So the lower the strike price—the deeper it is in the money—the better it is for me," repeated Lon. "In fact, that's exactly why we decided to call it *in the money* in the first place."

"Right," said Shorty. "The problem is, those in-the-money strike prices are not as good for me. Remember, since we set the strike price at $40, you will want to take my shares at the end of six months (if not before), if the stock price is something over $40. Of course, since you've already paid me $5, you actually need the stock price to go over $45 before you're profitable (the $40 per share plus the $5 you've already paid). But, in any case, the idea is simply that you make money by the stock price moving higher than the strike price, and the more it's over the strike price the more profit you make. Now *I* don't think the stock price will get over $40, but it might. Still, I'm willing to take that chance because you've already paid me $5.

"But if we set the strike price lower," Shorty continued, "say, at $35, then things are different: now you can take my shares when the stock is selling at a $5 *lower* price, and the chances of that happening are higher.

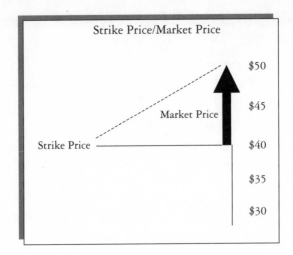

FIGURE 6.1 The Relationship of Strike Price to Market Price

Which means that the risk for me in this case is greater. And you know what? I still might be willing to take that risk—because I still think the stock will go down—but I won't take it for $5. I'll need more on the front end if I'm going to agree to a $35 strike price. Maybe $2 or $3 more. I don't know for sure, but it will certainly be more."

> *The lower the strike price, the more I will pay for it.*

"So the reverse will be true for me," observed Lon. "The higher the strike price—the more out of the money it is—the *harder* it is for me to make a profit. If I expect the stock price, currently at $40, to go to $55, and if I set the strike price at $50, I have much less room for error. The market price has to get above $50 before my strike price is in the money, or has any actual monetary value to me. That means it is less likely to happen—it is riskier. If it's riskier, it's less valuable to me, so I won't pay as much to make a deal at this strike price."

"Right. And the higher the strike price, the *less* risky the deal is for me," observed Shorty. "I won't need as much credit to make this kind of deal, because of the lowered risk. *You* want to pay less because the deal is more risky for you, and I can agree to *receive* less because the deal is *less* risky for me."

"So here's the relationship from my point of view," said Lon. *"The lower the strike price, the more valuable the deal is for me—the more likely the strike is to go in the money—and the more I will pay for it."*

"Right," said Shorty. "And from my point of view, it goes like this: *the lower the strike price, the riskier the deal is for me and the more I will* DEMAND *to be paid for it."*

"So let's put this in terms of the debit/credit stuff we talked about. Both of us can look at it this way: *the lower the strike price, the greater the debit/credit amount required to make a deal. The higher the strike price, the less the debit/credit amount required to make a deal.* It might look something like the relationship below." Lon sketched a quick table, and, in order to make them stand out, shaded the debit/credit amounts of all the strike prices that were in the money.

PLUM Stock Price: $40

Debit/Credit	Strike
14	25
11	30
8	35
5	40
3	45
2	50
1	55

"It's impossible to predict what the actual numbers would be," continued Lon, "because I think it would be pretty complicated to figure out exactly what the debit/credit amounts ought to be for each strike price. It would probably be different for every stock for a lot of different reasons, but the basic relationship would be the same."

"Right," Shorty jumped in. "There's an inverse relationship between the strike price and the debit/credit amount. The lower the strike price, the greater the credit I have to receive to make the deal worthwhile ... which automatically means the higher the debit you have to pay."

"While we're looking at this chart, there's something else to notice, too," added Lon. "Let's say that the stock price increases to $41 in the next week. At that point, the $40 strike would be in the money, because it would then be lower than the market price. And if the market price went to $46, then the $45 strike price would be in the money as well. As the stock price rises, more of the strikes go in the money. Then we would shade *their* debit/credit amounts too—like this."

PLUM Stock Price: $50

Debit/Credit	Strike
14	25
11	30
8	35
5	40
3	45
2	50
1	55

"And vice versa," added Shorty. "If the stock price were to go down to $34, say, then the $35 strike price would *no longer* be in the money because now it would no longer be *lower* than the market price. So the debit/credit amount at the $35 strike price would no longer be shaded. It would look like this."

PLUM Stock Price: $35

Debit/Credit	Strike
14	25
11	30
8	35
5	40
3	45
2	50
1	55

"Right," said Lon. "So strike prices being in the money, out of the money, and so on is something that moves with the stock price. If we made this deal next week or next month—or even later today—whether these strike prices would be in the money, out of the money, or at the money would all be different because the stock price would be different. For these call options we're talking about, all we have to remember is that, *at any given time*, if a strike price is lower than the market price, it is in the money."

"And if it's higher, it's out of the money," Shorty added.

"Right," agreed Lon, "and there's one more important point we have to be clear on, too. We made our deal at a $40 strike price, and that strike price doesn't change over time. If I want to call out your shares any time in the next six months, I can only do it at $40. That's what we agreed to. Now notice: that strike price was at the money at the time we made our deal. So we might say this was an at-the-money deal *at the time we made it.* But that will change over time, because the market price will obviously change over time. If the market price trends higher—to anything above $40 (say, $43), then we can say the strike price is *trending in the money* because it's now lower than the stock price. It now has actual, tangible monetary value; it's worth money to me immediately."

"But the strike price could also trend *out* of the money," said Shorty. "If the market price dropped below the strike price of $40 (say, to $37), then that's what would be happening. The strike price would now be *higher* than the market price. It would then be out of the money ... which means that if you exercised your option to call out my shares, you wouldn't be able to buy low and sell high; instead you would actually be buying high (at the strike of $40) and selling low (at $37)! And that would be really stupid."

"Right, which is exactly why I would never exercise my option when out of the money."

"Right, and that's why I hope the strike price *stays* out of the money," laughed Shorty. "If the market price stays at $40, or trends lower, our $40 strike price will never be in the money—you won't be able to buy low and sell high—and you will never call out my shares. I get to keep my shares *and* the credit you paid me."

"Yeah, and I'm expecting—and hoping for—just the opposite. I want the market price to move up so that our $40 strike trends *in* the money."

"Okay, got it. So let's construct another review to make sure we stay clear on all this. I'll do it this time," said Shorty.

REVIEW

"The _____ the strike price, the better the chance that the strike price will end up _____ on this trade. This means Lon is willing to _____ for lower strike prices.

"On my end, the _____ the strike price, the riskier the deal is for me: the _____ the chance that Lon will end up in the money and call out my shares. So the _____ the strike price, the _____ I will demand in a credit to make the trade.

"So it is the same for both of us: the _____ the strike price, the _____ the debit/credit amount will be involved in the trade.

"In call trades, there is an _____ relationship between _____ and _____ amount.

"For calls, at any given time, an in-the-money strike price is simply one that is _____ than the market price. An out-of-the-money strike price is simply one that is _____ than the market price. Whether a strike price is in or out of the money will _____ over time.

"For these calls, we can say that when the market price moves *above* the strike price, the strike price is _____ in the money. By the same token, when the market price moves *below* the strike price, the strike price is trending _____.

"Being in the long position, Lon wants the strike price to _____ in the money. Being in the short position, I want the strike price to _____."

"But you know, there's another thing we need to think about," said Shorty.

CHAPTER 7

Time Travel

"**W**e created this contract with a six-month time frame, but we didn't have to do that. We could have chosen one month, or three months, or nine months—any time frame we wanted. Right?"

"I guess that's right. How would we have thought about the deal then?"

> *We could have chosen any time frame we wanted.*

"Well, I don't know about you," answered Shorty, "but the more time you wanted to have to make your deal work—to have your stock price go up—the more money I would want in order to make the trade. The more time you have, the better the chances you have. Your risk goes down. But as always, I guess, the less risky something is for you, the more risky it is for me: the more time you have for a deal to go your way, the more risk I'm taking that it actually *will* go your way—and that's bad for me. So the longer you want the deal to be good for, the more I need you to pay me for the privilege."

"And the more time I want to have to reduce my risk, the more I will be *willing* to pay for the privilege," replied Lon.

"So I guess that's another relationship we can predict," said Shorty. "*The longer the time frame of the deal, the greater the debit/credit required to make the deal.*" So this is a direct, rather than an inverse, relationship.

Lon forced himself to complete the following statement to make sure he kept the ideas straight in his mind.

R E V I E W

"The longer the time frame I put around a trade, the _____ the chances I will be able to _____ low and _____ high. So the longer the time frame, the _____ my risk, and the _____ the debit I will be willing to pay for it.

"For Shorty, the longer the time frame for the trade, the _____ the risk in the trade: the more likely his shares will be _____ by me. So the _____ the time frame, the _____ the credit Shorty will _____."

CHAPTER 8

R&R and Time Travel for Lon

W ith the details of their deal wrapped up, and with a few realizations about their trade made along the way, Lon and Shorty hurriedly finished lunch (it was already well past 1:00), agreeing to stay in close touch over the next while.

As Lon drove home that night after work, he rehearsed to himself the deal he had struck with Shorty. Finally arriving after the 40-minute drive, he sought Cass excitedly.

"Look," he said upon finding her resting in the family room. "I made a *great* deal with Shorty today."

"A deal?"

"Yeah, a deal. See, we've been talking about the stock market for quite a while, and today we actually made our own deal, our own trade."

"Okaaaay," replied Cass apprehensively, not knowing where Lon might be headed with this "trade" thing.

Let's create a category that will help me keep track of my costs.

"Well, here's the deal. I recently bought 100 shares of Plum stock at $40 per share, which is about where they're still trading. Now I think that value is going to go up to around $55 per share. Well, Shorty also owns 100 shares of Plum stock. And we entered a contract with each other: I paid him $5 per share right now for the right to buy his 100 shares at $40 anytime in the next six months. That means if the stock price goes to $55,

I can still buy his shares at $40, and if I want to I can then turn around and sell them immediately on the open market for $55! Just think about it: I've made $15 per share."

"Well, I get your point, but that $15 isn't quite right," Cass remarked. "Remember, you just said you've already paid Shorty $5 per share. So those shares you're buying from him actually cost you $45, not just $40. That leads to a $10 profit, not $15."

"Right, I know that. I just got carried away. But the point is, I make $10 profit on those shares because I'm able to buy them below the market value. I think it's great."

"Well, I think it's great, too, but let's just make sure you don't get carried away again. If you go around thinking you're going to make $15 per share rather than $10, you're likely to make some bad decisions."

COST BASIS AND BREAKING EVEN

"You're right," agreed Lon. "So why don't we just create a category that will help me keep track of my costs. Let's call it my *cost basis*. My $40 stock by itself has a cost basis of $40; that's my total expense in buying the stock. But if I enter a trade to buy 100 more shares of stock at $40—and if I pay $5 per share for the right to be able to do that—then, if I exercise my option and actually buy Shorty's shares, my cost basis—my total expense—for those 100 shares is $45: the price we agreed to plus the $5 I paid for the option—what we call the *debit*."

"Alright, that makes sense to me—anything that will keep your mind right about your actual costs."

"I agree. In fact, this is important for another reason, too: knowing my cost basis tells me how much the stock price has to rise in order for me to break even on the deal. In other words, since my cost basis is $45, the stock price has to get over that for me to make any profit at all. Anything below $45 and I'm losing, and *at* $45, I'm only breaking even."

"That's kind of simple, actually, but it does seem important to keep in mind. The breakeven point on your deal is simply your cost basis."

My reward potential is theoretically unlimited.

"Good. So let me put all this in the terms Shorty and I developed for our contract," continued Lon. "I paid Shorty a *debit* of $5 per share to enter this trade. Now because I'm buying, we call that being *long*. Don't ask me why. But that's what we call it. *Long*. And since I'm buying the right to buy Shorty's shares later—to call them out, so to speak—we call this a long *call*. Now we made this deal at a *strike price* of $40. If the stock goes over $40, that strike price will be *in the money*. That means that the market price is higher than that strike price—which just means that I could immediately buy Shorty's shares for $40 and then sell them on the open market for more than that. And I guess we could add the term that you and I just came up with: *breakeven*. That's just my cost basis, or the amount I have to make on the deal if I'm not going to lose anything."

REWARD

"But now let me get to the best part of this deal with Shorty: if the stock price goes to $55, I've made $10 on this $45 investment. And that's 22 percent!" cried Lon. "It's fantastic. In fact, my reward potential is theoretically unlimited because the stock could go up to $1000 per share. Then I'd be making $955 on a $45 investment!"

"Yes, yes, but you know that's unrealistic. That's only a theoretical possibility. Still, 22 percent in six months is awfully good. But I can see something that's more important for you to have your mind on," cautioned Cass.

"What's that?"

"Your risk. What's the *risk* for you in this deal with Shorty?"

RISK

"Well, let's think about it. If the stock price goes to $55, then obviously I'll call out his shares and buy them at the $40 we agreed to. Of course—no, I haven't forgotten—I've already paid him $5, so again, my total cost basis for this trade is $45. That's my breakeven point. But, obviously, $55 is way over that, so I'll call out his shares and take ownership of them."

"Of course, but I asked you about the *risk*," reminded Cass.

"Right. So let's suppose the stock price stays below the strike price of $40. Say it goes down to $35 or even $30. In either case I won't call out Shorty's shares for $40; if I did, I'd be paying Shorty more for those shares than I'd have to pay for them on the open market. That would be stupid. So in that case, I just wouldn't exercise my option to buy his shares. The option would simply expire."

"And in that case you would forfeit the $5 you've already paid to Shorty. You can't reclaim it, so it's a loss. A $5 loss."

"Right. But that's also the *most* I could lose. I can't lose more than I've already paid. So that's my maximum risk: the $5 debit I paid to make the deal in the first place."

CALLING OUT SHORTY'S SHARES

"Okay, that makes sense. But that raises another question. What will you do if the market price goes over your strike price of $40, but stays under your *breakeven* price of $45? Say the market price goes to $43—what then?"

Lon was stumped. *What* WOULD *I do?* he asked himself. Finally, he thought he saw it.

"Well, as we've already said, in *any* circumstances, if I don't call out Shorty's shares I simply lose the whole $5 debit I paid to him. It's a $5 loss. But let's think about it. If the market price is at $43, as you say, I could still go ahead and call out Shorty's shares, buy them at $40, *and then turn around and sell them on the market for $43*. So on that part of the deal I actually *make* $3. That's what it means for a strike price to be in the money; because it's lower than the market price, it's worth money to me immediately. That's why this $40 strike price is in the money when the market price is $43."

"Okay, I get it! By calling out Shorty's shares and selling them for a profit, you at least recoup some of your losses on the deal. You're all set to lose $5, but because your strike price is in the money, as you call it, you can buy his shares and sell them for a $3 profit. Which means you at least reduce your losses on the overall deal by that $3. You end up losing $2 on the trade rather than $5."

"That's right. So it looks like these are the realities: (1) I won't call out Shorty's shares if the strike price never goes in the money (if the market price never goes higher than the strike price of $40). In that case, I realize the maximum risk; I lose my $5 debit. (2) I will definitely call out Shorty's shares at some point if the market price goes above my *break even* price. At that point I make a profit; I just want the market price to go as high as possible in the time I have so that I can make as much profit as possible. (3) If I run out of time—if the expiration date is close—I will call out Shorty's shares even if the market price is not above the breakeven price, as long as it's above the *strike price*. That way, I can at least reduce my losses."

"Okay, I see all that, but now I'm confused about the term *in the money*."

"What do you mean?"

"Well, it seems funny to call yourself 'in the money' simply by the stock price going higher than this $40 strike price. After all, we've just established that you don't even manage to break even until you get over your total cost basis of *$45*. So what's the deal with that?"

"Okay, look. By 'in the money' all we mean is that the *strike price* is in the money. That doesn't mean that the whole trade is profitable or in the money. You're right: with this long call we have to pass the breakeven point for that to be the case. So all we mean is that the strike price itself is worth money to us immediately. Now I have to admit that I might *talk* about myself being in the money or about the stock being in the money or about my option being in the money. I might use those expressions. But, in every case, all I mean is that the strike price itself is in the money. I don't mean that I've passed the breakeven point for the whole deal. Make sense?"

"Yes. Thank you."

"Okay. Now with all that said, what really matters here is the practical point: as I get close to our expiration date, I will call out Shorty's shares if my strike price is in the money—even if I haven't reached the breakeven point. Okay?"

"Okay."

"Good. Now let's review my reward potential on this deal. It's pretty simple. It's just a matter of how high the market price goes in the next six months. If it goes to $1,000 per share, I can still buy 100 shares from Shorty for $40. Of course, I've already paid him $5 per share, so my cost basis is $45. But still, my profit is the difference between $1,000 and my cost basis of $45. Pretty good! More realistically, however, if the stock goes to $55 in the next six months, my profit is the difference between that $55 and my cost basis of $45. That's $10 and that's still pretty good!"

"And your risk, again, depends on whether your strike price of $40 goes in the money or not. If it never goes in the money, you will realize the maximum risk; you will lose the $5 debit you paid up front. If it does go in the money—but you never pass the breakeven point—you will still lose some money, but not the whole $5. So the risk is minimal in either case."

"The good news," added Lon, "is that I have six months for this deal to work. The stock price might fluctuate some in that six months, but by the end I'm positive it will be up—way above even my breakeven price. Time is on my side. The more time I have to close this deal, the better my chances of the stock rising."

"And," he continued, "just to make sure I've explained everything clearly, let me create a review for you and see if you can fill in the blanks. If you can't, then I haven't explained the deal well enough. So here, take a shot."

REVIEW

"If I exercise my option and _____ Shorty's shares, my cost basis in this trade will be $_____. It is made up of the _____ plus the _____. This establishes my _____ point. This is the point I have to get over if I'm to make any _____ in the deal. My maximum potential reward is _____. The way I calculate my *realistic* potential reward is to ____ the agreed-upon _____ to the _____ I paid, and subtract this total from a realistic _____. In other words: _____ minus (strike price + _____).

"My maximum risk in this trade is $____. It is made up of _____ I paid to Shorty. I will lose this amount if the _____ stays _____ _____, which means that the market price doesn't get higher than the _____.

"I won't call out Shorty's shares if the strike price never goes ____ the money (if the market price never goes _____ than the strike price of $40). In that case, I realize the maximum ____; I lose my _____. I will definitely call out Shorty's shares at some point if the market price goes above my _____ point. At that point, I make a profit; I just want the _____ to go as high as possible in the time I have. If I run out of time—if the _____ date is close— I will call out Shorty's shares even if the _____ price is not above the _____ price, as long as it's above the *strike price*. That way I can at least reduce my _____.

"The more _____ I have on my side, the better my chances of the _____ getting higher than the _____, which means being ____ the money.

"The less _____ I have on my side, the better the chances of the _____ staying lower than the agreed-upon _____, which means it is ____ the money. Then I realize my maximum _____."

CHAPTER 9

R&R and Time Travel for Shorty

S horty left work at the end of the day and headed straight home. Eager to tell Sharon of the deal he had struck with Lon, he skipped his usual visit to the gym.

"You're early," said Sharon, greeting him at the door. "To what do I owe this great pleasure?"

"Well, something terrific happened today, and I couldn't wait to tell you about it."

"See," he continued as they entered the kitchen, "I just made a *great* deal." They took their normal seats facing each other around their small kitchen table. "As I've told you, I own 100 shares of Plum stock, which is currently trading at $40 per share—about the same I paid for it. But I think there's a decent chance that this stock is going to go down in value in the near term—maybe even to $25 or $30. Well, I had my usual monthly lunch with Lon today, and guess what? He was willing to pay me $5 per share right now for the right to buy my 100 shares later for the current $40 price! In other words, he's already paid me $5 and if he ever buys my shares he'll pay me $40 more."

I'll just get to keep the $5 credit per share he's already paid me. That's a 12.5 percent profit.

Sharon's brow was furrowed. "Okay, look at it this way," Shorty continued. "I sold something to Lon; I entered a contract with him. For the price of $5 per share I sold him the right to buy my shares any time in the next six months for $40. We call that $40 our *strike price*. Now because he has the right to call out my shares, we call this a *call*, and because I'm the seller, we call me *short*. Don't ask me why. But that's the word: *short*. I'm *shorting a call*. And the $5 per share I received from Lon is called a *credit*. So Lon is in this deal $45 worth, you might say. He can buy my shares if he wants to, but it will be at a cost of $45: the $40 strike price, plus the $5 he's already paid me. I guess we could call that his breakeven point. And here's the good news: if the stock price never gets over the $40 strike price, Lon won't call out my shares and buy them—and I still get to *keep* that $5 credit he's already paid me."

REWARD

"Look, two things can happen," Shorty continued, still seeing the quizzical expression on Sharon's face. "Let's suppose the stock price moves up and reaches a price higher than this $40 strike price. Let's say it goes even as high as $55. Well, Lon turns around and calls out my 100 shares and pays me $40 for them—and if he wants to, he can now sell them for $55. That's a great profit for him, and it's a profit I miss out on. But, remember, he's already paid me a $5 credit, so I still make $5 per share on that deal. That's not bad.

"But there's another thing that can happen, and it's very important. The price can *go down*, just like I think it will. Let's say it goes to $25 or $30—or *anything* below our $40 strike price. In that case, Lon won't call out my shares and buy them because he would be paying a higher price than he could pay on the open market. So in that case, he won't do anything. The six months will pass, he won't call out my shares, and I'll just keep the $5 per share credit he's already paid me. I've pocketed $5 per share—that's a 12.5 percent profit ($5/$40)—without doing anything! Then I just wait for the stock price to go back up. In fact, if I want to, I can take the credit he's paid me—$500 total—and buy more shares of Plum stock at the new lower market price."

"So let's be clear. The maximum reward you can make on this trade is that $5—12.5 percent, right?" asked Sharon.

"That's right. And there's no risk at all."

RISK

"Well, that's not exactly true. You own these shares of stock, and the stock price could go all the way down to zero, right?"

"Yes."

"Well, then, isn't that a big risk?" she insisted.

> *I will make $5 per share and I have no risk of losing that.*

"Well, yes and no. Yes, it's a *theoretical* risk. I wouldn't let that happen, but, yes, it *could* happen. But notice: I had *that* risk long before I ever talked to Lon. That's a risk of simply owning stock. But my specific deal with Lon—this *short call* as we're calling it—doesn't *itself* have any risk. And that's my point: in my specific deal with Lon, I'll make $5 per share and I have no risk of losing *that*.

"See," he continued, "even if the stock price goes to $1,000 per share . . . well, I already own the stock so I will just sell my 100 shares to Lon for $40—just like I'm obligated to do. I don't *lose* anything. Of course, I don't make the huge profit he makes, but I do keep the $5 he's already paid me. And, actually, there won't be this kind of discrepancy anyway. Let's suppose, to be more realistic, that the stock price goes to $55. Well, then Lon exercises his option to buy my shares for $40 and I'm obligated to sell them at that price. He makes $10 on the trade ($55 minus the total of $45 he pays me), but *I* still make $5. That seems fair since he's taking more risk than I am—he could lose the $5 he's paid me, after all—and I'm taking no risk at all. It's true that I make less, but I'm also risking less."

"But there's one thing you haven't thought about enough," said Sharon.

"What's that? What haven't I thought about?"

"Well, I'm not sure you've thought enough about the time frame in this deal," she answered matter-of-factly. "It seems to me that time is on *Lon's* side in this trade. I know you think the stock price will go down, but the more time that's available, the more likely it is that the stock price will also go up. Didn't you say that Lon has the right to exercise his option *anytime* in the next six months?"

"Yes."

"Well, all it has to do is go up once, for a little while, past his breakeven price and Lon could call out his shares from you for $40. Anything past his breakeven price and he's profitable . . . and he could decide to exercise his option anytime. But that's not all. If I understand correctly, it would work for Lon to call out your shares even if the market price *didn't* rise higher than the breakeven price, but only rose higher than the *strike* price—say, to $43. Even in that case Lon could buy shares from you for $40 and sell them for $43. And I think that's exactly what he would do if time were running out on your expiration period: he would make the best deal he could before it was too late."

"I see," answered Shorty, "In either case—whether the stock price rises above Lon's breakeven price, or whether time is running out and it just gets over the strike price—Lon will call out my shares and I will have to sell them. So, yes, that's a risk. But in either case I don't *lose* money. I sell my 100 shares for the $40 strike price we agreed to, plus I get to keep the $5 he's already paid me."

"It's true you haven't lost any money on the deal, but what if you'd rather not lose your shares?" she answered. "Then it's a risk, at least to some degree. It seems to me that, typically at least, you'd like to collect the $5 credit and still keep your shares. But the more time you give Lon, the less likely that is to happen. With six months to play with, the stock price could well go up enough for him to call out your shares. You keep the credit, sure, but you lose the shares you own. I'm not saying there's anything wrong, exactly, with accepting a six-month deal, or even with losing shares. It just seems that you didn't consider all this—especially the time frame—like you should have."

"That's true about the time frame. The problem is that Lon and I have already decided that the shorter the time frame, the less the deal is worth. He wouldn't pay $5 if the deal lasted only three months. He might only pay $2.50. Part of the attraction in the deal is getting this high credit."

"Right. I see that, and that *is* important to consider. I'm just saying that you also ought to consider what a shorter time frame would do for you. I guess you always have to balance (1) the size of the credit you can get, with (2) the chances of having to sell your shares."

"Yeah," agreed Shorty, "and now that you mention it, I can even imagine making a deal with a 12-month time frame. I would just pick a good out-of-the-money strike price—one that I would feel good about selling my shares for, if it came to that, and one that would bring a high credit amount to me. But I could also see making a deal with a 3-month time frame—and a smaller credit—in order to decrease the chances of having to sell my shares."

"Right. So it's a balance. I'm just saying that you ought to consider all of these factors every time, and not just accept a time frame because it's the one that's offered. That's what happened, isn't it?"

"Yeah, you're right. That's what happened. I'll be more alert next time. I'll consider the time frame as carefully as I consider the credit amount."

"Now, to make sure I've explained this whole deal well enough," he added, "I'm going to create a review for you. See if you can fill in the blanks."

"Let's suppose the Plum stock price moves up and goes higher than our strike price. In that case, Lon will _____. So I will lose those _____, but I will keep the _____. So if Lon exercises his option and _____ my shares, my reward in this trade will be $_____. If the stock price never moves higher than our strike price, Lon won't _____. His option will _____. In that case, I will keep the _____, plus I won't lose _____.

"So my maximum risk in this trade is to lose _____. But, even then, he pays me a total of _____ for them.

"The shorter the time frame for this trade, the _____ my chances of the market price staying higher than the _____. If that happens, I won't _____ my shares.

"I ought to consider _____ as well as _____ in determining the value of a trade."

CHAPTER 10

How Lon and Shorty Came Out on Their Deal

"Okay, Shorty," Lon laughed, "I'm ready to call out your shares."

Nine weeks had passed since they had entered their option contract. In that time, Plum stock had risen to $51.50 per share and had now fallen back to $49. Lon had hoped to get to $55, and he still had nearly four months left for that to happen, but the drop had made him hesitant. *What if Shorty turns out to be right? Why not take my profits and call it a day?* Thus, the call to Shorty.

"Alright," answered Shorty. "So, where do we stand?"

"Well, nothing's changed. I'm ready to buy 100 shares of Plum stock from you at our strike price of $40. I had thought about waiting longer, but I'm in a decent position right now, so I've decided to pull the trigger."

"Okay. Done. I'll get my shares transferred to you. I don't know how that's done, but I'll figure it out."

"Fine. It's more important to me right now to review where we've ended up on this trade," answered Lon. "I paid you $5 per share to make the deal in the first place. That was my debit."

"Right, and my credit."

"Yes. Now, in the market, I've made $9 per share on this stock. I'm buying these shares from you at $40 (our strike price), and I'll be able to sell them for $49 on the open market. That's a $9 profit. Of course, I paid you $5 per share up front, which gives me a cost basis of $45 in the stock. So, obviously, I end up making a net profit of $4: $49 – $45. That works out to 10 percent in nine weeks. Not bad."

"Funny thing—I made out even better," observed Shorty. "It's true that I missed out on the $9 profit I might have had, and it's true that I'm selling my shares to you when I might have wanted to hang onto them. But you paid me $5 per share for this deal, so I'm actually selling you my shares for $45, or a $5 profit. That $5 profit works out to 12.5 percent in nine weeks."

"In other words, we both came out winners on this deal."

"Yeah, it's just like you said at the very beginning, Lon. You thought it would work out for both of us, and it has."

"Right. So . . . do you want to try another deal?"

"Why not? Let's go for it."

Understanding the Long and Short of "Put" Options in the Market

CHAPTER 11

Bulls, Bears, and Stags

As the months passed, Shorty and Lon made a number of additional trades. Lon found that he liked the idea of always being long in these deals. He liked the psychology of being in the buying position—of purchasing rights. It gave him a sense of freedom to be able to call out Shorty's shares within a fixed time frame at a fixed price. It also gave him a definable risk that he knew at the outset and that wouldn't change: the debit he paid to make the deal in the first place.

The problem was that this worked only for stocks that were increasing in value—stocks that were *bullish*. In such bullish cases, Lon could always do a long call—buy the right to buy shares at a strike price that would eventually turn out to be below the stock price because the stock price would rise. That higher stock price thus puts the strike price in the money: he could *buy low* by calling out his shares at the lower strike price, and *sell high* by then selling those shares on the open market at the higher market price.

How could he protect himself from downturns in stock price? And how could he do this by buying, rather than selling?

But stocks weren't always bullish. They often went down in value, at least in the short term. Lon owned stock in Nextall (NXL), for example—100 shares he had bought at $40 and that were currently at $40—and he noticed that when Nextall had a bad earnings report its stock price would normally decline, or go *bearish*. (Incidentally, try as he might, Lon could never discover where the terms *bullish* and *bearish* actually came from. He had heard some possibilities—for example, that the terms referred to the nature of bulls to attack upward with their horns while bears swipe downward with their paws, or that they referred to two old banking families called the Barings and the Bulstrodes. But none of the stories seemed plausible to Lon, and he finally decided that no one really knew and that he would simply have to use the terms without really understanding why. In other words, he would have to do what everyone else does!)

Lon wondered how he could possibly reduce this bearish risk. How could he protect himself from such downturns in stock price? And how could he do this by buying, rather than selling?

Finally a possibility dawned on him: *What if I could buy the right to SELL shares rather than buy them? For example, let's suppose the Nextall stock price dropped to $25 or so in the next month or two. Wouldn't it be great if I had a deal where I could actually sell my 100 shares at $40? That would be a way of making a profit even when a stock is going down: I could sell my shares at $40, compared to a market price of $25, and, if I wanted to, I could then actually turn around and buy more shares at $25! I would own more shares of Nextall, and my cost basis would be lower because I would be investing less in them.*

At the same time, Shorty was pondering his own situation. He liked being short—always being on the selling end of deals. That way, he always took in a credit up front, and all he had to do was settle on a high *out-of-the-money* strike price—one that the market price would probably stay below—because then his shares would never be called out (again, Lon wouldn't call out and buy Shorty's shares in that case because he could buy them more cheaply on the open market). The pattern fit him like a glove.

Shorty realized that this strategy worked great for stocks that were either bearish—going down in value—or that were *stagnant*—that were just hanging around a certain price for weeks at a time. If he had an out-of-the-money strike price—and if the market price never went above it—it didn't matter much whether the stock price fell or just stayed in one place. Either way, his shares were never called out and he just collected his credit. So his selling strategy was a great way to make money with bearish or stagnant stocks.

How could he take advantage of those many bullish times, and yet do so by selling rather than buying?

But Shorty knew that many stocks were actually bullish long term, and many more at least had bullish periods. He also knew that he had no good strategy for maximizing profits in these situations. How could he take advantage of those many bullish times, and yet do so by selling rather than buying?

So Shorty found himself wondering: *Wouldn't it be great if I could find a way to take a credit on a stock that was actually increasing in value—one that was bullish? Then I wouldn't be restricted to trading just bearish or stagnant stocks; I could then do better on more deals and I could still do it by selling and taking in a credit.*

So Shorty wanted a selling strategy that would allow him to do something he couldn't do with short calls: make money in a bullish trend. He decided to call Lon.

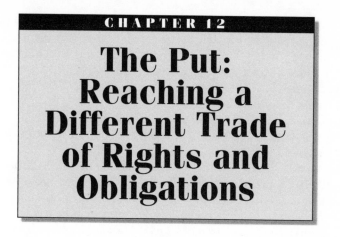

CHAPTER 12

The Put: Reaching a Different Trade of Rights and Obligations

As they talked, Shorty and Lon discovered that they both held 100 shares of Nextall at $40 per share. Expecting that the stock price might fall to $25, Lon thought through a deal this way: *What if I offer to buy the right to SELL Shorty my 100 shares of Nextall stock? I could pay him $5 per share right now, and have the option of selling him my 100 shares later at $40. If the stock price goes to $25, I have saved myself from a $15 loss because I can still sell my shares to Shorty at $40. And if I want to, I can actually buy more shares at this lower price with the money I take in from selling. This deal really pays off for me if the stock goes bearish. I'm also helped by having enough time for all this to happen, so I'll offer a six-month expiration period again.*

> *The only thing that's different is that I won't be calling out shares from you. I will actually be putting shares of mine to you.*

And that's what Lon offered. "Let's enter a different kind of option contract, Shorty. I'll pay you $5 per share right now to have the right to sell you 100 shares later at $40. Let's say within six months. Now in this case, I'm not buying the right to *buy* 100 shares from you. I'm doing something different: I'm buying the right to make *you* buy 100 shares from *me*. I'm still shelling out money to make this deal and that means I'm still *long*, if we keep to our earlier terminology. The only thing that's different is that I won't be *calling out* shares from you. I will actually be *putting* shares of mine *on* you, or *to* you. I will put them over to you, and you will have to buy them from me."

"I suppose you're telling me we ought to call this kind of trade a *put*," remarked Shorty with a trace of sarcasm.

"I guess so. If I'm calling out your shares, it's a call. If I'm putting shares over to you, it's a put. Makes sense to me."

"*Everything* makes sense to you, Lon. I think we could come up with something better if we worked at it, but it really doesn't matter that much, so I'll go with it. *Put* it is."

Now it was Shorty's turn to think through the deal. Expecting the stock price to actually increase, Shorty thought it through this way: *If the stock price goes up, say, to $55, like I think it will, Lon will never exercise his option to force me to buy his shares. If he did, he would be forcing me to buy his shares at $40 when he could sell them on the open market at $55! That would be stupid. So if the market price does go up, it would be great for me. Then Lon would never exercise his option to put his shares to me and force me to buy them, and I just get to keep the $5 credit he's paid me. Here's my chance to make money on a bullish stock—at least it looks bullish to me, given everything I've studied—and I get to do it by being short, by selling. Still, I learned my lesson about time. I need to consider the odds of the stock going down and Lon's forcing me to buy his shares at this $40 strike price when the stock price is actually lower than that. I think I should be careful here and only agree to a one-month expiration period.*

Finally, Shorty said: "Before actually entering a deal, let's make a chart like we did for calls to try to keep everything straight. Have a look at this." Shorty pulled out a piece of paper and drew the table seen in Figure 12.1.

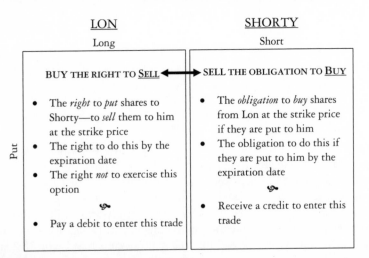

FIGURE 12.1 Rights and Obligations for Puts

"That looks right," said Lon. "Let me create a review to make sure we fully understand what we're considering."

REVIEW

"I will _____ a certain dollar amount to enter this trade. By doing so, I will have the right to _____ to you for $40 if I want to. I will also have the right to do this by whatever _____ we agree on. I also have the right _____ if I don't want to; I can let my option _____. If I do, I _____ the amount I paid to you.

"You will _____ a certain dollar amount, or _____, from me to enter this trade. By taking my money, you will have the obligation to _____ of my shares at the _____ price of $40 if I _____. You will have to do this if I exercise my option any time in _____. If I never exercise my option, you still get to _____."

"But look, Lon," said Shorty. "Before I respond to your offer, I want to point something out."

CHAPTER 13

Strike One . . .

"Yes?"

"Well, see, it looks to me like the strike price works one way for calls and exactly the opposite way for puts. Look at the chart again that we created for call options."

Stock Price: $40

Debit/Credit	Strike
14	25
11	30
8	35
5	40
3	45
2	50
1	55

"In this chart, which we created for Plum, the lower the strike price, the higher the debit/credit involved in making the deal. That's because, in the long call position, you want to be in a position to buy low and sell high, and you do so in that sequence. When the strike price is lower than the market price, you can buy my shares *at* that lower strike price (after all, you paid for the right to do that), and you can then turn around and sell them on the open market at the higher market price. So, as we learned, it's the *lower* strike prices that are worth money to you right out of the gate."

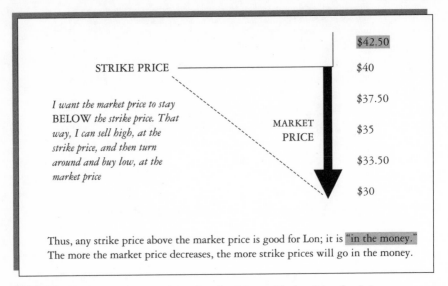

FIGURE 13.1   The Relationship of Strike Price to Market Price for Puts

"I see where you're headed," interrupted Lon. "In the case of long puts, it's just the opposite: it's the *higher* strike prices that have monetary value to me right out of the gate. I want the market price of the stock to move *lower* than the strike price. The idea here is that I pay you a debit for the right to sell you my shares at the strike price of $40. Then, if the stock moves lower, say to $30, I still get to sell you my shares at $40 and then turn around and *buy* shares on the market *for $30!* I'm still buying low and selling high; I just do it in reverse order: I first *sell to you* (at the high strike price), and then I can *buy from the market* at the lower market price. So when it comes to my long put, it's the higher strike prices that are good for me—that have tangible monetary value immediately. So here's what I want in a long put." (See Figure 13.1.)

"In fact," said Lon, "this whole buy low/sell high business is one way to remember the difference between long calls and long puts. In the long call, I'm setting myself up to *buy*, so I want to be able to buy low. Of course, it's the strike price I'm buying at, so obviously I want the *strike price* to be low in comparison to the market price—which means it is the *lower* strike prices that are in the money. And with puts, it's the opposite. In the long put, I'm setting myself up to *sell*, so I want to be able to sell *high*. Again, it's the strike price I'm selling at, so obviously I want the *strike price* to be high in comparison to the market price. I actually want the market price to move lower because that's how the strike price stays high, and allows me to *sell high*. Remembering, in general, that I want to buy low and sell high reminds me that I want low strikes for calls and high strikes for puts—low strikes for when I'm setting myself up to buy and high strikes for when I'm setting myself up to sell. And for our purposes here, that simply means that for puts the *higher* strike prices are the ones that are in the money."

"You know what this means, don't you—that strike directions are reversed for calls and puts?" asked Shorty.

"No, what?"

"It means that the relationship between the debit/credit amounts and strike prices will also be reversed," explained Shorty. "Since with puts the *higher* strike prices are worth money to you immediately, they're also the ones that are more valuable to you. And since higher strike prices are riskier for me, I will *demand* a higher credit to be willing to make a deal at a higher strike. So we can identify this relationship regarding puts: *the higher the strike price, the greater the debit/credit required to make a deal. The lower the strike price, the less the debit/credit required to make a deal.* Of course, as I said, that's exactly the opposite of the relationship with calls.

"So we have to amend our chart to show both calls *and* puts," he added. "Let's try this."

Stock Price: $40

CALLS		PUTS
Debit/Credit	Strike	Debit/Credit
$14	$25	$2
11	30	3
8	35	4
5	40	5
3	45	8
2	50	11
1	55	14

"Since calls and puts work just the opposite of each other," Shorty explained, "we have to show that in our chart and label them appropriately. Long *calls* are in the money when the strike price is lower than the market price (these debit/credit amounts are shaded). Long *puts* are in the money when the strike price is higher than the market price (these debit/credit amounts are shaded, too). Again, we define *in the money* in terms of what's good for you, since you're in the long position, and are therefore the one shelling out money to make the deal in the first place."

I'm still buying low and selling high: I'm just doing it in reverse order.

"Got it," affirmed Lon. "I get the relationship, and the chart seems to capture it. But I'm going to suggest a change in our terminology."

"What now?"

"All these elements of the chart are linked, so let's call it a chain. An *option chain*. What do you think?"

"Whatever," replied Shorty, too tired to argue. "If it works for you, it works for me. But let me make a point of my own about terminology. Again, you're buying this put from me, so you're long. It's a *long put* from your standpoint. As you said, you're buying the right to put your shares over to me to buy. And that means that I'm selling you this option, just like last time. I'm selling you the right to do that. So I guess we want to say that I'm short again. From my vantage point, this is a *short put*. I'm selling, or *shorting*, a put. And that means, like always, that this is a debit trade for you and a credit trade for me."

"Got it. Now let's create another review," said Lon.

REVIEW

"Again, the chart of strike prices is based on the idea of the _____ strike price appearing _____ on the list. So as we read more strike prices, down the list, the strike prices get _____. Now we decided to name strike prices in terms of what is good for the person who is _____. In the case of puts, strike prices that are higher than the market price of the stock are called _____. This is because they are worth _____ to me immediately. If the stock price moves _____ than the strike price, then I am able to _____ low and sell _____, *but in reverse order:* I first _____ to you at the _____ strike price, and then I'm able to _____ shares on the open market at the _____ market price. So an 'in-the-money' strike price, for puts, is one that is _____ the market price of the stock. By this same logic, a strike price that is _____ than the market price is _____. A strike price that is the same as the market price is _____.

"The _____ the strike price, the better the chance that it will end up in the money on this put trade. This means I am willing to _____ for higher strike prices.

"On your end, the _____ the strike price, the riskier the deal is: the _____ the chance that it will end up in the money and I will call out your shares. So the _____ the strike price, the _____ you will demand in a credit to make the trade.

"So it is the same for both of us when it comes to put trades: the _____ the strike price, the _____ the debit/credit amount will be involved in the trade.

"And this chart showing the relationship between strike prices and debit/credit amounts, for both calls and puts, is now called an _____.

"Finally, because I am doing a debit trade—I am buying—we can say I am placing a _____. And since you are doing a credit trade—you are selling—we can say you are placing a _____."

"Okay, now about the deal itself," continued Shorty. "Everything's fine except for one thing."

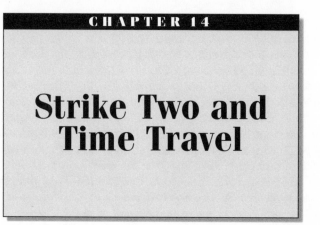

CHAPTER 14

Strike Two and Time Travel

"**W**hat's that?"

"Well, the time frame is a problem. I'll accept the $5-per-share credit and the $40 strike price, but I won't make a trade for longer than one month."

"Well, if the expiration period is only one month long, I'm not willing to pay $5 for it," replied Lon. "This is the same as with calls. The longer the time frame, the better my chances are, and the more I will be willing to pay to make a deal."

"Right. And because my risk *goes up* with longer time frames, I will *demand* more money to make a deal," replied Shorty. "So I guess this is a relationship we can predict for puts as well as for calls: *the longer the time frame of the deal, the greater the debit/credit required to make the deal.*"

"That's right. So where do we end up?" asked Lon. "What if I offer you a one-month expiration period, but a $2 credit. Will you take that?"

Shorty thought it through. *Over the next month, if the Nextall stock drops below the strike price of $40, say to $30, Lon will exercise his option, put his 100 shares to me, and force me to buy them at $40. I'll own his shares at a high price. Good deal for him; bad for me. But if the stock rises and stays above the strike price of $40, say around $45, then he won't exercise his option—again, he would be stupid to force me to buy his shares at our strike price of $40 when he can sell them on the market for $45. So I want a strike price that will stay lower than the market price for a month. The stock is selling at $40 right now; I think the stock will move up, but I have to be sure it stays above whatever strike price I agree to. That means I would be smart to pick a strike that* *will stay out of the money. I should go for a strike of, say, $35. Lon will probably insist on a credit of only $1.50 for a strike that low. But I'm sure the market price won't go that low, certainly not in a month, and I make a guaranteed $1.50 credit. The credit is small, but it's guaranteed, and the short amount of time is working in my favor: it increases the probability of the strike price staying out of the money—lower than the market price—and in that case I won't have to buy Lon's shares.*

"Tell you what," Shorty offered. "I'll agree to a strike price of $35 for a credit of $1.50 with a one-month expiration period. What do you think?"

Now Lon thought it through. *Over the next month, if the stock drops below the strike price of $35—and I think it will—I can put my shares to Shorty and force him to buy my 100 shares at $35. Say it drops to $30. If I pay Shorty $1.50 to make this deal, I make $3.50 per share: I sell the shares to Shorty at $35, and I can turn around and buy them on the market at $30; that's a $5 pick-up in my position. Of course, I have to subtract the $1.50 debit I paid Shorty to make the deal in the first place, but that still leaves a $3.50 net profit. That's a good return for one month. Time is working against me, but my debit is small, so my risk is small.*

"I'll take it," he announced. "So let's take a test for this idea, too."

REVIEW

"The longer the time frame I put around a trade, the _____ the chances I will be able to _____ high and _____ low. So the longer the time frame, the _____ my risk, and the _____ the debit I will be willing to pay for it.

"For you, the longer the time frame for the trade, the _____ the risk in the trade: the more likely I am to _____ to you and force _____. So the _____ the time frame, the _____ the credit you will _____."

CHAPTER 15

R&R for Lon

L on was eager to find Cass and explain the new trade he had made with Shorty.

"Look," he said, "I've done this option contract a different way this time. Doing only long calls, I was never able to find a way to make money, or at least reduce risk, when stocks went down. Long calls were great for bullish stocks, but not for bearish ones. But I've found a way around that now.

"Here's the deal we just made," he continued. "I expect Nextall stock to go down. The shares are now at $40 but could go as low as $30 or even $25. I've paid Shorty $1.50 per share to have the right to sell my shares to him anytime in the next month at $35! So even if the stock goes down, I can still sell my 100 shares at this $35 strike price."

It looks like the same principle as buying insurance on our home and cars. If something bad happens, we're protected.

"It looks like the same principle as buying insurance on our home and cars," observed Cass. "If something bad happens, we're protected. We pay a premium, sure, but it's worth it. Is this something like that?"

"Exactly. In this case, the debit I pay is like an insurance premium. Paying this debit to Shorty, I have the right to sell shares to him at a certain price even if the market price is lower. It's financial protection. We call this a *long put* (don't ask me why—there's a reason, but don't ask me), so I might even call this a *protective put.* It's a put that protects my investment."

COST BASIS

"What's your cost basis for this long put? Remember that category we created to help you keep track of your costs?" Cass asked.

"Right. Cost basis. Well, my cost basis would be the price I initially paid for the stock—$40—plus the debit I paid to Shorty—$1.50; $40 plus $1.50 is $41.50. That's how much I have invested in this trade; that's my cost basis."

REWARD

"And what's your maximum reward potential in this trade?" she asked.

"Well, first of all, I protect myself from losing. I paid $40 per share for this stock, so if the price goes to $25 I'll have a paper loss of $15. But with this long put, that won't happen. See, with this long put I can sell my shares at the $35 strike price, and if I want to, I can then turn around and buy more shares at the $25 market price! If you want to feel even better, think of it this way: the stock might go to zero in the next month, and if it does . . . I can still sell *my* shares for $35! Now, of course, I paid a $1.50 debit for the ability to do this, so my reward—if the stock did go to zero—would be $35 minus the $1.50 debit I paid, or $33.50."

> But with this long put, I'm insured. I'm still guaranteed to be able to sell my *shares to Shorty* for $35.

"That's your reward?"

"Well, that seems like one good way to look at my reward potential. See, in the real world—in the market—the stock is now worth zero. That's the value everyone else is stuck with. If they originally paid $40 like I did, *that's a $40 loss per share.* But with this long put, I'm insured. I'm still guaranteed to be able to sell *my* shares to Shorty *for $35.* Subtract the $1.50 debit I paid to guarantee this right and, in this scenario, I'm still ahead $33.50. At least compared to everyone else.

"It might help to show what actually happened to one company. So, let's take Bear Stearns, for example." (See Figure 15.1.)

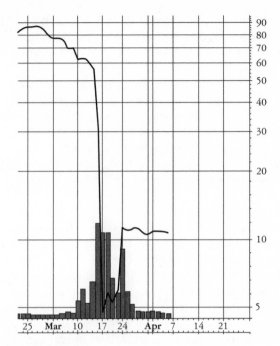

FIGURE 15.1 Bear Stearns
Source: Chart courtesy of StockCharts.com.

"On February 25, 2008, the stock was selling for nearly $90 per share. Less than a month later, on March 17, it was selling for $2 per share! That's an $88 loss, per share, in one month. That's 98 percent! If someone had bought 100 shares at that $90 price, their investment would have been $9,000, and by March 17 it would have plummeted in value to a mere $200. That's serious pain."

"Oh, I get it! What you're saying, then, is that if that same person had created a long put at the same time they bought their stock—at a strike price, say, of $85—they would still have been able to sell their shares *for $85* on March 17, even though everyone else was selling them for $2. That's how you're figuring the reward. You're comparing the strike price—what you can sell your shares for—with the actual market price."

"Right. That seems a good way to look at it to me. And since the share price, at least theoretically, can go all the way to zero, my profit *potential* in my deal with Shorty would be figured by comparing my strike price (minus whatever debit I paid for this long put) to zero."

"Okay, so it looks like your maximum reward in a deal of this type is (1) based on the possibility of the market price going to zero (which I can now see is actually possible), and (2) the strike price, whatever it is, minus the debit, whatever *that* is: in your deal with Shorty it's $35 minus $1.50, for a total reward potential of $33.50. Do I have it right?" asked Cass.

"That's how I'm thinking about it. Now notice, that's still an overall loss from where I started with Shorty. My cost basis is still $41.50 and I'm selling at $35. So I'm down $6.50. But, again, I'm calculating my reward by comparing what I can sell *my* shares for with what everyone else can sell *their* shares for. It's the same for that Bear Stearns investor. Suppose she had paid a $10 debit for her long put. With a strike price of $85, she could sell her shares for $85, which was $83 above the market price! We just subtract the $10 debit she paid to buy the put in the first place, and we have a $73 net reward. She comes out $73 better than the market. That's impressive."

"Makes long puts look pretty good!"

"Right. What Bear Stearns investor couldn't have benefited from this kind of trade? And I mean *hugely* benefited. Well, anyway, it's this kind of thing I'm doing in my latest deal with Shorty."

"Something I notice," said Cass, "is that in the case of this long put, or protective put as you called it, your reward is really capped: it's capped by the strike price you agreed to. You have a guarantee to be able to sell your Nextall shares at $35—but not at $40 or $50 or anything else. Thirty-five dollars is the maximum because that's what you agreed to when you agreed to the $35 strike price. Shorty is not obligated to pay you any more than that."

"Right," agreed Lon. "With the long calls, my reward potential was un-limited because the stock could go up dramatically in the time frame. In those deals, the strike price set the price at which I could *buy*. With this long put, on the other hand, the strike price sets the price at which I can *sell*. And that naturally caps my reward."

"But let's think about that a minute," said Cass. She was now focused intently on everything Lon was saying. "If you think about it, what you just said is true only if the stock actually goes down like you expect, and if you actually exercise your option to put your shares over to Shorty. In that case you can sell to *him* at no higher than the strike price. In that sense, true, you're capped. But what if you're wrong in your expectation and the stock price goes *up*? What if all your worry about protection is a mistake? In that case you still own the stock—and *it's growing* in value. *It's* not capped at all. As long as it's higher than the strike price, you can sell it to anyone, anytime you want, for whatever they'll pay."

"Oh, I see where you're headed. You're saying that there's a sense in which my potential reward is actually unlimited—at least theoretically—just because I own the stock. After all, the stock price could go up dramat-ically, just as you say. And in that case I would have a high stock price and only be out the debit of $1.50 I paid to Shorty to buy the put in the first place. I get it."

"Yep, that's true," Cass observed. She paused and pondered the matter for a full minute. Maybe longer. Lon waited.

Finally, she spoke. "But you know, as I think about it, your original way of describing the reward might be better. After all, if I understand everything correctly, you're buying this put for protection. That's the purpose. And if that's the case, then it really makes the most sense to think of the reward potential in terms of this purpose, namely, to provide protection. So it probably is best to do what you did just a minute ago: assume that the stock price could go to zero and compare that to the long put strike price—the amount of protection you've bought. Then you just subtract the debit you paid for the put, and that's your reward potential."

"Yeah, I guess you're right. I suppose we need to acknowledge that there's a sense in which the reward potential is unlimited—just by virtue of owning the stock—but given what I'm trying to *do* with this put, this other sense of reward is more relevant to me. It's the one I should always keep in mind."

RISK

"Okay, got it. That all makes sense now. But now tell me about your risk," she insisted. "Basically, you think of your reward potential in terms of the stock going down—of dropping below your $35 strike price. But what if the stock stays at $40 or goes above that—to $45 or $50? You think you're going to get a bearish trend, but suppose it turns bullish? What's the risk if that happens?"

> It's the same as with the long call: my only risk is the debit I pay to make the deal in the first place.

"Well, look. If the stock price stays stagnant or moves up, I just won't put my shares to Shorty and make him buy them. If I want to sell those shares, I'll do it on the open market where the price is higher than the $35 Shorty and I agreed to. In that case, I'm out the $1.50 I paid Shorty to make the deal. It's the same as with the long call: my only risk is the debit I pay to make the deal in the first place."

"Let me make sure we're together on this. Here's a review of our deal."

REVIEW

"Another term for my long put is a _____, because it _____ the stock I own. The _____ for my trade with Shorty is calculated by adding the _____ I paid to Shorty to the price of _____ I already own.

"Because I am paying a _____, this might be called a _____ trade.

"My maximum possible reward is calculated by considering what would happen if the market price of the stock went to _____. Based on that, I calculate my maximum possible reward by starting with my _____ and subtracting from it the _____ I paid to Shorty.

"My potential reward is _____ by the _____ Shorty and I agreed to. He is not obligated to _____ my shares at a price _____ than that. The reward potential for a long call is _____, but for a long put it is _____. The difference is that with a long put the _____ determines where I _____ and with a long call the _____ determines where I _____.

"My maximum risk in this trade is $_____. It is made up of _____ I paid to Shorty. I will lose this if the _____ stays _____, which means that the _____ price doesn't get higher than the _____ price."

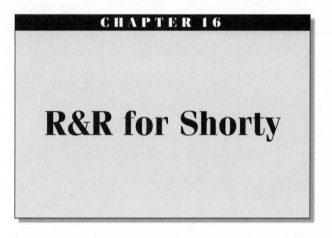

CHAPTER 16

R&R for Shorty

S horty was equally anxious to find Sharon.

"Look," he exclaimed, "I found a new way to make money. Lon and I call it *shorting put options.*"

"Doing *what?*"

"I know it sounds funny. All I mean is that I've found a new way to make money on deals where I'm selling something and taking in a credit. Here's what happened. I talked to Lon, and he wanted to enter a trade on Nextall, one of the stocks I own. I paid $40 for my 100 shares and they're currently trading at that. Well, Lon thinks the stock price might go down quite a bit, so he offered to pay me $1.50 per share to have the right to sell me his 100 shares at a strike price of $35. We decided to call this a *put* because he's buying the right to put his shares over to me, or on to me, and to force me to buy them. He's *long* just like last time because he's *buying* the right to do this; he's paying me in advance. I'm short because I'm *selling* him the right to do this. It's just a different kind of option contract.

"See," he continued, "Lon thinks the stock is going to move like this." Shorty took a piece of scrap paper and sketched a quick graph. "The solid line represents his expectation. The dotted line represents mine." (See Figure 16.1.)

REWARD

"Because Lon thinks Nextall's stock price is going to fall like this, he wants insurance against it. At a minimum he wants to be able to sell his shares for

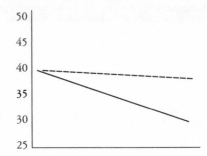

FIGURE 16.1 Lon's and Shorty's Expectations

$35 no matter what they happen to be selling for on the market, whether $25 or $20 or even $5.

"Well," Shorty continued, "as you can see, I don't think the stock price will go down that much, if at all, so we entered a deal where *I'm* the one selling Lon the insurance he wants. And I do that by promising him, for a fee of $1.50, that I will buy his shares at the $35 strike price if he puts them over to me anytime in the next month. Now think about it. If the strike price stays out of the money—if the market price stays higher than $35—Lon won't do this; he won't exercise his option. After all, why would he make me buy his shares at $35 if he could sell them on the open market for more than that? So if the stock stays higher than the $35 strike, I lose nothing and I gain the $1.50 per share he paid me. And it's all over in a month."

> *I lose nothing and gain the $1.50 per share he paid me. And it's all over in a month.*

"Okay, I see your reward here," replied Sharon, "you pocket the credit, and you do it in a short time period."

RISK

"But what about your risk? Based on what you're telling me, if the stock drops below $35, Lon can put his shares over to you and force you to buy them at $35—even though they're worth less. In fact, even if the stock goes to zero, you're still obligated to buy his shares for $35. That's an extreme possibility, but the general idea is still true: if the stock falls below $35, you will have to buy the stock at $35—which will be higher than the market price. That seems pretty bad to me."

> *I get more shares of a stock I like, and I get them at a pretty good price. And on top of all that, I get to keep the $1.50 credit Lon paid me in the first place.*

"You're right," he agreed. "That is my risk. I might be forced to buy Lon's 100 shares at $35. Of course, he's paid me $1.50 for the right to be able to do that, so that's a credit I've taken in. So my actual risk is the $35 minus the $1.50, for a total risk of $33.50.

"But look," Shorty continued, "that's precisely why I went for a low strike price—an *out-of-the-money* strike price. Notice, for example, that the lower the strike price, the less likely it is to go in the money in one month. Again, just as with my short calls, the short time frame is on my side. In addition, let's say the stock price drops significantly, say, to $30; well, then it *is* in the money, just as you've said, and Lon will exercise his option ... and I'll have to buy his shares at $35. But notice, I already own 100 shares of this stock at $40, because I think it's a good stock; I think it will increase over time. So if Lon puts his shares to me and forces me to buy them, I'm still getting them for less ($35) than I paid for my original shares ($40). It's actually not too bad. I get more shares of a stock I like, and I get them at a pretty good price. And on top of all that, I get to keep the $1.50 credit Lon paid me in the first place. So in a way I'm getting his 100 shares for $33.50—the $35 he's charging me minus the $1.50 credit he's already paid me. It's actually pretty good!"

"In other words, the only risk is that you might end up owning new shares of a stock you like, at a pretty good price, and pocketing the credit to boot. It does sound pretty good," she mused.

"Yes, but it all depends on getting the right strike price and a short time frame, not to mention doing this kind of deal only with a stock I like—one I wouldn't mind owning more shares of. Having all these in place is the only way to reach an acceptable level of risk. And you know what? That's exactly what I did in this case."

"Now let me create another review to make sure I've explained everything clearly."

REVIEW

"Because I am taking in a _____ from Lon, this might be called a _____ trade. My maximum reward is this _____. If the strike price stays out of the money, it will be _____ than the market price. In that case, Lon won't _____ to me and I will still get to keep _____. If the strike price trends in the money, then it will be _____ than the market price. In that case, Lon can _____ to me for a price of _____. So my risk in this trade is calculated by subtracting the _____ from our _____ price, which just means that I can end up owning _____ I _____ at a price of _____."

"Okay, I think I get this, but can you give me the big picture of what's going on in these trades you're making?" asked Sharon.

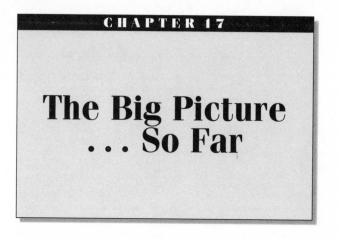

CHAPTER 17

The Big Picture ... So Far

66 **I** 'm getting the ideas piece by piece, but it would help to have some kind of picture or table I can refer to that will help me understand the *whole* better."

"Sure," replied Shorty. "Let me draw this table for you. See if it helps." (See Figure 17.1.)

"Now let's see if we can fill in the blanks," suggested Shorty. (See Figure 17.2.)

"When you look at it this way, you might say we've developed four option 'instruments,'" said Shorty.

"I see," agreed Sharon. "If you think a stock is going to trend either stagnant or bearish—stay even or go down in value—you can *optimize* that trend, so to speak, by doing a short call, or, you might say, by shorting a call. Since you like being in the selling position, this is great for you."

Between the two of us, we have four instruments to choose from: long call, short call, long put, short put.

"But that's not all," Shorty jumped in. "I can also optimize a bullish trend—a stock that is going up in value—by creating a short put, or by 'shorting a put.' I'm still in the selling position and taking in a credit, but I'm now able to profit on stocks that are bullish. As long as I'm willing to buy the stock, I'm okay."

<table>
<tr><td></td><td align="center">**Lon**
Long</td><td align="center">**Shorty**
Short</td></tr>
<tr>
<td>Call</td>
<td>

BUY THE RIGHT TO BUY ◄───────► **SELL THE OBLIGATION TO SELL**

- The *right* to call out and *buy* Shorty's shares at strike price
- The right to do this by the expiration date
- The right *not* to exercise this option

ℂ

- Pay a debit to enter this trade
- Good for bullish trends
- Good when stock trends ITM: when stock price is *higher* than strike price
- Good in longer time frames
- Goal: *be able to* BUY *Shorty's shares at lower than market price*
- Risk: the debit I pay to Shorty
- Reward: theoretically unlimited

</td>
<td>

- The *obligation* to *sell* shares at the strike price if called out by Lon
- The obligation to do this if called out by the expiration date

ℂ

- Receive a credit to enter this trade
- Good for bearish/stagnant trends
- Good when stock trends OTM: when stock price is *lower* than strike price
- Good in short time frames
- Goal: *have option* EXPIRE—*keep the credit and not have to sell shares to Lon at lower than market price*
- Risk: forced to sell shares at strike price (i.e., lower than market)
- Reward: the credit I take in from Lon

</td>
</tr>
<tr>
<td>Put</td>
<td>

BUY THE RIGHT TO SELL ◄───────► **SELL THE OBLIGATION TO BUY**

- The *right* to *put, or sell,* shares over to Shorty at the strike price
- The right to do this by the expiration date
- The right *not* to exercise this option

ℂ

- Pay a debit to enter this trade
- Good for bearish trends
- Good when stock trends ITM: when stock price is *lower* than strike price
- Good in longer time frames
- Goal: *be able to* SELL *shares to Shorty at higher than market price*
- Risk: the debit I pay to Shorty
- Reward: the strike I agreed to sell shares for, minus the debit I've already paid to Shorty

</td>
<td>

- The *obligation* to *buy* Lon's shares at the strike price if they are put to him
- The obligation to do this if they are put to him by the expiration date

ℂ

- Receive a credit to enter this trade
- Good for bullish trends
- Good when stock trends OTM: when stock price is *higher* than strike price
- Good in short time frames
- Goal: *have option* EXPIRE—*keep the credit and not have to buy shares from Lon at higher than market price*
- Risk: forced to buy shares at strike price (i.e., higher than market)
- Reward: the credit I take in from Lon

</td>
</tr>
</table>

FIGURE 17.1 Summary of Calls and Puts

	Lon Long	**Shorty** Short
Call	_____ ____ _______ ___ _____ • The *right* to _____ and _____ Shorty's shares at __________ • The right to do this by ___________ ________ • The right ______________ this option • Pay _________ to enter this trade • Good for _________ trends • Good when stock trends ___: when stock price is ______ than strike price • Good in _________ time frames • Goal: *be able to* _____ *Shorty's shares at* __________ *than market price* • Risk: _________ to ___________ • Reward: ______________________	_____ ___ ___________ ___ _____ • The *obligation* to ____ shares at the ________ if __________ by Lon • The obligation to do this if called out by ____________________ • Receive _______ to enter this trade • Good for _______________ trends • Good when stock trends ____: when stock price is ______ than strike price • Good in ______ time frames • Goal: *have option* _______—*keep the* ______ *and not have to* ___________ *at* __________ *than market price* Risk: forced to ________ at _______ _______ (i.e., _______ than _______) • Reward: the ________ I _________ from _______________
Put	______ _____ _________ ____ _______ • The *right* to ___, *or* ____, shares over to Shorty at _________________ • The right to do this by _____________ ______________________ • The right _______________ this option • Pay _________ to enter this trade • Good for _________ trends • Good when stock trends _____: when stock price is _______ than strike price • Good in ________ time frames • Goal: *be able to* ____ *shares to Shorty at* __________ *than market price* • Risk: __________ to ___________ • Reward: _________ I agreed to ______ ________ for, ______ the _____ I've _____________________	_______ _____ ___________ ___ ___ • The *obligation* to ____ Lon's shares at the __________ if _________ to him • The obligation to do this if they are put to him by ________________ • Receive a ________ to enter this trade • Good for ________ trends • Good when stock trends ____: when stock price is ______ than strike price • Good in ______ time frames • Goal: *have option* ______—*keep the* _______ *and not have to* ___________ *at* ________ *than market price* Risk: forced to ________ at _______ _______ (i.e., _______ than _____) • Reward: the ________ I _________ from ______________

FIGURE 17.2 Review of Calls and Puts

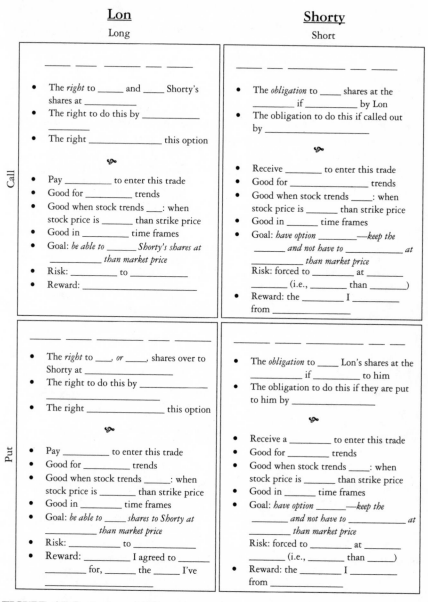

"And for Lon," said Sharon, "since he likes being in the buying position, he can profit on bullish stocks by doing long calls. And he can optimize bearish stocks by creating long puts. In both cases, he's buying something—the right either to buy stock or to sell it. Apparently, this type of option suits him perfectly."

"Between the two of us," observed Shorty, "we have four instruments to choose from: long call, short call, long put, short put. I guess someone who wasn't committed to just buying or selling all the time could actually use all four, depending what was best for them at the time."

"That seems right," she agreed.

"But you know, I think Lon's always gonna be long. And me, I think I'm always gonna be short."

CHAPTER 18

How Lon and Shorty Came Out on Their Deal

"Okay, Shorty," Lon laughed, "there's nothing I can do this time." One month had passed since they had entered their most recent option contract. In that time, Nextall stock had fallen from $40 to $37.50 but had not fallen below the strike price of $35. That meant Lon had no reason to put his shares over to Shorty and force him to buy them at $35: after all, Lon could sell those shares on the market for $37.50 if he wanted to. Since the one-month expiration period had passed, the option had simply expired.

"All right," answered Shorty. "So, let's review where we stand. I received a credit from you of $1.50, for a total of $150. If Nextall stock had dropped below $35 as you expected, you could have forced me to buy your shares for $35 and pocketed the difference as profit."

"As it is, though," replied Lon, "that didn't happen, so my option just ran out; obviously, you get to keep the $1.50 and you don't have to buy my shares. That makes it a good deal for you. You made 3.75 percent on your money ($1.50 / your $40 stock price), in one month, for doing nothing! But it was still a good deal for me, too, because during that month I had protection in case the stock fell as I expected it to. Insurance always costs a little money, but it's always worth it, and it sure didn't cost me much this time."

"I think you're right. It was a good deal for both of us. I made a little money in a short time, and you didn't have to pay much for your insurance. We both came out fine."

"And," said Lon, "we both would have come out fine even if the stock price had fallen below $35 and I had put my shares over to you. Let's suppose the price had fallen to $30. In that case I would have sold you my shares for $35—a $5 profit. Of course, since I already paid you $1.50, my profit would have been reduced by that much, leaving me a net profit of $3.50. That's a return of nearly 9 percent ($3.50/$40 investment). Pretty good in one month."

"Right," answered Shorty, "and in that case I would have bought your shares for $35. But notice, I like this stock for the long term, and I already paid $40 for my own shares earlier, so I would actually be getting these new shares at a lower price than I had paid before. In addition, I would still have the $1.50 you paid me up front—my credit. So I actually would have been buying your shares at a net cost of $33.50—$35 minus $1.50. So it would have been a good deal for me, too, even in that case."

"You know what?" said Lon. "I think we've found a way to trade with each other that allows us both to come out ahead. I thought that might be possible, but we're actually doing it. It's really kind of amazing."

"I agree. Let's keep it up."

STEP THREE

Ramping Up the Possibilities

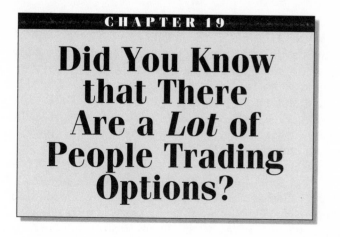

CHAPTER 19

Did You Know that There Are a *Lot* of People Trading Options?

"You guys have done a great job of figuring out how to trade with each other."

The speaker was Nathan (though he usually went by "Nate"), a roommate of Lon's from college. Lon smiled when he spoke, because his tone said, "I can't believe my goofy roommate, the one who couldn't do his trigonometry without asking me for help, has actually managed to figure out the stock market!" Nate was always too polite to say so, but Lon didn't mind his thinking it. It was true.

Lon had been scouring the Internet for information on investing and had happened across an intriguing site that, to his surprise, had featured his old friend. He knew that Nate had always been sort of an economics whiz, but he had never expected this kind of public profile. Eager to see all that Nate was up to, and to find out what he could learn about investing from him firsthand, Lon had finally made contact. After just a minute of explaining to Nate what he and Shorty were doing, Nate couldn't help laughing. "You don't know what you've gotten yourselves into," he had chuckled. "It's all good, believe me, but you're stepping into a whole new world. And you're going to need some help."

"Oh no, that sounds familiar. Just like when I was taking trig, right?"

"Something like that. Look, Lon, why don't we get together? I'll be near Wichita for a conference next month; I can take a couple of extra days and we can catch up. Then I can tell you a lot more about the kind of trades you and your friend are making. And, frankly, I want to hear more about how you two worked it all out."

And here he was. A famous financial expert impressed with him, project manager Lon, and his accountant friend Shorty. Surprised, yes, but also impressed. He now sat in Lon's study with his business partner, Aaron. Nate and Aaron had agreed to spend three evenings with Lon and Shorty, helping them use their ideas in the larger market. The four of them—Lon, Shorty, Nate, and Aaron—now sat around Lon's small office table.

"Option trading isn't actually as complicated as everyone thinks," Nate continued, "but it's pretty unusual to figure it out for yourselves. So we want to hear how you did it."

Lon and Shorty took turns describing their experience. Shorty had kept Lon's notes, so they went through the whole process. They were excited and rather proud of themselves, and they noticed that Nate and Aaron kept exchanging looks—of amazement, Lon hoped. Along the way, Lon shared the story of his brother-in-law, Bruce. He even mentioned the London, Nebraska, faux pas and his embarrassing blunders in China. Part of his motivation—he couldn't deny it—was to redeem himself with Cass . . . so he could start winning arguments again—at least some of them.

As they finished, Nate spoke.

"As I said, you've done a great job of figuring this out on your own, and it's impressive. Very creative and solid. But—I don't know how you'll take this—there are actually a lot of people already doing the same thing you're doing."

"At least, a lot of people compared to the two of you," said Aaron. "They're only a fraction of the total number of people with money in the market, but that fraction is growing. Fast. In fact, there's a whole industry that's grown up around option trading."

"Aargh," Lon threw his hands up. "You mean we didn't invent it?"

"Well, no, not really," Nate put in. "It's been done for years. But actually that's better. There's a well-developed, regulated system that lets people enter option contracts online with people they never see. You're not limited to trades that you both agree to; you can enter almost any trade because there will be someone wanting to make it. So, really, it's better this way. After all, you invest so you can make more money, not so you can be an inventor."

Speak for yourself, Lon thought.

"Yes, of course," Shorty agreed, but he was a little disappointed, too. They'd invested a lot of time and effort into something that turned out to be old news. "But to enter that system we'll have to learn all about how it works and a lot of new language, right? That's why you two are here."

To his surprise, Nate and Aaron both chuckled. Aaron said, "No, not exactly," while Nate chimed in, "I'm just here for old time's sake." He slapped Lon on the shoulder. Lon and Shorty exchanged questioning glances.

"What's funny," said Aaron, "is that you guys came up with the same chart, and even *precisely* the same terms, that the option market uses. So we're here to teach you how to use the real market and add knowledge to what you're already doing, but you actually don't need to change any of the terms you've got so far."

"You mean they use our words? *Long calls* and *short puts* and *option chains* and all that?"

"Yes, exactly."

"I don't believe it," said Lon. "Some of those terms hardly even made sense." Shorty grinned triumphantly.

"But you came up with *strike price*," he offered generously.

"It's the only decent term we use," he muttered under his breath. But Nate and Aaron had already moved on and pulled out some charts of their own.

"It really is amazing what you've done," said Nate. "Let me show you what a formal option chain looks like, for example." He pulled up on his laptop screen an actual option chain. (See Figure 19.1.)

"An option chain looks complicated, but it's actually easy to figure out if we learn one piece at a time," Nate continued. "We're not ready to examine every element of this option chain yet, but notice a few central features. Near the top of the page, for example, in the center, you see the current market price for this stock, $23.65. Now extending down the center of the page are the various strike prices. Notice how they go from low to high as you move down the page, just as you two did it."

Now it was Shorty's turn to object. "They really go from low to high? Unbelievable." And Lon grinned.

"So you can see," Nate went on, "that traders don't just come up with whatever strike price they want; *these* are the strike prices they choose from."

"Who decides what those prices will be?" asked Lon.

	Calls							Puts						
Symbol	Last	Chg	Bid	Ask	Imp. Vol	Delta	Strike	Symbol	Last	Chg	Bid	Ask	Imp. Vol	Delta
Dec 08 Calls		(211 days to expiration)			NVDA@23.65								Dec 08 Puts	
UVALC	7.80	0	9.30	9.50	57.0	.90	15.00	UVAXC	0.55	0	0.55	0.65	57.8	-.10
UVALT	7.53	+0.33	7.30	7.60	54.8	.83	17.50	UVAXT	1.10	0	1.05	1.15	54.9	-.17
UVALD	5.50	0	5.70	5.90	53.9	.74	20.00	UVAXD	1.95	-0.10	1.85	1.95	53.6	-.26
UVALX	4.30	+0.10	4.30	4.50	52.7	.64	22.50	UVAXX	3.00	0	2.90	3.00	52.1	-.36
UVALE	3.30	-0.10	3.20	3.40	52.1	.54	25.00	UVAXE	4.50	0	4.20	4.40	51.3	-.47
UVALY	2.50	+0.10	2.30	2.45	50.7	.43	27.50	UVAXY	6.00	+0.10	5.80	6.00	50.6	-.57
UVALF	1.70	+0.20	1.65	1.75	49.9	.34	30.00	UVAXF	6.50	0	7.60	7.80	49.9	-.66
UVALZ	1.15	0	1.15	1.25	49.3	.27	32.50	UVAXZ	9.80	+0.10	9.60	9.80	49.8	-.73

FIGURE 19.1 Option Chain
Source: Screenshot courtesy of optionsXpress, Inc. © 2008.

		Calls					**Strike**			**Puts**				
Symbol	Last	Chg	Bid	Ask	Imp. Vol	Delta	Strike	Symbol	Last	Chg	Bid	Ask	Imp. Vol	Delta
Dec 08 Calls			(211 days to expiration)				NVDA @ 23.65						**Dec 08 Puts**	
UVALC	7.80	0	9.30	9.50	57.0	.90	15.00	UVAXC	0.55	0	0.55	0.65	57.8	-.10
UVALT	7.53	+0.33	7.30	7.60	54.8	.83	17.50	UVAXT	1.10	0	1.05	1.15	54.9	-.17
UVALD	5.50	0	5.70	5.90	53.9	.74	20.00	UVAXD	1.95	-0.10	1.85	1.95	53.6	-.26
UVALX	4.30	+0.10	4.30	4.50	52.7	.64	22.50	UVAXX	3.00	0	2.90	3.00	52.1	-.36
UVALE	3.30	-0.10	3.20	3.40	52.1	.54	25.00	UVAXE	4.50	0	4.20	4.40	51.3	-.47
UVALY	2.50	+0.10	2.30	2.45	50.7	.43	27.50	UVAXY	6.00	+0.10	5.80	6.00	50.6	-.57
UVALF	1.70	+0.20	1.65	1.75	49.9	.34	30.00	UVAXF	6.50	0	7.60	7.80	49.9	-.66
UVALZ	1.15	0	1.15	1.25	49.3	.27	32.50	UVAXZ	9.80	+0.10	9.60	9.80	49.8	-.73

FIGURE 19.2 Elements of an Option Chain
Source: Screenshot courtesy of optionsXpress, Inc. © 2008.

"We'll get to that," said Aaron. "But first, let's go over the elements of the chart. (See Figure 19.2.)

"As you two have already figured out, the option chain needs to capture both calls and puts, because they behave differently. Calls are on the left and puts are on the right. Now you two have been talking in terms of debits and credits, and that's exactly right. When you're buying an option, Lon, you're paying a debit, and you're right to call that a debit trade. And when you're selling an option, Shorty, you are taking in a credit and that's called a credit trade, just as you have called it."

"But the language here is different," Shorty jumped in. "I don't see *credit* and *debit*. I see terms like *bid* and *ask*.

"Right. That's exactly where I was headed," replied Aaron. "The terms *bid* and *ask* refer to the same concept that *credit* and *debit* refer to. See, in the market in general, there is always this interaction between what buyers are *bidding* for a share of stock and what sellers are *asking* for a share of stock. That's why you always see these terms in reporting the action of any stock: bid price and ask price. It reflects the negotiation that is going on between buyers and sellers."

"So think of it this way," said Nate. "When we're trading options we're also dealing with bid and ask prices. Here, in the option industry, when we buy, we buy at the price that is being *asked*. When we want to be long, for example, we are buying, so the price we want to pay attention to is the *ask* price. This ask price is simply what our debit is in buying this option. And when we want to be short, we are selling, so the price we want to pay attention to is the *bid* price. That bid price is simply the credit we take in when we sell this option."

Nate saw furrowed brows on both Shorty and Lon.

"In our charts the debit and the credit amounts were always identical," Lon finally said, "but in this option chain, the bid and ask amounts are always different. Sometimes they're a nickel apart, and sometimes more, but they're never identical. Just look at the bid and ask amounts for any strike price, for either calls or puts. They're always different. Why is that? Where does that difference go?"

"Well," said Aaron, "there are many costs that go into facilitating these trades. As Nate mentioned a few minutes ago, there's a whole industry that has grown up around option trading. The industry works because there are people who bring all us traders together and provide the information we need to make our trades. The reason we can go online and trade with strangers instead of having to call up our buddies one at a time, is that these people—they're called market makers—set it all up, so to speak. They're the ones who set those prices we were talking about before, and otherwise handle the logistics of it all. Anyway, the upshot is that they take a cut of the transaction. That's where that nickel goes."

"Okay, that makes sense."

"Good. Now let's draw attention to just two more elements of the chain. Then, once we do an example or two, everything will click for you."

"The first," said Aaron, "is that the option chain identifies the month of expiration (December 2008). The second is that it also identifies the days *remaining* until expiration (211). Those are important. We won't talk about other elements of the option chain until later, but you should be familiar with these now."

"Based on this chain," said Nate, "let's suppose you want to place a long call at a strike of $25. The price you pay will be the ask price of $3.40. That's what the chain shows you. And Lon, that identifies your debit: $3.40. So see? The ask price simply tells you what your debit will be." (See Figure 19.3.)

"I get it," Shorty jumped in. "So if I want to sell an option—place a short call, for example—then I would sell at the *bid* price. I sell for the price that is being bid. Right?"

"That's right," replied Nate. "If you wanted to place a short call at a strike of $27.50 you would sell at the bid price of $2.30. And that's your credit: $2.30. The bid price simply tells you what credit you will take in." (See Figure 19.4.)

"One way to remember this is that you always buy on the right and sell on the left," said Aaron. "Another way to remember it is that you never put two 'Bs' together: you buy at the ask, and sell at the bid. You never 'buy at the bid'—two Bs together. You buy at the ask and sell at the bid." (See Figure 19.5.)

"I'll try to remember that," replied Lon. "No Bs together . . ." he murmured as he wrote it down. "I hope you don't mind, but I usually create

Symbol	Last	Chg	Bid	Ask	Imp. Vol	Delta	Strike	Symbol	Last	Chg	Bid	Ask	Imp. Vol	Delta
Calls								**Puts**						
Dec 08 Calls			(211 days to expiration)		NVDA@23.65								Dec 08 Puts	
UVALC	7.80	0	9.30	9.50	57.0	.90	15.00	UVAXC	0.55	0	0.55	0.65	57.8	-.10
UVALT	7.53	+0.33	7.30	7.60	54.8	.83	17.50	UVAXT	1.10	0	1.05	1.15	54.9	-.17
UVALD	5.50	0	5.70	5.90	53.9	.74	20.00	UVAXD	1.95	-0.10	1.85	1.95	53.6	-.26
UVALX	4.30	+0.10	4.30	4.50	52.7	.64	22.50	UVAXX	3.00	0	2.90	3.00	52.1	-.36
UVALE	3.30	-0.10	3.20	3.40	52.1	.54	25.00	UVAXE	4.50	0	4.20	4.40	51.3	-.47
UVALY	2.50	+0.10	2.30	2.45	50.7	.43	27.50	UVAXY	6.00	+0.10	5.80	6.00	50.6	-.57
UVALF	1.70	+0.20	1.65	1.75	49.9	.34	30.00	UVAXF	6.50	0	7.60	7.80	49.9	-.66
UVALZ	1.15	0	1.15	1.25	49.3	.27	32.50	UVAXZ	9.80	+0.10	9.60	9.80	49.8	-.73

FIGURE 19.3 Ask Price and the Debit
Source: Screenshot courtesy of optionsXpress, Inc. © 2008.

Symbol	Last	Chg	Bid	Ask	Imp. Vol	Delta	Strike	Symbol	Last	Chg	Bid	Ask	Imp. Vol	Delta
Calls								**Puts**						
Dec 08 Calls			(211 days to expiration)		NVDA@23.65								Dec 08 Puts	
UVALC	7.80	0	9.30	9.50	57.0	.90	15.00	UVAXC	0.55	0	0.55	0.65	57.8	-.10
UVALT	7.53	+0.33	7.30	7.60	54.8	.83	17.50	UVAXT	1.10	0	1.05	1.15	54.9	-.17
UVALD	5.50	0	5.70	5.90	53.9	.74	20.00	UVAXD	1.95	-0.10	1.85	1.95	53.6	-.26
UVALX	4.30	+0.10	4.30	4.50	52.7	.64	22.50	UVAXX	3.00	0	2.90	3.00	52.1	-.36
UVALE	3.30	-0.10	3.20	3.40	52.1	.54	25.00	UVAXE	4.50	0	4.20	4.40	51.3	-.47
UVALY	2.50	+0.10	2.30	2.45	50.7	.43	27.50	UVAXY	6.00	+0.10	5.80	6.00	50.6	-.57
UVALF	1.70	+0.20	1.65	1.75	49.9	.34	30.00	UVAXF	6.50	0	7.60	7.80	49.9	-.66
UVALZ	1.15	0	1.15	1.25	49.3	.27	32.50	UVAXZ	9.80	+0.10	9.60	9.80	49.8	-.73

FIGURE 19.4 Bid Price and Credit
Source: Screenshot courtesy of optionsXpress, Inc. © 2008.

Symbol	Last	Chg	Bid	Ask	Imp. Vol	Delta	Strike	Symbol	Last	Chg	Bid	Ask	Imp. Vol	Delta
Calls								**Puts**						
Dec 08 Calls			(211 days to expiration)		NVDA@23.65								Dec 08 Puts	
UVALC	7.80	0	9.30	9.50	57.0	.90	15.00	UVAXC	0.55	0	0.55	0.65	57.8	-.10
UVALT	7.53	0.33	7.30	7.60	54.8	.83	17.50	UVAXT	1.10	0	1.05	1.15	54.9	-.17
UVALD	5.50	0	5.70	5.90		.74	20.00	UVAXD	1.95	-0.10	1.85	1.95	53.6	-.26
UV		.10	4.30	4.50			22.50	UVAXX	3.00	0	2.90	3.00	52.1	-.36
U	"Short" Sell on the Left Sell at the Bid	10	3.20	3.4	"Long" Buy on the Right Buy at the Ask		25.00	UVAXE	4.50	0	4.20	4.40	51.3	-.47
U		10	2.30	2.45		43	27.50	UVAXY	6.00	+0.10	5.80	6.00	50.6	-.57
UVA		+0.20	1.65	1.75		.34	30.00	UVAXF	6.50	0	7.60	7.80	49.9	-.66
UVALZ	1.15	0	1.15	1.25	49.3	.27	32.50	UVAXZ	9.80	+0.10	9.60	9.80	49.8	-.73

FIGURE 19.5 Short: Bid Price/Long: Ask Price
Source: Screenshot courtesy of optionsXpress, Inc. © 2008.

a review for myself when we've developed something new. I'll want to do that tonight, too."

"Of course," said Aaron. "That's very important; it's probably why you two were able to work this out so well. Trading options may not be as difficult as some think, but there's a lot to keep track of, and if you hadn't been careful about memorizing the basics, you probably wouldn't have gotten this far."

"So here's a way to designate our long and short calls," added Nate. "The short call at a bid of $2.30 and the long call at an ask of $3.40." (See Figure 19.6.)

"In other words," continued Nate, "this chain tells us that if we chose a $25 strike price and wanted to place a long call, we would *buy* at the ask price of $3.40. If we chose a $27.50 strike price, and wanted to place a short call, we would *sell* at the bid price of $2.30."

"Right," said Shorty. "And if we wanted to place a long call at a strike of $27.50, we would buy at the ask price of $2.45. And if we wanted to place a short call at a strike of $25, we would sell at the bid price of $3.20. It's all there on the chain. We just read over to the correct column (bid or ask), based on the strike price we choose."

"Okay, good," said Aaron. "Now notice that the same thing happens on the put side of the option chain." (See Figure 19.7.)

"I see," said Lon. "If I want to place a long put, I'm buying, so the price I pay is the ask price. If I place a long put at a strike of $22.50, I will pay the ask price of $3. That's my debit."

"And if I want to place a short put at a strike price of $25, I will sell at the bid price of $4.20," Shorty jumped in. "That's the credit I take in."

	Calls							Puts						
Symbol	Last	Chg	Bid	Ask	Imp.Vol	Delta	Strike	Symbol	Last	Chg	Bid	Ask	Imp.Vol	Delta
Dec 08 Calls			(211 days to expiration)		NVDA@23.65								Dec 08 Puts	
UVALC	7.80	0	9.30	9.50	57.0	.90	15.00	UVAXC	0.55	0	0.55	0.65	57.8	-.10
UVALT	7.53	+0.33	7.30	7.60	54.8	.83	17.50	UVAXT	1.10	0	1.05	1.15	54.9	-.17
UVALD	5.50	0	5.70	5.90	53.9	.74	20.00	UVAXD	1.95	-0.10	1.85	1.95	53.6	-.26
UVALX	4.30	+0.10	4.30	4.50	52.7	.64	22.50	UVAXX	3.00	0	2.90	3.00	52.1	-.36
UVALE	3.30	-0.10	3.20	3.40	52.1	.54	25.00		Long Call				51.3	-.47
UVALY	2.50	+0.10	2.30	2.45	50.7	.43	27.50		Short Call				50.6	-.57
UVALF	1.70	+0.20	1.65	1.75	49.9	.34	30.00	UVAXF	6.50	0	7.60	7.80	49.9	-.66
UVALZ	1.15	0	1.15	1.25	49.3	.27	32.50	UVAXZ	9.80	+0.10	9.60	9.80	49.8	-.73

FIGURE 19.6 Long and Short Calls
Source: Screenshot courtesy of optionsXpress, Inc. © 2008.

	Calls						Puts						
Symbol	Last	Chg	Bid	Ask	Imp. Vol	Delta	Strike	Symbol	Last	Chg	Bid	Ask	Imp. Vol	Delta
Dec 08 Calls			(211 days to expiration)			NVDA@23.65							Dec 08 Puts	
UVALC	7.80	0	9.30	9.50	57.0	.90	15.00	UVAXC	0.55	0	0.55	0.65	57.8	-.10
UVALT	7.53	+0.33	7.30	7.60	54.8	.83	17.50	UVAXT	1.10	0	1.05	1.15	54.9	-.17
UVALD	5.50	0	5.70	5.90	53.9	.74	20.00	UVAXD	1.95	-0.10	1.85	1.95	53.6	-.26
UVALX	4.30		**Long Put**				22.50	UVAXX	3.00	0	2.90	(3.00)	52.1	-.36
UVALE	3.30		**Short Put**				25.00	UVAXE	4.50	0	(4.20)	4.40	51.3	-.47
UVALY	2.50	+0.10	2.30	2.45	50.7	.43	27.50	UVAXY	6.00	+0.10	5.80	6.00	50.6	-.57
UVALF	1.70	+0.20	1.65	1.75	49.9	.34	30.00	UVAXF	6.50	0	7.60	7.80	49.9	-.66
UVALZ	1.15	0	1.15	1.25	49.3	.27	32.50	UVAXZ	9.80	+0.10	9.60	9.80	49.8	-.73

FIGURE 19.7 Long and Short Puts
Source: Screenshot courtesy of optionsXpress, Inc. © 2008.

"That's exactly right," Aaron agreed. "Again: buy at the ask, sell at the bid; buy to the right, sell to the left. As you just said, Shorty, you just pick the strike price you want and then read over to the correct column—bid or ask."

"I notice," said Lon, "that these bid/ask prices are shaded, just like Shorty and I shaded these numbers."

"And for exactly the same reason," said Nate. "The shading tells you which strike prices are currently in the money."

"Right," said Shorty. "And on the call side of the page—the left side—all the bid/ask amounts corresponding to the strike prices *below* the current market price are in the money: they're shaded. That's exactly how we did it."

"And the put side of the page—the right side—is just the opposite," interjected Lon. "The bid/ask amounts corresponding to the strike prices *above* the current market price are all in the money and are therefore shaded."

"Yes, and *in the money, out of the money,* and *at the money* are defined just as you defined them," said Aaron. "Whatever strike prices have immediate monetary value for the *long* person are called *in the money,* for both calls and puts. They're the strike prices that are worth money to him immediately."

"Notice, too," said Nate, "that *in-the-money* strike prices have higher bid/ask prices. The more in the money a strike price is, the more valuable it is to the person in the long position and the more he will be willing to pay for it. At the same time, the more in the money a strike price is, the riskier it is to the person shorting the option, so the more he will demand to be paid for it. That's why you see this relationship for both calls and puts." (See Figure 19.8.)

	Calls						Strike		Puts					
Symbol	Last	Chg	(Bid)	(Ask)	Imp. Vol	Delta	Strike	Symbol	Last	Chg	(Bid)	(Ask)	Imp. Vol	Delta
Dec 08 Calls			(211 days to expiration)				NVDA@23.65						**Dec 08 Puts**	
UVALC	7.80	0	9.30	9.50	57.0	.90	15.00	UVAXC	0.55	0	0.55	0.65	57.8	-.10
UVALT	7.53	+0.33	7.30	7.60	54.8	.83	17.50	UVAXT	1.10	0	1.05	1.15	54.9	-.17
UVALD	5.50	0	5.70	5.90	53.9	.74	20.00	UVAXD	1.95	-0.10	1.85	1.95	53.6	-.26
UVALX	4.30	+0.10	4.30	4.50	52.7	.64	22.50	UVAXX	3.00	0	2.90	3.00	52.1	-.36
UVALE	3.30	-0.10	3.20	3.40	52.1	.54	25.00	UVAXE	4.50	0	4.20	4.40	51.3	-.47
UVALY	2.50	+0.10	2.30	2.45	50.7	.43	27.50	UVAXY	6.00	+0.10	5.80	6.00	50.6	-.57
UVALF	1.70	+0.20	1.65	1.75	49.9	.34	30.00	UVAXF	6.50	0	7.60	7.80	49.9	-.66
UVALZ	1.15	0	1.15	1.25	49.3	.27	32.50	UVAXZ	9.80	+0.10	9.60	9.80	49.8	-.73

FIGURE 19.8   Strike Prices and Bid/Ask Amounts
Source: Screenshot courtesy of optionsXpress, Inc. © 2008.

"Okay, I think I get it," said Lon. "It's pretty much like our own chart, but we've also learned about bid and ask prices. I think I'd like a quick review at this point, if you don't mind."

"Of course not," said Aaron. "I'll ask you some questions about this chart," he said, pulling out a new one, "and we'll see how you do."

REVIEW

Symbol	Last	Chg	Bid	Ask	Imp. Vol	Delta	Strike	Symbol	Last	Chg	Bid	Ask	Imp. Vol	Delta
Jun 08 Calls			(29 days to expiration)				NOK@28.94						**Jun 08 Puts**	
NAYFE	3.90	0	3.90	4.10	26.3	.98	25.00	NAYRE	0.15	+0.03	0.05	0.15	36.5	-.07
NAYFZ	3.80	0	3.00	3.20	30.1	.90	26.00	NAYRZ	0.20	-0.05	0.15	0.25	35.3	-.13
NAYFA	2.25	0	2.25	2.40	32.8	.79	27.00	NAYRA	0.35	-0.05	0.35	0.40	34.2	-.22
NAYFB	1.60	+0.05	1.55	1.65	31.8	.67	28.00	NAYRB	0.65	-0.15	0.60	0.70	32.9	-.34
NAYFC	0.96	-0.09	1.00	1.10	31.8	.52	29.00	NAYRC	1.10	-0.15	1.05	1.10	32.2	-.48
NAYFF	0.60	0	0.60	0.65	31.3	.37	30.00	NAYRF	1.60	+0.10	1.65	1.75	33.4	-.62
NAYFW	0.35	-0.05	0.30	0.40	31.2	.24	31.00	NAYRW	2.30	+0.10	2.35	2.50	33.7	-.74
NAYFS	0.23	-0.02	0.15	0.25	32.0	.15	32.00	NAYRS	3.20	+0.35	3.20	3.50	38.7	-.80
NAYFT	0.10	-0.05	0.05	0.15	31.9	.09	33.00	NAYRT	3.70	0	4.10	4.40	40.9	-.85
NAYFV	0.10	0	0.05	0.10	34.9	.06	34.00	NAYRV	4.10	0	5.00	5.30	40.8	-.90
NAYFG	0.05	0	0	0.10	36.8	.04	35.00	NAYRG	5.80	0	6.00	6.30	46.2	-.91

Source: Screenshot courtesy of optionsXpress, Inc. © 2008.
Review

1. Where is the call information found on this page?
2. Where is the put information found?
3. What would I pay for a call at a $30 strike?
4. What would I receive for a call at a $31 strike price?
5. What would I pay for a put at a $27 strike?
6. What would I receive for a put at a $28 strike?
7. What strikes are in the money for calls? Why are they called "in the money"?
8. What strikes are in the money for puts? Why are they called "in the money"?
9. Just for grins: if I bought a put at a strike of $28 and sold a put at a strike of $26, what would be the difference between what I pay out and what I take in?
10. Just for grins: if I bought a call at a strike of $29 and sold a call at a strike of $31, what would be the difference between what I pay out and what I take in?

"Now let me show you something that you two thought about a little bit—and that is really important in the option industry."

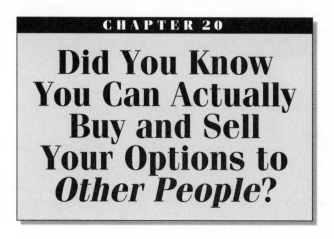

CHAPTER 20

Did You Know You Can Actually Buy and Sell Your Options to *Other People*?

Nate pulled up additional option chains on his laptop screen. "Look at these chains for different months," he said. "What do you notice about the relationship between time frame and the bid/ask amounts? I've helped by identifying one strike price over three months." (See Figure 20.1.)

"Well, the bid/ask amounts are different for the same strike price in different months," answered Shorty. "And that's true for both calls and puts."

"Specifically," added Shorty, "the further out you go in time, the higher the bid/ask amounts get. Again, for both calls and puts. It's just like we thought."

"Yeah, but we were just speculating about what would happen if you and I were negotiating. This looks a lot more systematic than that."

"And it is," said Aaron. "The whole relationship between strike prices, stock prices, bid/ask amounts, and time frame is systematic—*and* complicated. But for now it's sufficient to understand that time is critical in determining the value of an option . . . so you have to pay attention to it. Other things equal, the more time an option has before expiration, the more valuable it is."

"There's something else you should know at this stage of the game that is extremely important," added Nate. "In fact, it's the central fact that drives option trading. It's the relationship between movement in the stock price and movement in the option price. Think, for example, of a long call. Let's say you place an October long call on this stock at a strike price of $50. You pay a $4.50 debit for that—the ask price of that long call.

Symbol	Last	Chg	Bid	Ask	Imp. Vol	Delta	Strike	Symbol	Last	Chg	Bid	Ask	Imp. Vol	Delta
Jun 08 Calls		(29 days to expiration)			GRMN@46.28								Jun 08 Puts	
GQRFX	19.50	0	23.50	24.00		1.00	22.50	GQRRX	0	0	0	0.05	105.4	-.01
GQRFE	17.30	0	21.00	21.50		1.00	25.00	GQRRE	0.10	0	0	0.05	91.1	-.01
GQRFF	16.50	-0.70	16.00	16.50		1.00	30.00	GQRRF	0.05	0	0	0.10	72.6	-.01
GQRFG	11.05	+0.04	11.10	11.60	41.1	.99	35.00	GQRRG	0.10	-0.04	0.05	0.10	52.7	-.03
GQRFH	6.70	+0.20	6.70	7.00	50.7	.88	40.00	GQRRH	0.50	0	0.45	0.55	50.6	-.14
GQRFI	3.05	+0.15	3.00	3.20	45.4	.62	45.00	GQRRI	1.75	-0.20	1.75	1.85	46.4	-.39
GQRFJ	0.95	0	0.95	1.05	43.5	.29	50.00	GQRRJ	4.78	-0.32	4.50	4.70	42.7	-.71
GQRFK	0.25	0	0.20	0.30	43.7	.10	55.00	GQRRK	9.80	0	8.70	9.00	42.3	-.91
GQRFL	0.05	-0.05	0.05	0.10	47.0	.03	60.00	GQRRL	13.68	0	13.50	14.10	55.0	-.94
GQRFM	0.05	0	0	0.05	50.6	.01	65.00	GQRRM	18.70	+3.81	18.50	18.90	60.0	-.97
Jul 08 Calls		(57 days to expiration)			GRMN@46.28								Jul 08 Puts	
GQRGE	18.57	0	21.10	21.60		1.00	25.00	GQRSE	0.05	+0.03	0	0.10	71.7	-.01
GQRGF	16.60	0	16.20	16.70	55.6	.98	30.00	GQRSF	0.11	0	0.05	0.20	60.5	-.03
GQRGG	11.10	0	11.60	11.90	53.1	.93	35.00	GQRSG	0.40	-0.10	0.35	0.45	54.7	-.08
GQRGH	7.30	+0.30	7.40	7.70	50.4	.80	40.00	GQRSH	1.15	-0.15	1.15	1.25	51.4	-.20
GQRGI	4.20	+0.30	4.10	4.30	47.6	.60	45.00	GQRSI	2.81	-0.19	2.75	2.90	48.3	-.40
GQRGJ	1.90	0	1.90	2.00	45.1	.37	50.00	GQRSJ	5.50	-0.50	5.50	5.70	46.4	-.62
GQRGK	0.80	0	0.75	0.90	44.9	.20	55.00	GQRSK	9.50	-0.70	9.30	9.60	46.4	-.79
GQRGL	0.35	+0.05	0.30	0.40	45.8	.09	60.00	GQRSL	11.50	0	13.70	14.30	49.5	-.89
GQRGM	0.15	0	0.10	0.20	47.1	.04	65.00	GQRSM	19.00	+1.50	18.60	19.00	53.4	-.93
GQRGN	0.15	0	0	0.15	49.5	.02	70.00	GQRSN	23.30	0	23.50	24.10	62.8	-.94
Oct 08 Calls		(148 days to expiration)			GRMN@46.28								Oct 08 Puts	
GQRJE	18.50	0	21.20	21.70		1.00	25.00	GQRVE	0.30	0	0.25	0.35	60.8	-.04
GQRJF	16.70	-2.50	16.60	17.20	47.9	.94	30.00	GQRVF	0.85	0	0.80	0.90	59.6	-.09
GQRJG	12.30	0	12.50	13.00	48.7	.86	35.00	GQRVG	1.85	0	1.70	1.85	57.1	-.17
GQRJH	8.80	+0.20	9.00	9.50	48.7	.74	40.00	GQRVH	3.40	0	3.20	3.40	55.5	-.27
GQRJI	6.30	+0.20	6.20	6.60	48.0	.61	45.00	GQRVI	5.40	-0.10	5.40	5.70	55.0	-.39
GQRJJ	4.20	+0.02	4.10	4.50	47.8	.47	50.00	GQRVJ	8.50	-0.30	8.20	8.60	54.4	-.51
GQRJK	2.75	+0.11	2.75	2.95	47.9	.35	55.00	GQRVK	12.10	-0.10	11.70	12.10	54.8	-.62
GQRJL	1.65	0	1.70	1.85	47.2	.25	60.00	GQRVL	15.07	0	15.60	16.10	55.7	-.70
GQRJM	1.05	+0.05	1.00	1.15	46.6	.17	65.00	GQRVM	18.70	0	19.90	20.40	57.2	-.77
GQRJN	0.60	-0.05	0.60	0.75	46.7	.11	70.00	GQRVN	22.70	0	24.50	25.00	60.0	-.81

FIGURE 20.1 Time Frame and Bid/Ask Amounts
Source: Screenshot courtesy of optionsXpress, Inc. © 2008.

> *If the market price of the stock moves up, the price of that long call will move up, too.*

"Now if the market price of the stock moves up," continued Nate, "*the price of that long call will move up, too.* There are exceptions to this, but this basic relationship is all you need to know right now: generally speaking, as the value of the stock increases, the value of the call will increase, too. And that means it will become more expensive to buy a call at that strike price. If the stock price has moved to $60, then a $50 strike price is way in the money. It is now very attractive to pay the strike price of $50 for shares of stock because the stock is actually worth $60. And as you two discovered, more money will always be involved in trading options when the strike price is in the money: an in-the-money strike price is more valuable to the person in the long position, and it's riskier for the person in the short position. The first will be *willing* to pay more for it, and the second will *demand* more for it."

"Now let's be explicit about what this means," said Aaron. "It means that that long call, generally speaking, becomes more valuable as the stock becomes more valuable. In a month, if the stock price has moved up, say, to $60, then the price of a long call at a strike of $50 will also move up. Then it will cost more to buy this long call than it would cost today. *The long call itself has become more expensive.*"

"And notice what this means," Nate added. "(1) If I place this long call today at a price of $4.50, and (2) if the market price of the stock goes to $60, then (3) the price of this same long call will also increase—perhaps to $6 or $7, which means (4) that I can actually turn around and *sell my option to someone else—at the* NEW *option price.*"

"You mean I have the right to actually sell my long call to someone else? I entered a contract with Shorty, and I can actually turn around and sell that contract to someone else for a profit?" asked Lon.

"Exactly," said Aaron. "See, you did a good job of identifying your rights before, because you didn't realize that there's a whole industry of option trading out there and that there are thousands of people you can make deals with. So you actually have a right you didn't know you had: the right to sell your option to someone else. You pocket the profit, and now they have the rights that you have had up to now—including the right to *re*sell the option to someone else *themselves.*"

> *I can actually turn around and sell my option to someone else—at the* new *option price.*

"This is overwhelming," remarked Lon. "On a long call, as the stock price moves up, the value of the option itself moves up, which means I can actually sell the option to someone else and make a profit on it—all without touching the stock itself. And *they* can do the same thing. Amazing."

"Okay, I think I get this on long calls," said Shorty a bit impatiently. "If I make a deal with Lon—for example, on this stock for a $50 strike price, and if the market price moves up—he might actually sell his part of our contract to someone else to make a profit on *that*. So it might be this next person who actually exercises the option to buy my shares at the $50 strike price."

"Right. The value of the option increases, and becomes an opportunity to make a profit. Of course, the opposite must be true if the value of the stock goes *down*: the value of the option will go down, too," said Lon.

"Yes," assured Aaron. "If you pay $4.50 to be able to buy shares at a $50 strike, and the stock price goes down to $40, the right to buy shares for a $50 strike price is no longer attractive. That means, generally speaking at least, that the price of this option will go down, too, because its value has gone down. On the option chain, it will no longer be listed at $4.50, but at something much lower."

"And in that case, I wouldn't be able to sell it for a profit," said Lon. "I would be stuck with a stock that has gone down in value and with an option that has gone down in value, too."

"And that means that no one will exercise their right to buy my shares at $50," said Shorty. "I get to keep the credit that Lon paid me to enter the trade *and* I get to keep my shares of stock."

"Right," said Nate, "and for now that's the main thing to remember about your short call. Lon is looking for his long call to increase in value so he can sell it for a profit. But that's not what you're doing; you've structured a deal where you make money if *nothing* happens. Basically, you just want time to run out so you can keep your shares and the credit you received. As we say, you want the option to 'expire worthless.' You already figured this out on your own. It works the same way in the wider option industry."

"Okay, all that's clear," said Lon, "but what about puts? How does all this work with puts?"

"Well, think about it," said Nate. "Lon, you like to do long puts. Why is that?"

> *The basic strategy of trading options, is . . . well, trading options. You make money by buying and selling the options themselves.*

"Because they offer protection. Let's say I own this stock, which is trading today at about $46 and I think it could go down—maybe an earnings report is coming up or something like that. Well, then I could place a July long put at a strike price of perhaps $45, and pay a $2.90 debit for it (the ask price). Then, if the market price actually went down to $35 or whatever, I would have the right to sell my shares at $45."

"Okay, good," answered Nate, "but what then do you think happens to the value of that option itself—the option to be able to sell at $45? Do you think it would be more valuable, or less, if the stock were trading at $35?"

"It would be more valuable," answered Lon, suddenly seeing the point. "To put it simply, the worse the stock is doing, the more valuable the insurance on it would be."

"That's right," said Nate. "Again, there can be exceptions, but right now the general relationship is what's important: with puts, the value of the long put goes up as the value of the stock goes down. The more such insurance is needed, the more valuable it is—and the higher its price. Whereas you paid $2.90 for it initially, it might now be worth $5 or $6."

"I get it!" exclaimed Shorty. "And now Lon could turn around *and sell the long put for a profit*. He bought it for $2.90 and could now sell it for $5 or $6. And all without touching the underlying stock."

"Yes, you're beginning to get it," remarked Nate. "The basic strategy of trading options is . . . well, *trading options*. You make money by buying and selling the options themselves."

"And as far as increasing and decreasing value goes, notice that the situation with puts mirrors the situation with calls," said Aaron. "Generally speaking, if the stock price goes up, the value of the long put will *go down*. If the stock price stays around $46, or perhaps rises above it, the value of being able to *sell* it at $45 goes way down. And that would be reflected in the option chain. You wouldn't be able to sell this insurance for as much as you paid for it."

"But that's not a problem," Nate jumped in, "because the main thing is that the put protected you *while* you had it. And now if you do sell your put, you at least recoup some of what you paid for it. So suppose you paid $2.90 for the put initially and you now sell it for $1; well, that $1 at least recoups some of your original investment. You paid $2.90 and now you get $1 of that back. And that means that the cost of your insurance actually turns out to be $1.90 rather than $2.90. Right? $2.90 minus $1 equals $1.90. That's a pretty good deal."

"Right," said Aaron. "The cost of the put is not a problem. But it's important for you to understand that long puts can lose value just as long calls can. They just lose value for opposite reasons: generally speaking, long puts lose value when the stock goes up (because insurance is then less needed and is therefore less valuable) and long *calls* lose value when the stock goes down (because the strike price I have the right to buy at is now closer to—or perhaps even higher than—the stock price for which I can buy shares on the open market)."

"Unfortunately," Nate added, "we can't tell you how to predict exactly how an option price will change over time as the stock price changes. There's a mathematical relationship, called a *delta*, that identifies the exact amount an option value will change as the stock value changes: for

Symbol	Last	Chg	Bid	Ask	Imp. Vol	Delta	Strike	Symbol	Last	Chg	Bid	Ask	Imp. Vol	Delta
Jun 08 Calls			(29 days to expiration)				GRMN@46.28							Jun 08 Puts
GQRFX	19.50	0	23.50	24.00		1.00	22.50	GQRRX	0	0	0	0.05	105.4	-.01
GQRFE	17.30	0	21.00	21.50		1.00	25.00	GQRRE	0.10	0	0	0.05	91.1	-.01
GQRFF	16.50	-0.70	16.00	16.50		1.00	30.00	GQRRF	0.05	0	0	0.10	72.6	-.01
GQRFG	11.05	+0.04	11.10	11.60	41.1	.99	35.00	GQRRG	0.10	-0.04	0.05	0.10	52.7	-.03
GQRFH	6.70	+0.20	6.70	7.00	50.7	.86	40.00	GQRRH	0.50	0	0.45	0.55	50.6	-.14
GQRFI	3.05	+0.15	3.00	3.20	45.4	.62	45.00	GQRRI	1.75	-0.20	1.75	1.85	46.4	-.39
GQRFJ	0.95	0	0.95	1.05	43.5	.29	50.00	GQRRJ	4.78	-0.32	4.50	4.70	42.7	-.71
GQRFK	0.25	0	0.20	0.30	43.7	.10	55.00	GQRRK	9.80	0	8.70	9.00	42.3	-.91
GQRFL	0.05	-0.05	0.05	0.10	47.0	.03	60.00	GQRRL	13.68	0	13.50	14.10	55.0	-.94
GQRFM	0.05	0	0	0.05	50.6	.01	65.00	GQRRM	18.70	+3.81	18.50	18.90	60.0	-.97

FIGURE 20.2   Delta
Source: Screenshot courtesy of optionsXpress, Inc. © 2008.

example, a delta of 0.5 would mean that the option value would change $0.50 for every $1 change in the stock price. In fact, the delta appears on the option chains we have been showing you. Have a look." (See Figure 20.2.)

"The delta for calls is expressed as a positive decimal, while the delta for puts is expressed as a negative decimal. That difference doesn't matter. In both cases the delta simply identifies the exact amount an option value will change as the stock value changes. For example, if the delta is .29, as it is for calls at the $50 strike, it means that the value of the call option will change $0.29 for every $1 change in the stock price. If the stock price goes up $1, the option value will go up $0.29. And if the stock price goes down $1, the option value will go *down* $0.29. That's what the delta tells us: how much the option will change as the stock value changes."

"Now there's one thing you have to know about this delta," added Aaron. "*It changes all the time.* The delta for a particular option doesn't stay at 0.29 or 0.62 or −0.14—or anything else. It changes as a function both of stock price movement and of time, and the whole thing is pretty complicated. Fortunately, you can find out the *current* delta on any given strike price, but, as I said, the delta itself changes and that makes predictions inexact."

"Okay, I think I've got that. But I want to get back to how I make a profit. Lon can sell his long puts just like he can sell his long calls. What about my short puts; are they the same as my short calls? It seems like it; I just want to make sure."

In a long put, the value of the put increases as the stock decreases—this is just the nature of insurance.

"Yes," answered Aaron. "Just as with his long calls, Lon can make a profit by selling his long puts. But, just like with your short calls, you've structured a different kind of deal, based on a different expectation: you have a deal that will make money if *nothing* happens. Here, as with your short call, you just want time to run out. Then you get to keep the credit you took in and no one forces you to buy any shares of stock. Again, we say that the option 'expires worthless.' That's good for you, and that's the starting point for thinking about your short puts. Again, this is no different than what you already figured out on your own."

"Okay, give me a minute to summarize what I've learned," said Lon. "First, time is an important factor in determining the value of an option. I need to pay close attention to that. I don't know exactly how to pay attention to time yet, but I know it's crucial. Second, I've learned that the option value changes with stock value. In a long call, the value of the call increases as the stock increases. In a long put, the value of the put increases as the stock *decreases*—this is just the nature of insurance. Third, I've learned that I can actually sell my options to others. Because options can grow in value over time, I can actually sell them to others for a profit. Finally, I've learned that there's something called a delta that identifies how an option value will change in relation to the stock value. The delta itself changes all the time, but at least I can learn what it is at any given point in time. Have I got it?"

"Yes, that's a good summary," answered Nate.

"And I've learned all that," interrupted Shorty, "plus that I'm basically not looking to do anything with the short call or short put I have. I'm just wanting time to run out. When it does, I get to keep the credit I took in *plus* I'm not called out and forced to sell shares in the case of a short call, and I'm not forced to *buy* shares in the case of a short put. Right?"

"That's what you discovered on your own, and that's the fundamental way it works for everyone," assured Aaron. "There are nuances, but what you've described is certainly the right starting point."

"So Lon has discovered a new right," said Nate. "It's the right for option traders to buy and sell their options. Let's build that into the table he and Shorty have created."

"Okay," agreed Aaron. "And then, because this table is so important, let's make a test out of it."

"But we've already done that," objected Lon. "I'm not sure I want to do it again."

"Okay. Fair enough. But let me ask you a question: Has the information become second nature to you yet?"

"Well, I can't say *that*."

"Neither can I," muttered Shorty. "I'd like to say it has, but it hasn't."

"Well, then, let's do it again. It's not complicated and you can learn it. But you have to do it enough times that the answers begin to seep into your bones. You're getting there, but you're not completely there yet."

"Fair enough," they agreed. "We'll do it again." (See Figure 20.3.)

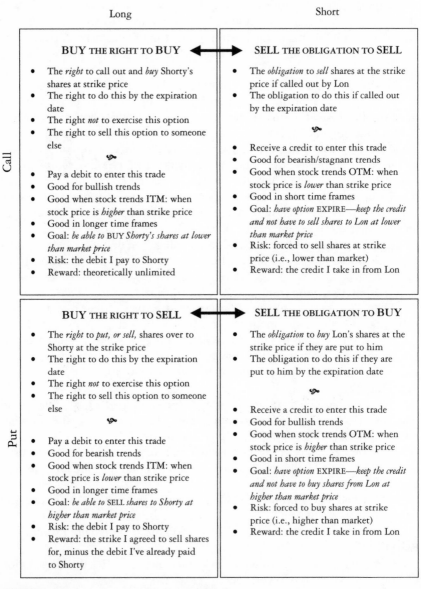

Long   Short

Call

BUY THE RIGHT TO **BUY** ⬅➡ **SELL** THE OBLIGATION TO **SELL**

- The *right* to call out and *buy* Shorty's shares at strike price
- The right to do this by the expiration date
- The right *not* to exercise this option
- The right to sell this option to someone else

❧

- Pay a debit to enter this trade
- Good for bullish trends
- Good when stock trends ITM: when stock price is *higher* than strike price
- Good in longer time frames
- Goal: *be able to* BUY *Shorty's shares at lower than market price*
- Risk: the debit I pay to Shorty
- Reward: theoretically unlimited

- The *obligation* to *sell* shares at the strike price if called out by Lon
- The obligation to do this if called out by the expiration date

❧

- Receive a credit to enter this trade
- Good for bearish/stagnant trends
- Good when stock trends OTM: when stock price is *lower* than strike price
- Good in short time frames
- Goal: *have option* EXPIRE—*keep the credit and not have to sell shares to Lon at lower than market price*
- Risk: forced to sell shares at strike price (i.e., lower than market)
- Reward: the credit I take in from Lon

Put

BUY THE RIGHT TO **SELL** ⬅➡ **SELL** THE OBLIGATION TO **BUY**

- The *right* to *put, or sell,* shares over to Shorty at the strike price
- The right to do this by the expiration date
- The right *not* to exercise this option
- The right to sell this option to someone else

❧

- Pay a debit to enter this trade
- Good for bearish trends
- Good when stock trends ITM: when stock price is *lower* than strike price
- Good in longer time frames
- Goal: *be able to* SELL *shares to Shorty at higher than market price*
- Risk: the debit I pay to Shorty
- Reward: the strike I agreed to sell shares for, minus the debit I've already paid to Shorty

- The *obligation* to *buy* Lon's shares at the strike price if they are put to him
- The obligation to do this if they are put to him by the expiration date

❧

- Receive a credit to enter this trade
- Good for bullish trends
- Good when stock trends OTM: when stock price is *higher* than strike price
- Good in short time frames
- Goal: *have option* EXPIRE—*keep the credit and not have to buy shares from Lon at higher than market price*
- Risk: forced to buy shares at strike price (i.e., higher than market)
- Reward: the credit I take in from Lon

FIGURE 20.3 Summary of Calls and Puts

Now some people can figure out all the details," said Aaron, "if they can just keep the big picture in mind—what each option is trying to do with the underlying stock and how the options relate to each other. Like this." (See Figure 20.4.)

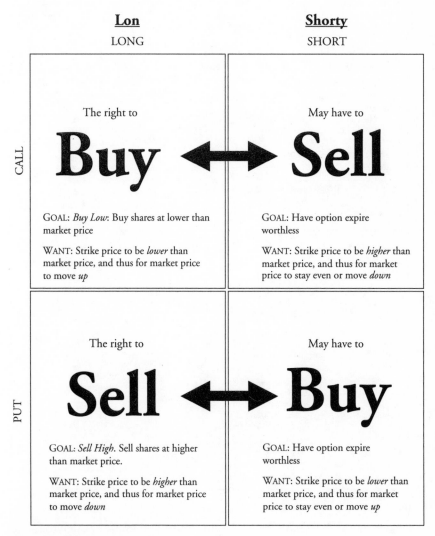

FIGURE 20.4 The Big Picture

"So here you go," said Nate. "Fill in the blanks."

REVIEW

| | Long | Short |

<table>
<tr><td rowspan="2">Call</td><td>

BUY THE RIGHT TO **BUY** ◀━━

- The *right* to _____ and ____ Shorty's shares at _____
- The right to do this by _____ _____
- The right _____ this option
- The right _____ this option to _____

❧

- Pay _____ to enter this trade
- Good for _____ trends
- Good when stock trends ____: when stock price is _____ than strike price
- Good in _____ time frames
- Goal: *be able to _____ Shorty's shares at _____ than market price*
- Risk: _____ to _____
- Reward: _____

</td><td>

━━▶ **SELL** THE OBLIGATION TO **SELL**

- The *obligation* to ____ shares at the _____ if _____ by Lon
- The obligation to do this if called out by _____

❧

- Receive _____ to enter this trade
- Good for _____ trends
- Good when stock trends ____: when stock price is _____ than strike price
- Good in _____ time frames
- Goal: *have option _____ᐧ___ keep the _____ and not have to _____ at _____ than market price*
- Risk: forced to _____ at _____ _____ (i.e., _____ than _____)
- Reward: the _____ I _____ from _____

</td></tr>
<tr><td>

BUY THE RIGHT TO **SELL** ◀━━

- The *right* to ____, *or* _____, shares over to Shorty at _____
- The right to do this by _____ _____
- The right _____ this option

❧

- Pay _____ to enter this trade
- Good for _____ trends
- Good when stock trends _____: when stock price is _____ than strike price
- Good in _____ time frames
- Goal: *be able to _____ shares to Shorty at _____ than market price*
- Risk: _____ to _____
- Reward: _____ I agreed to _____ _____ for, _____ the _____ I've _____

</td><td>

━━▶ **SELL** THE OBLIGATION TO **BUY**

- The *obligation* to _____ Lon's shares at the _____ if _____ to him
- The obligation to do this if they are put to him by _____

❧

- Receive a _____ to enter this trade
- Good for _____ trends
- Good when stock trends ____: when stock price is _____ than strike price
- Good in _____ time frames
- Goal: *have option _____ keep the _____ and not have to _____ at _____ than market price*
- Risk: forced to _____ at _____ _____ (i.e., _____ than _____)
- Reward: the _____ I _____ from _____

</td></tr>
</table>

Review

    "Sorry, guys, but that's not all," said Nate. "You know enough to figure out some answers based on the option chain—more than you could figure out before. So look at the imaginary option chain immediately below, and then imagine two months later it looks like the second chain. Based on these two chains, answer the questions that follow."

		PLUM $39		
		Strike		
6.50	6.70	35.00	0.75	0.85
5.80	6.00	37.50	2.0	2.50
3.80	4.00	40.00	3.00	3.80
2.90	3.00	42.50	4.20	4.70
2.00	2.50	45.00	5.00	5.60
0.80	0.90	47.50	6.10	6.40

Current chain (two months later):

		PLUM $44.50		
		Strike		
9.50	9.70	35.00	0.75	0.85
6.80	7.00	37.50	1.50	1.75
4.80	5.00	40.00	2.00	2.25
3.90	4.00	42.50	3.00	3.25
3.00	3.50	45.00	5.00	5.25
1.80	1.90	47.50	7.00	7.50

Review

1. What call strikes were in the money two months ago? How about today?
2. What put strikes were in the money two months ago? How about today?
3. If I bought a call at a $37.50 strike two months ago and sell it now, two months later:
   (a) What did I pay for it?
   (b) What will I receive for it now?
   (c) How much profit will I make?

4. If I bought a put two months ago at a $40 strike and sell it now:

   (a) What did I pay for it?

   (b) What will I receive for it now?

   (c) So how much of my original cost do I recoup?

5. If I shorted a call two months ago at a $45 strike:

   (a) How much credit did I receive?

   (b) What will happen if nothing changes and the option expires?

6. If I shorted a put two months ago at a $35 strike:

   (a) How much credit did I receive?

   (b) What will happen if the option expires today—with the chain looking as it does right now?

7. If I shorted a put two months ago at a $40 strike:

   (a) How much did I receive?

   (b) What will happen if the option expires today—with the chain looking as it does right now?

"Okay, thanks for this, but I want to go back to an earlier point," said Lon eagerly. "You said that we can buy and sell options without touching the underlying stock. Right?"

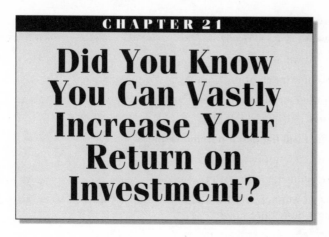

CHAPTER 21

Did You Know You Can Vastly Increase Your Return on Investment?

"That's right."

"Well, that raises this question: In order to buy and sell options on a particular stock, do you first have to own the stock? Or can you just buy and sell options *without* owning the stock?"

"No, you don't have to own stock at all to buy and sell options," answered Nate. "And that's a significant advantage. If the only way to be in the stock market were to own shares, you'd have to shell out thousands of dollars to barely get started. Look at our AAPL chain for example. (See Figure 21.1.)

"The stock is trading at $177.05 per share, so if you bought 100 shares, you would have to come up with $17,705. But you can buy an option—place a long call at a strike of $180—for *$7.10 per share*, or a total investment of $710 for 100 shares. With that $710 purchase of options (long calls), you would have these rights:

- The right to exercise your option and buy the 100 shares if you wanted to:

  (a) at the strike price of $180, and

  (b) within the expiration period

- The right to let the option expire rather than exercising it.
- The right to *sell* the option to someone else.

"Now let's suppose," said Aaron, "that the stock price goes up, say, to $200 by June, and let's say the option value (depending on the delta) goes up to $12 per share. Now of course you have the *right* to let your option

Jun 08 Calls								Jun 08 Puts					
			(29 days to expiration)			AAPL @ 177.05						Jun 08 Puts	
APVFK	23.95	0	23.85	24.10	45.4	.86	155.00	APVRK	1.62	0	1.59	1.66	45.0	-.13
APVFL	19.65	0	19.65	19.65	43.7	.81	160.00	APVRL	2.42	0	2.38	2.47	43.6	-.19
APVFM	15.90	0	15.75	15.95	42.3	.74	165.00	APVRM	3.60	0	3.50	3.65	42.6	-.26
APVFN	12.40	0	12.35	12.45	41.5	.66	170.00	APVRN	5.10	0	5.05	5.15	41.6	-.34
APVFO	9.55	0	9.40	9.55	41.1	.57	175.00	APVRO	7.15	0	7.10	7.20	41.1	-.43
APVFP	7.00	0	6.95	7.10	40.7	.47	180.00	APVRP	9.55	0	9.65	9.80	40.9	-.53
APVFQ	5.15	0	5.05	5.15	40.5	.38	185.00	APVRQ	12.75	0	12.70	12.85	40.6	-.62
APVFR	3.60	0	3.55	3.65	40.3	.30	190.00	APVRR	16.45	0	16.15	16.35	40.4	-.70
APVFS	2.59	0	2.48	2.54	40.5	.22	195.00	APVRS	20.15	0	20.00	20.25	40.4	-.78
APVFT	1.75	0	1.71	1.77	40.9	.17	200.00	APVRT	25.40	0	24.25	24.50	41.0	-.83

FIGURE 21.1 Long Call vs. Buying Shares
Source: Screenshot courtesy of optionsXpress, Inc. © 2008.

expire ... but why would you do that in this case? You have a chance to make money, so you can't just let the option expire and forfeit the debit you paid to make the trade in the first place.

"So look at another right you have," he continued. "You have the right to buy 100 shares at your strike of $180. If you use this right, and exercise your option to buy these shares at $180, you can then turn around and sell them at $200. So you buy for a total cost of $18,000 and sell the same shares for $20,000. That's $20 per share profit, for a total profit of $2,000. Of course, we have to subtract the $7.10 (or $710) debit you paid to make the trade in the first place, so you make $20 minus $7.10, or $12.90 per share, for a total dollar profit of $1,290. That's a 7 percent return (our net profit of $1,290 divided by our investment of $17,705)—and that's pretty good, especially if the expiration period is relatively short."

> *So two of the advantages of trading in options are: (1) options require less capital and (2) return on investment for options is much higher.*

"The problem," said Nate, "is that perhaps the reason you didn't buy shares in the first place is because you didn't have $17,705 to spend. If so, you probably don't have the $18,000 to spend in order to exercise your option now—even if you could make a decent return on your money by doing so. So exercising your option to actually buy shares may present a problem."

"But look what happens," Aaron jumped in, "if you simply sell your option to someone else for its current value of $12. You paid $7.10 for it, and you sell it for $12, so you realize a profit of $4.90 . . . and that's a return of almost 70 percent ($4.90 / $7.10)!

"So two of the advantages of trading options are: (1) options require less capital and (2) return on investment for options is much higher."

"Well, what about me?" asked Shorty.

"What do you mean?" asked Aaron.

"Remind me how I make money *selling* options—always being in the short position."

"Well, while Lon cares a lot about fluctuating options value, you don't. The amount you can make is capped by the credit you received in the first place. All you want is for the strike to stay out of the money. Remember what you figured out earlier by yourself: the way you make money is by taking in a credit from someone like Lon. In the case of short *calls*, you pick a favorable strike price—one that ought to stay higher than the market price of the stock—and you pick a favorable combination of time frame and credit amount. In the chart below, for example, suppose you pick a strike price of $78, to expire at the end of April. As long as that strike of $78 stays out of the money—that is, the market price stays lower than that strike price—for that time period, Lon won't exercise his option to buy your shares. The option will expire worthless, and you simply keep the credit Lon paid you in the first place. That's the maximum reward you can receive." (See Figure 21.2.)

"In the case of short *puts*," added Nate, "you do the same. You pick a favorable strike price—one that ought to stay *lower than* the market price of the stock—and again you pick a favorable combination of time frame and credit amount. In the chart in Figure 21.3, for example, suppose you pick a strike price of $28.50, to expire at the end of April. As long as that strike of $28.50 stays out of the money—that is, the market price stays higher than that strike price—for that time period, Lon won't exercise his option to put his shares to you and force you to buy them. The option will expire worthless, and you simply keep the credit Lon paid you in the first place." (See Figure 21.3.)

"Got it. Lon's trying to make as much as he can. He'd like his strikes to get as far in the money as he can, for both calls and puts. The further they're in the money, the more his option is worth, and the more he makes in profit. But for me it's different. I can't make any more than the credit I received to make the deal in the first place. I just want the option to expire worthless—without Lon exercising it."

"We're going to correct one thing you just said—and it's very important—but it's okay for now. Just complete this review and then we'll come back to it."

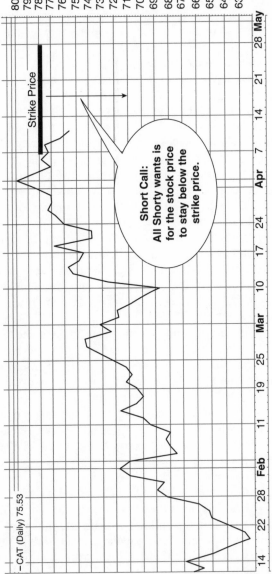

FIGURE 21.2 What Shorty Wants in His Short Call

Source: Chart courtesy of StockCharts.com.

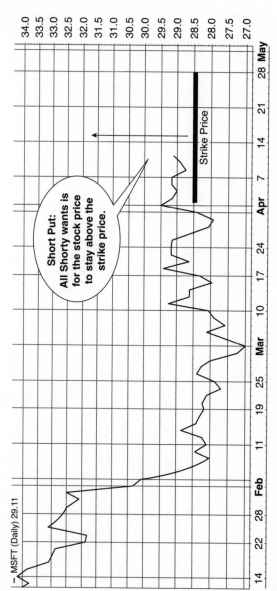

FIGURE 21.3 What Shorty Wants in His Short Put

Source: Chart courtesy of StockCharts.com.

Sell at a put option at 28.50

REVIEW

Jan 09 Calls			(402 days to expiration)			ADBE@44.35					Jan 09 Puts		
VAEAG	11.90	0	12.30	12.60	30.0	.86	35.00	VAEMG	1.60	0	1.50	1.60	33.9	-.16
VAEAH	9.10	+0.30	8.80	9.10	29.0	.75	40.00	VAEMH	2.85	0	2.85	2.95	32.7	-.26
VAEAI	6.20	-0.10	6.00	6.20	28.2	.62	45.00	VAEMI	4.90	0	4.90	5.10	32.6	-.38
VAEAJ	4.00	0	3.80	4.00	27.2	.47	50.00	VAEMJ	7.50	0	7.60	7.90	32.7	-.50
VAEAK	2.29	0	2.30	2.45	26.5	.34	55.00	VAEMK	12.10	0	11.20	11.50	34.6	-.60

Source: Screenshot courtesy of optionsXpress, Inc. © 2008.
Review

1. If you bought 100 shares of this stock at its current price, how much would you pay in total dollars?
   If the stock price went to $50 and you sold:
2. How much profit would you make in total dollars?
3. What percent profit would this be?
4. If you bought a call (opened a long call) for 100 shares on this stock, at a $45 strike price, how much would you pay in total dollars?
   If the stock price went to $50, and the long call price went to $11, and you sold your long call:
5. How much profit would you make in total dollars?
6. What percent profit would this be?

"Now there are two things we have to make absolutely clear before we move on," said Nate. "They are critical."

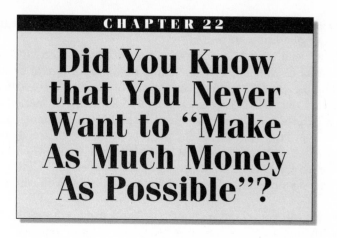

CHAPTER 22

Did You Know that You Never Want to "Make As Much Money As Possible"?

"**F**irst, Shorty, I want to address something you just said. You said that Lon is trying to make as much money as possible on his long calls and puts."

"Yes, that's the way it seems to me," answered Shorty.

"Yeah, me too!" exclaimed Lon.

"Unfortunately, that's exactly how you go broke in the market. Your goal is NEVER to make as much money as you can on any one deal. Think about it, Lon. Suppose at the end of a month you happen to be up 20 percent on a long call on Plum. Suppose you paid $6 for it, and now you could sell it for $7.20—a 20 percent return. What should you do? Should you hope it just goes up more and wait for that to happen? That's tempting, but what happens if the stock goes down and the value of the option goes down? Suppose you end up out of the money at the end of the expiration period, so you're forced to just let the option expire worthless? Then Shorty gets to keep the debit you paid and you get nothing! How does that 20 percent return on investment look to you now?"

There are a million deals out there. It's far better to make a lot of 20 percent deals than to hold out for one or two big payouts.

"So here's the deal," Aaron chimed in. "You never make a deal—on a trade like this long call we're discussing—unless you decide *in advance* the percentage profit you want to make on it. Then, when you reach that percentage profit (and it should always be something reasonable like 20 to 25 percent), *you sell your option.*"

"Right," said Nate. "There are a million deals out there. It's far better to make a lot of 20 percent deals than to hold out for one or two big payouts. The problem with holding out for one or two big payouts is that you can't predict the market precisely enough to do that. The market can turn on a dime. Far better to take good profits when you have them than run the risk—the very large risk—of losing them because you're greedy for something even better. Nope. Take your profits and run. Go make another deal. There are a million deals out there; don't get trapped into banking on just one. Greed is your enemy, in more ways than one, and you can never give in to it."

"Let me tell you about a friend," added Aaron, "who did this sort of thing. Early in his trading career he reached a point on one deal where, in six weeks, he was up 25 percent both in the stock he owned and in the long call he held on it. Everything looked bullish, not only for the market, but especially for this stock. Well, he should have ignored this bullish trend and closed his positions with these 25 percent gains. But he didn't. Like a knucklehead—that's what he calls himself looking back—he decided there was no better place to put his money, so why not just let it ride and accumulate more gains? Well, he'd tell you now that that was a stupid mistake. Within days, the market—and this stock—plummeted. If he had sold when he should have he would have been flush with cash and he could have taken advantage of a lot of buying opportunities—lots of low prices. As it was, he had no cash and the value of both his stock and his long call had evaporated. Painful lesson . . . but he's never made that mistake since."

"So what you're both telling me is that I'm *not* trying simply to make as much money as I can on a deal. I'm trying to make 20 to 25 percent."

"Right."

"And I'm certainly not trying to make as much money as *I* can," said Shorty. "I just set up a trade that gives me a great chance of keeping the credit I've taken in—and being forced neither to sell, nor buy, any shares of stock that I don't want to."

"That's right, too."

"Which brings us to the second point," said Aaron, "that is absolutely critical. Remember, Lon, you asked if it's possible to buy and sell options without owning the underlying stock."

"Right, and you said that that was possible and that it even had two major advantages," said Lon.

"That's correct," replied Aaron, "except that Shorty's case is different from yours. Shorty, you're always shorting calls and puts—giving someone else rights over you."

"That's right. If I short a call, I give Lon, or someone like him, the right to buy shares from me at the strike price. They will do that if the market price goes higher than the strike—if it goes in the money."

"Okay, stop there," said Aaron. "Now ask yourself what that means for you—selling stock at lower than the market price—if you don't already own the stock."

"Well, if I don't already own the stock, it means I would have to go out and buy the stock in order to be able to sell it to Lon like I'm obligated to do."

"Which means," Aaron said with emphasis, "that you would have to go out and buy stock at the higher market price in order to be able to sell it to Lon at the *lower* strike price that you've guaranteed him! So let's say the strike price is $155 and the market price is $180. If you don't already own the stock, you will have to buy shares at $180 to be able to sell them to Lon at $155—which is a loss of $25 per share automatically!"

"That's a world of hurt," muttered Shorty.

"Right," said Aaron. "And that's why you can't ever put yourself in that position. When you place a short call on stock you already own, your call is 'covered' by the stock; you already own it, and you probably paid a lower price for it. So this is called a *covered call*. But when you place a short call on stock you *don't* own, your call is not covered—it is 'naked,' so to speak. So this is called a *naked call*. And you never want to do it. Understand?"

"I understand," answered Shorty.

"Okay, so let's review to make sure you have everything."

REVIEW

"It's far better to make a lot of _____ deals than to hold out for one or two _____ deals. Your goal is _____ to make as much money as you can on _____ deal.

"If I place a short call on stock I _____ already own, and if the _____ goes in the money—if the market price goes _____ than the _____—then I will have to go out on the market and _____ shares at the _____ market price and turn around and sell them at the _____ strike price I agreed to. I _____ want to do that."

"Okay, now I have to tell you two something fundamental that you're both doing wrong," said Nate. "It's a mistake you're both making."

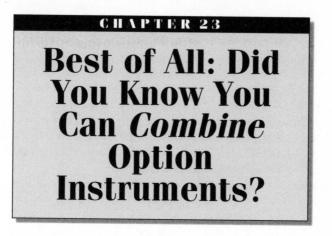

CHAPTER 23

Best of All: Did You Know You Can *Combine* Option Instruments?

"What's that?" challenged Lon. "I think we're doing pretty well. What are we doing wrong?"

"Well, you're both far too limited," answered Nate, "and that means you're both taking far too much *risk*. Lon, you like doing long trades, or debit trades. You like shelling out money to buy rights. For bullish trends you place long calls, and for bearish trends you place long puts."

"And Shorty," said Aaron, "you like doing short trades, or credit trades. You like taking in money and then waiting out the expiration period. For stagnant/bearish trends you create short calls, and for bullish trends you create short puts."

> *You're both far too limited and that means you're taking far too much* risk.

"Unfortunately, this isn't very flexible. In addition, it requires you to be good at calling trends . . . and how good are you at that? There are valuable technical signals you can use to help, and we will cover them tomorrow night, but even they can't account for the effects of earnings reports, economic data, and pronouncements by the Fed. Any one of those factors can *rapidly* turn a trend in the opposite direction from the one you are expecting. Then how good is your option strategy?"

"Right," added Aaron. "Suppose you have a long call on Plum because you expect a bullish trend, and then an earnings report scares the market and the stock turns bearish. What happens to your long call then?"

"Well, it goes down in value," answered Lon.

"Exactly. And then you're stuck with an option that's declining in value, and you can't sell it without taking a loss."

"And Shorty," said Nate, "you're sitting there, say, with a short call, waiting out the expiration period and hoping the stock price doesn't go higher than the strike price you've agreed to. If it doesn't, great; you get to keep your credit without losing any shares. But if the stock price does go higher than the strike price, Lon or someone like him will force you to sell your shares to him at lower than market value ... and, for our purposes right now, you normally don't want that."

"The point," emphasized Aaron, "is that you can have much more flexibility than you have right now ... and much less *risk*. You don't have to stick to just going long or going short. You should be able to do both. But more than that: you can actually do both ... *on any trade*."

"Right," said Nate. "The beauty of option trading is that you can combine option instruments on a single trade. Then you can take advantage of any trend that happens to occur."

"You mean I can do a long call *and* a short call on a single trade?" asked Lon.

"Or both a long put *and* a short put on a single trade?" queried Shorty.

> *The beauty of trading options is that you can combine option instruments on a single trade. Then you can take advantage of any trend that happens to occur.*

"Sure. And not only that: you can also do a *short call* and a *long put* on a single trade," said Aaron. "Again, the beauty of trading options lies in the *combinations* available to you. The more combinations that are available, and the more you understand them, the better you can use them to take advantage of any market trend. Creating these combinations is called spread trading. We're not ready to talk about that yet, but we will once we get the foundation laid."

TRENDS

"Knowing that you can combine option instruments," added Nate, "means that you will want to do different combinations on different stocks, because different stocks will have different trends. Think about the trends that are possible: slightly bearish, bearish, stagnant, slightly bullish, and bullish. You want to be able to take advantage of any of these trends ... and combining options permits you to do that."

"It may help if you get a feel for what we mean by these trends," said Aaron. "Here's a simple way to look at them." (See Figure 23.1.)

OPTION INSTRUMENTS: BASIC CHARACTERISTICS

"With all this in mind," he continued, "it's a good time to review each option instrument and remind ourselves what each of them does for us. We'll learn some things later that will add to our knowledge, but let's review the basics now."

"So let's start with the long call," said Nate. "As a rule, it increases in value as the stock increases in value. That means it's good in a bullish trend: as long as the stock is going up, the long call will be going up too, at a rate determined by the delta. At the same time, as we saw a few minutes ago, this long call is always *cheaper* than the stock. That means we can use less money and still get benefit from a rising stock. So we might say that a long call 'leverages' a bullish trend. We can make money without spending a lot of money."

"Right," added Aaron, "that's the good news. But we have to keep in mind the risk as well. And the risk in a long call is that if the stock stops going up, the value of the long call will stop going up too. In fact, as we'll learn, it will even *fall*. And that means we can lose the entire amount we spent to buy the call in the first place—the entire debit we paid."

"Now with a short call," said Nate, "the idea is different. Here, we just want to bring in cash by selling the call and receiving a credit for it. This strategy is great for a stagnant trend because it allows us to generate income even when nothing is happening with the stock. The same is true for a slightly bearish trend: we generate income even when the stock is dipping."

"Well, what about bullish or bearish trends?" asked Lon. "Why not a short call then?"

"The main problem with using a short call in a bullish or bearish trend is that there are *better* instruments to use at those times. Think about a bullish trend, for example. Remember that with a short call, what we make is simply what we receive in a credit. Once we choose a strike price and an expiration date, the bid amount we will receive is determined. That's the most we can make. But if a stock is bullish we don't want a limit like that. We want to make more as the stock continues to move upward, which, unlike a short call, is exactly what a *long call* will do for us. So a long call is a better instrument in a bullish trend than a short call. Make sense?"

"Sure."

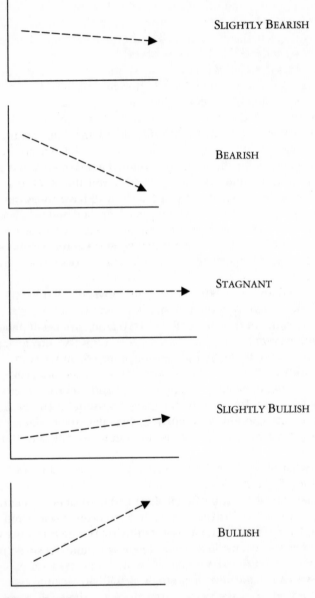

FIGURE 23.1 Trends

"And in a bearish trend," added Aaron, "the same principle applies. A long put is a much better way to make money than a short call, because the long put will continue to grow in value as long as the stock keeps falling—which is exactly what it's doing in a bearish trend. A short call, on the other hand, limits *at the outset* how much we can make. That's why it's not as good."

"So the main reason we don't use short calls in bullish or bearish trends is simply because there are better instruments to use in those trends. Get it?"

"Got it."

"Good. So now let's look at the risk in a short call," said Nate. "On one hand, as Aaron said a few minutes ago, we can have a short call without owning any stock. As he said, that's called a *naked call*, and we never do it precisely *because of* the risk. Remember: if the stock goes bullish, we will get called out, which means that we will have to go out and buy shares at a high market price so we can turn around and sell them, as we are obligated to do, at the lower strike price we agreed to. That's a guaranteed way to lose money, and, theoretically at least, the risk is unlimited. After all, the stock price could rise dramatically and put us in a position to have to buy at an impossibly high price in order to be able to meet our obligation to sell at the lower one. So with a naked call, the risk is really unlimited."

"Which is why we never do that," added Aaron. "We never place a short call without owning the stock. In that case—when we own the stock—if the stock price goes bullish, we already *own* shares, and they're shares we bought earlier at a lower price. Thus, when we're called out, we simply sell our shares at the strike price we agreed to and pocket the profit we made on them. *And* we obviously keep the credit we took in to make the deal in the first place. None of this is particularly negative, of course, but if we have to call something a risk with this kind of short call, this would be it. Make sense?"

"Sure."

"Okay, so now let's look at the long put," said Nate. "And, as Aaron just said a second ago, we use a long put in bearish trends. That's when it grows. And the *reason* we use it, typically, is to protect ourselves. If we're worried that a stock will go down we can protect our investment by buying puts. Then, if the stock price does go down, our puts will be going up . . . offsetting the loss in the stock."

"I've got to say, this never ceases to amaze me," said Lon in wonder. "The whole thing is so ingenious it's unbelievable."

"I agree," replied Nate, "but we also have to remember the risk in a long put. After all, if the stock doesn't do what we expect—if it goes bullish rather than bearish—our long put *won't* grow in value; in fact, as we'll see a little later, it will even *drop* in value. Then we lose the entire amount we paid to buy the put in the first place—the entire debit. Got it?"

"Yeah. The long put's easy."

"So finally," said Aaron, "let's turn to the short put. Now, basically, we use the short put for the same reason we use the short call: to bring in cash through the credit we receive. The short put thus generates cash in either a stagnant or slightly bullish trend. By taking in a credit, we make money even when the stock isn't doing anything or at least much of anything."

"And I guess," volunteered Shorty, "that we don't use a short put in a bullish trend because there's a much better instrument to use: the long call. And, of course, the long put is a much better instrument for a bearish trend. Neither limits what we can make, while the short put does. Once we choose a strike price and an expiration date for the short put, the bid amount we will receive is determined. And that's the most we can make *no matter what the stock does*. That's why it's limiting."

"Right," said Nate. "That's why the short put is valuable in stagnant and slightly bullish trends, but not so valuable in other trends. But now let's look at the risk in a short put. It's simply that the strike price goes in the money, which means that we will have shares put over to us . . . which means that we have to buy those shares at the strike price we agreed to. That's it."

"Now obviously," added Aaron, "that's not the worst thing in the world. After all, we simply choose a strike price that we are willing to buy the stock at . . . and then, if we *have* to buy shares at that price, what's the harm? It's the price *we* chose. Still, if we have to call something a risk for a short put, this would be it: meeting our obligation to buy shares at the price we chose."

"Alright," said Nate, "let's create a summary of these instruments in a table. Then we can get the big picture at a glance." (See Figure 23.2.)

Instrument	What it does for us	Trend	Risk
Long Call	Leverages a bullish trend	Bullish	Lose entire debit
Short Call	Brings in cash	Stagnant to slightly bearish	Unlimited (if naked), or have to sell shares
Long Put	Protects us	Bearish	Lose entire debit
Short Put	Brings in cash	Stagnant to slightly bullish	Have to buy shares

FIGURE 23.2 Option Instruments: Basic Characteristics.

"That's helpful," said Shorty. "We've really talked about all thes before, but we've never collected them in one place. This helps me.

"Good," replied Nate. "See, we have to understand these instrum we're going to know how and when to combine them to get the best results. In fact, including these instruments, there are eight basic variables we need to look at as we think about combining."

Eight Variables in Combining

1. Stock ownership ("long in the stock")
2. Trend, or expected trend, of the stock

3–6. The four option instruments:

  3. Long Call
  4. Short Call
  5. Long Put
  6. Short Put

7. Strike price (at the money, near the money, in the money, out of the money)
8. Time frame

"So you can see that there are a lot of things to consider," said Nate. "The key to trading options is understanding all these matters and then getting good at combining them. That's what we do in spread trading; it's why we're able to take advantage of all the different trends. Not only that, but it's also possible to *adjust* trades once we're in them. We're not locked in once and for all once we make a trade; we can actually make adjustments as we go.

"Now we'll never be able to cover all the combinations and all the adjustments in the time we have together. There's too much—but do you get the idea?"

"Sure," answered Lon. "There are a lot of variations, a lot of possibilities in option trading."

The more combinations that are available, and the more you understand them, the better you can use them to take advantage of any market trend.

"And which combinations and variations we choose has a lot to do with what trends we expect," added Shorty. "And I guess the same goes for adjustments."

"That's right," answered Aaron. "We have to be smart, but if we are, there are a lot of ways to make the most out of the market. We have many tools to use—and that's one of the beauties of option trading. We have an answer for everything. What we're trying to do in these three evenings together is give you a foundation. In fact, before we're through we'll share with you five important spread trades where we combine these instruments in different ways.

"To begin, though," he continued, "these are the types of questions that we want to ask in determining what to do in a particular option trade."

Questions to Ask
- Should I be long in the stock?
- What is the trend of this stock, and what do I *expect* the trend to be?
- What combination of option instruments should I use?
- What should the strike price be for each instrument I use in the trade?
- What time frame should I use for each instrument I use in the trade?
- What are my exit points for each trade? How do I decide when to "get out"?
- What are my possible adjustments?

"The answers to these questions are very important," said Nate, "because, as we've already seen, different answers will lead to different results. Now as I just said, we can't cover all of these in detail in the time we have. But we *can* get you started. In fact, by the end of our third night we will have laid a foundation that can genuinely change your life."

> *Smart combining of option instruments can reduce your risk and make you money in every market trend—and all at the same time.*

"The main point," Aaron continued, "is simply this: smart combining of option instruments can reduce your risk and make you money in every market trend—and all at the same time."

"There are a number of basics we need to cover before we show you this, however, and it's getting late. So let's just start a little earlier tomorrow night. Then we can get some of the basics in place."

"Great. Is it okay with everyone if we meet here again?" Lon asked.

"Sure. No problem."

"Before we break, though, you first have to do your review."

REVIEW

"Fill in the following table."

INSTRUMENT	WHAT IT DOES FOR US	TREND	RISK
Long Call	Leverages a bullish trend	Bullish	
		Stagnant to slightly bearish	Unlimited (if naked), or have to sell shares
Short Put			Have to buy shares

Review

Questions to consider in making any option trade:

1. Should I be _____ in the stock?

2. What is the _____ of this stock, and what do I _____ the trend to be?

3. What combination of _____ should I use?

4. What should the _____ be for each _____ I use in the trade?

5. What _____ should I use for each _____ I use in the trade?

6. What are my _____ for each trade? How do I decide when to _____?

STEP FOUR

Getting a Few Basics in Place

CHAPTER 24

More Time Travel

I t was 7:30 by the time everyone had gathered in Lon's study the next evening. Aaron began the discussion.

"The first thing we need to talk about tonight has to do with time frames. It's something you have to have in mind from this point forward.

"Let's start," he continued, "by remembering that you, Lon, always like a lot of time built into your trades. That's because you like to be long. In a long call you want the market price to go higher than the strike price, and the more time you have, the more likely that is to happen. Same thing for a long put. You want the market price to go lower than your strike price, and, again, the more time you have, the more likely that is to happen."

"So," added Nate, "it's like time is part of the *value* of the option. The more time an option has, the more value it has. So think of time itself as having value. In fact, we call it *time value.*"

"That's why, by the way," said Aaron, "the further we go out in time, the higher the bid/ask amounts are. Remember that?"

Other things equal, the price of this option will drop day by day just because of the passage of time.

"Sure. We figured that out ourselves. And then you showed it to us on an option chain."

"Good. And the point is that this happens because the further out in time that we place, say, a long call or a long put, the greater the chance it has of going in the money: it has more time available to it to do so. That makes it more valuable to Lon, which means he will be willing pay a higher price for it."

"Right," said Shorty. "And all that makes it riskier for me, which means I will *demand* a higher price for it."

"All of which simply adds up to make such options more costly. It's due to what I said just a second ago: the value of *time*. That's why it's called *time value*."

"Now notice what all this means," added Aaron. "*As time runs out, so does the value!* In other words, as we get closer and closer to the expiration date for Lon's long call, the less time value it has. And that means the less *total value* it has. Other things equal, the price of this option will drop day by day just because of the passage of time."

"Right," said Nate. "Think of it this way: each day that goes by without the stock going up enough to put that long call strike in the money, the lower the chances are that it will *ever* go in the money. It now has one less day to do so—so the odds are reduced one day's worth."

"So think of time value as like a piece of wood, or a home or a building—or even the Sphinx," said Aaron. "It decays over time. It just sort of deteriorates. And it's for the reason Nate said: the chances of an option going in the money go down as the amount of time *available* to go in the money goes down. The value of the option *decays* as time goes by."

"And it gets even more interesting than that," Nate chimed in.

"Oh, no. What now?"

"Well, let's suppose you've placed a nine-month long call," answered Nate. "As we've just said, the time value of that option will decay as time goes by ... *but the decay won't be spread out evenly over those nine months*: most of the decay will occur in the last three months, and most of *that* in the *last* month. So time decay isn't steady; it accelerates toward the end.

"Now it's possible to get very technical about all this," said Aaron. "In fact, based on the market price, the strike price, and the expiration period, you can calculate the actual dollar amount that a particular option will drop in value, every day, due to time decay. This dollar amount even has a name; it's called the *theta*.

"But those details don't matter for now," he continued. "The main thing for you to know is that the value of an option goes down due to the passage of time, and it goes down more rapidly as it gets closer to expiration. Got it?"

"Got it."

"Good. So there are three main things to remember about time, and the first two you discovered on your own.

"First, for both calls and puts, the longer the time frame, the greater the likelihood that the option—the strike price—will go in the money. This means, other things equal, that longer time frames are *less* risky for Lon and *more* risky for Shorty.

"Second, for both calls and puts, the longer the time frame, the higher the debit/credit amounts for strike prices.

"And third, option value decays over time, and the decay accelerates toward the end of the expiration period."

"Good," said Shorty. "But the stuff about time decay raises another question."

"We'll wait for your question. First, the review."

REVIEW

"Each _____ that goes by without the stock going up enough to put the strike _____, the _____ the chances are that it will _____ go _____.

It now has one less _____ to do so—so the odds are _____ one day's worth.

"Most _____ will occur in the _____ three months, and most of *that* in the _____ month. So _____ isn't steady; it _____ toward the _____."

"For both calls and puts, the greater the time frame, the _____ the likelihood that the option will go in the money. This means, other things equal, that _____ time frames are _____ risky for Lon and _____ risky for Shorty.

"For both calls and puts, the _____ the time frame, the higher the _____ amounts for strike prices."

"Okay, now. What was your question?"

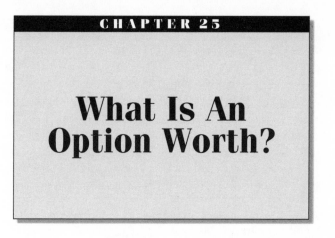

CHAPTER 25

What Is An Option Worth?

"Well," said Shorty, "with all this talk about time being part of the value of an option, it makes me wonder what else makes up the value of an option. Time can't be the only factor."

"That's right," said Aaron. "So let me tell you: for our purposes, it helps to think of four basic elements that determine the value of an option.

"The first element," he continued, "is the relationship between the strike price and the market price. Look, for example, at the option chain. (See Figure 25.1.)

"The market price of the stock is $34.53. And look at all of the in-the-money strike prices for calls. Obviously, all of them are lower than the market price, ranging from $25 to $32.50. As we've learned, these strikes are in the money precisely because they're lower than the market price: an option bought at any one of these strike prices would permit us to buy shares for lower than the market price and then turn around and sell them at the higher market price. They have this monetary value for us immediately."

"And now look at the out-of-the-money calls," said Nate. "Obviously, they're all *higher* than the market price. Which means if we bought and exercised call options at those strikes right now, we would have the right to buy shares at *higher* than the market price—and we would be losing money if we did that."

"So which set of call strike prices do you think would be more valuable—those that are in the money or those that are out of the money—those that are worth money to us right now or those that aren't?" asked Aaron.

Jul 08 Calls			(224 days to expiration)			MSFT@34.53			Jul 08 Puts					
MSQGE	9.60	0	10.30	10.40	20.8	.99	25.00	MSQSE	0.42	-0.03	0.40	0.41	36.0	-.08
MSQGY	7.75	0	8.15	8.20	25.3	.92	27.50	MSQSY	0.68	-0.06	0.68	0.69	33.7	-.13
MSQGF	6.00	-0.15	6.15	6.20	25.7	.83	30.00	MSQSF	1.18	0	1.12	1.14	31.7	-.21
MSQGZ	4.45	+0.05	4.40	4.45	25.3	.71	32.50	MSQSZ	1.83	-0.04	1.82	1.85	30.4	-.31
MSQGG	2.96	+0.01	2.97	3.00	24.8	.58	35.00	MSQSG	2.88	-0.06	2.85	2.87	29.7	-.42
MSQGU	1.90	-0.01	1.87	1.89	24.2	.43	37.50	MSQSU	4.37	-1.03	4.20	4.25	29.5	-.54
MSQGH	1.13	0	1.10	1.13	23.7	.30	40.00	MSQSH	6.00	-0.20	5.95	6.05	30.7	-.64
MSQGV	0.63	-0.02	0.61	0.63	23.3	.19	42.50	MSQSV	8.30	0	8.05	8.15	33.4	-.70
MSQGI	0.33	-0.01	0.32	0.34	23.1	.12	45.00	MSQSI	10.65	0	10.30	10.50	37.2	-.74

FIGURE 25.1 Looking at the Market Price and the Strike Price
Source: Screenshot courtesy of optionsXpress, Inc. © 2008.

"Obviously, the in-the-money strikes are more valuable," said Lon. "And that's exactly what the option chain shows: the bid/ask amounts for the in-the-money call options are all higher than the out-of-the-money call options. In fact, the *deeper* the strike price is in the money, the higher its bid/ask amounts."

For our purposes, it helps to think of four basic elements that determine the value of an option.

"And I see that the same is true for the put options," added Shorty. "The bid/ask amounts for the in-the-money put options (ranging from $35 to $45) are all higher than the out-of-the-money put options. And, just as with calls, the deeper the strike price is in the money, the higher are its bid/ask amounts."

"Okay, so that's one element," said Aaron. "You've got it. It's the relationship between the strike price and the market price. For both calls and puts, in-the-money options are more valuable than out-of-the-money options; and the more in the money they are, the more valuable they are, which means the higher priced they are."

"Which brings us to the second element in determining the value of an option," said Nate. "It's simply the *expectation* of how much the price of a stock will move. If a stock is expected to move a lot—to be volatile—then its options values will be higher. If a stock is not expected to move—to be nonvolatile—then its options values will be lower. All of this seems to be more a function of hype than anything else, but, for what it's worth, what a stock is *expected* to do, looking forward, is an important element in determining the value of its options."

"The third important element," said Aaron, "is what we've already talked about: time value. Other things equal, the more time that is built into an option the more valuable it is, and this value decays as time passes."

"There are a couple of other elements that figure into the value of an option," interjected Nate, "but they're not important right now. Let's just call them *other stuff*. So that's the fourth dimension: 'other stuff.'"

"So let's see if I've got this," said Lon. "Someone somewhere determines the value of any given option. They do this by considering four basic elements: (1) how far in the money or out of the money the strike price is; (2) how much movement is expected in the market price of the stock—how volatile it is expected to be; (3) the amount of time left before expiration; and (4) other stuff. Right?"

"That's right," answered Nate. "And for what it's worth, I should tell you that this second element—the expectation of movement—is called *implied volatility*. You'll run into this term, so you should know it."

"But that's a stupid term!" exploded Lon. "Why be so technical about it?"

"I know what you mean, but think about it this way," replied Aaron. "*Volatility* is just another name for *movement*. It means essentially the same thing. So when you hear 'volatility,' just think 'movement.' And the term *implied* suggests that this expectation we're talking about isn't *certain*. It's merely suggested, or implied, by what is happening to the stock. Like Nate said, this expectation may be closer to hype than anything, but in any case, there you have it: *implied volatility*—expected movement."

"Given all this it helps to divide the value of an option into two major categories," said Nate. "To help me explain, look at the option chain again." (See Figure 25.2.)

Jul 08 Calls			(224 days to expiration)			MSFT@ 34.53		Jul 08 Puts					
MSQGE	9.60	0	10.30	10.40	20.8	.99	25.00	MSQSE	0.42	-0.03	0.40	0.41	36.0	-.08
MSQGY	7.75	0	8.15	8.20	25.3	.92	27.50	MSQSY	0.68	-0.06	0.68	0.69	33.7	-.13
MSQGF	6.00	-0.15	6.15	6.20	25.7	.83	30.00	MSQSF	1.18	0	1.12	1.14	31.7	-.21
MSQGZ	4.45	+0.05	4.40	(4.45)	25.3	.71	32.50	MSQSZ	1.83	-0.04	1.82	1.85	30.4	-.31
MSQGG	2.96	+0.01	2.97	3.00	24.8	.58	35.00	MSQSG	2.88	-0.06	2.85	2.87	29.7	-.42
MSQGU	1.90	-0.01	1.87	1.89	24.2	.43	37.50	MSQSU	4.37	-1.03	4.20	4.25	29.5	-.54
MSQGH	1.13	0	1.10	1.13	23.7	.30	40.00	MSQSH	6.00	-0.20	5.95	6.05	30.7	-.64
MSQGV	0.63	-0.02	0.61	0.63	23.3	.19	42.50	MSQSV	8.30	0	8.05	8.15	33.4	-.70
MSQGI	0.33	-0.01	0.32	0.34	23.1	.12	45.00	MSQSI	10.65	0	10.30	10.50	37.2	-.74

FIGURE 25.2 Identifying "Intrinsic Value"
Source: Screenshot courtesy of optionsXpress, Inc. © 2008.

"This stock is currently selling at $34.53," he continued. "If I do an in-the-money long call at a $32.50 strike, notice that the difference between the market price and the strike price is $2.03 ($34.53 − $32.50). In other words, if I owned this option I could buy shares for $2.03 less than the current market price. That's what being in the money is all about. It's an actual, tangible value."

"Now notice," said Aaron, "what I would pay to buy this call: $4.45. Someone has determined that that's the value of this long call: $4.45. So now the question is how much of the value of this long call is due to the actual, tangible value we just identified?"

"Well, the actual, tangible result we identified was $2.03," answered Shorty. "So that must be the answer: of this total value of $4.45, $2.03 of it is due to this actual, tangible value."

"That's right," answered Nate. "And notice that this $2.03 is simply the amount that this strike price is in the money. A $32.50 strike for this call is $2.03 less than the market price of $34.53, so we would say it is *$2.03 in the money*. It's the dollar advantage that the strike price *intrinsically* gives us over the market price. That's why we usually call this the *intrinsic value* of the option. It's *built in* to the relationship between the market price and the strike price."

"So in this case," added Aaron, "the total value of the option is $4.45, but the *intrinsic* part of this value is $2.03. That's the amount it's in the money; it's the dollar advantage that the strike price intrinsically gives us over the market price."

"Well, that leaves a difference of $2.42," interrupted Lon. "If we have a total value for this option of $4.45, and the intrinsic value is $2.03, then that leaves $2.43 in value that *isn't* intrinsic. So what's that part of the total value called? 'Extrinsic value?'"

"Exactly," replied Nate. "The remaining $2.43 is not due to the difference in strike and market price; it's *not* made up of this actual, tangible advantage. It's due instead to the other elements we talked about. Together they make up what we call *extrinsic value*. So we might draw a table like the one in Figure 25.3."

"I didn't say it before," said Nate, "but obviously only a strike that's in the money has intrinsic value. Remember, intrinsic value *just is* the amount a strike price is in the money. Out-of-the-money strikes don't have any intrinsic value: that's precisely *why* they're called *out of the money*. All the value they have is based on expectation, time value, and the like."

"Now obviously all this works the same for puts," said Aaron. "Look again at the option chain. Suppose we wanted to buy a put at a strike of $35. Someone has determined that the value of this option is $2.87. (See Figure 25.4.)

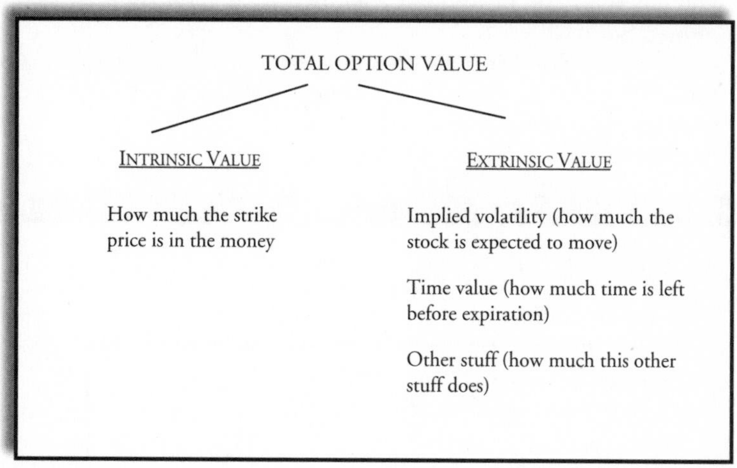

FIGURE 25.3 Option Value

"Now compare the current market price of $34.53 to the strike price of $35," he continued. "That's a $0.47 difference. The strike price is $0.47 higher than the market price. And that means that if I bought this option I would have the right, immediately, to sell shares at $35 even though the market price is $34.53. I'm $0.47 in the money, and that means the option has $0.47 of intrinsic value. The remaining value of the option, $2.40 ($2.87 − $0.47), is all extrinsic value."

Jul 08 Calls		(224 days to expiration)		MSFT@34.53								Jul 08 Puts	
MSQGE	9.60	0	10.30	10.40	20.8	.99	25.00	MSQSE	0.42	-0.03	0.40	0.41	36.0	-.08
MSQGY	7.75	0	8.15	8.20	25.3	.92	27.50	MSQSY	0.68	-0.06	0.68	0.69	33.7	-.13
MSQGF	6.00	-0.15	6.15	6.20	25.7	.83	30.00	MSQSF	1.18	0	1.12	1.14	31.7	-.21
MSQGZ	4.45	+0.05	4.40	4.45	25.3	.71	32.50	MSQSZ	1.83	-0.04	1.82	1.85	30.4	-.31
MSQGG	2.96	+0.01	2.97	3.00	24.8	.58	35.00	MSQSG	2.88	-0.06	2.85	2.87	29.7	-.42
MSQGU	1.90	-0.01	1.87	1.89	24.2	.43	37.50	MSQSU	4.37	-1.03	4.20	4.25	29.5	-.54
MSQGH	1.13	0	1.10	1.13	23.7	.30	40.00	MSQSH	6.00	-0.20	5.95	6.05	30.7	-.64
MSQGV	0.63	-0.02	0.61	0.63	23.3	.19	42.50	MSQSV	8.30	0	8.05	8.15	33.4	-.70
MSQGI	0.33	-0.01	0.32	0.34	23.1	.12	45.00	MSQSI	10.65	0	10.30	10.50	37.2	-.74

FIGURE 25.4 Identifying "Intrinsic" and "Extrinsic" Value for Puts
Source: Screenshot courtesy of optionsXpress, Inc. © 2008.

"Which is made up of implied volatility, time value, and all that other stuff," added Shorty.

"Right," said Nate. "So now take this review to make sure you've got these ideas."

REVIEW

"First, fill in this chart."

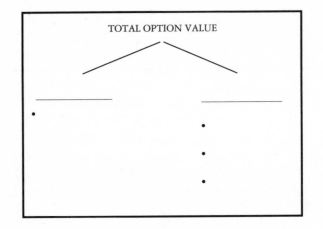

Review

"Now answer some questions based on the option chain." (See page 141.)

1. If your only consideration were to avoid time decay, which month would you choose for placing your option?

2. If you bought an April 2008 call at a strike of $30:

   (a) What would you pay for the option?

   (b) How much of that would be intrinsic value? How much would be extrinsic value?

3. If you bought a January 2009 put at a strike of $35:

   (a) What would you pay for the option?

   (b) How much of that would be intrinsic value? How much would be extrinsic value?

Apr 08 Calls		(133 days to expiration)		EBAY @ 33.73			Strike	Apr 08 Puts						
QXBDE	9.30	0	9.50	9.70	42.8	.91	25.00	QXBPE	0.60	0	0.45	0.55	46.0	-.10
QXBDY	7.80	0	7.40	7.60	40.9	.85	27.50	QXBPY	0.95	0	0.85	0.95	44.1	-.17
XBADF	5.80	+0.20	5.60	5.70	39.7	.75	30.00	XBAPF	1.50	-0.10	1.45	1.50	41.7	-.25
XBADZ	3.95	-0.15	4.00	4.10	38.4	.64	32.50	XBAPZ	2.30	-0.20	2.30	2.40	40.4	-.36
XBADG	2.75	-0.05	2.70	2.80	37.0	.51	35.00	XBAPG	3.60	0	3.50	3.60	39.5	-.48
XBADU	1.70	-0.10	1.75	1.80	36.0	.39	37.50	XBAPU	5.20	0	5.00	5.10	38.8	-.60
XBADH	1.05	-0.15	1.05	1.15	35.4	.27	40.00	XBAPH	7.30	0	6.90	7.00	40.2	-.69
XBADV	0.70	+0.05	0.65	0.70	35.3	.19	42.50	XBAPV	8.91	0	9.00	9.10	42.2	-.76
Jul 08 Calls		(224 days to expiration)		EBAY @ 33.73				Jul 08 Puts						
QXBGE	10.50	0	10.10	10.30	40.2	.89	25.00	QXBSE	1.05	0	0.85	0.95	44.4	-.13
QXBGY	8.20	0	8.20	8.40	39.6	.82	27.50	QXBSY	1.45	0	1.40	1.45	42.9	-.19
XBAGF	6.70	+0.20	6.50	6.70	38.9	.74	30.00	XBASF	2.20	0	2.10	2.15	41.4	-.27
XBAGZ	5.10	-0.20	5.00	5.10	37.5	.65	32.50	XBASZ	3.10	-0.10	3.00	3.10	40.2	-.35
XBAGG	3.90	0	3.70	3.80	36.2	.55	35.00	XBASG	4.30	0	4.20	4.30	39.5	-.44
XBAGU	2.75	+0.10	2.70	2.80	35.7	.45	37.50	XBASU	5.80	0	5.60	5.80	39.3	-.53
XBAGH	1.90	-0.05	1.85	1.95	34.5	.35	40.00	XBASH	7.30	-1.50	7.30	7.50	39.5	-.61
XBAGV	1.30	-0.15	1.30	1.40	34.4	.27	42.50	XBASV	9.60	0	9.30	9.50	41.3	-.67
Jan 09 Calls		(406 days to expiration)		EBAY @ 33.73				Jan 09 Puts						
OYIAE	11.20	-0.30	11.30	11.50	39.4	.86	25.00	OYIME	1.70	-0.20	1.65	1.75	44.8	-.16
OYIAY	9.50	0	9.60	9.80	39.0	.80	27.50	OYIMY	2.50	0	2.30	2.45	43.6	-.21
OYIAF	7.90	-0.30	8.00	8.20	37.9	.74	30.00	OYIMF	3.30	-0.10	3.10	3.30	42.5	-.27
OYIAG	5.40	-0.30	5.30	5.50	36.0	.60	35.00	OYIMG	5.50	-0.20	5.30	5.50	41.3	-.39
OYIAU	4.60	+0.20	4.30	4.50	35.8	.53	37.50	OYIMU	7.30	0	6.70	6.90	41.2	-.46
OYIAH	3.40	-0.10	3.40	3.60	35.2	.45	40.00	OYIMH	9.50	0	8.30	8.50	41.6	-.51

Source: Screenshot courtesy of optionsXpress, Inc. © 2008.
Review

4. If you bought a July 2008 call at a strike of $35:

(a) What would you pay for the option?

(b) How much of that would be intrinsic value? How much would be extrinsic value?

"Now there's another general principle we need to share that will be important in making trades," announced Nate.

Sell 60 Call $2

by 50 Call $5

Risk of Loss = 3 $

10 lots = 3000 Risk

potential gain 7K

plus $2000 premium

on sale

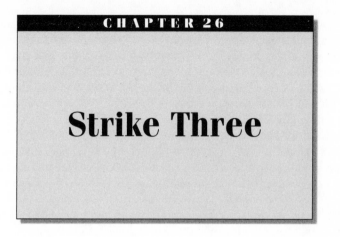

CHAPTER 26

Strike Three

"The principle is that, for the kind of trades we will be making, we will usually be placing strike prices *out of the money*. We may want them near the money, or even at the money, but usually not *in* the money."

"Why's that?" asked Lon.

"Well, there are two basic parts to the answer," answered Nate. "First, remember that some of the time we want to *finish* out of the money. Suppose Shorty, for example, wants to place a short call on 100 of his shares that are trading at $45 per share because he wants to receive a credit. But suppose he wants to be able to *keep* the shares that he owns: he doesn't want to be called out and have to sell them. In that case he'll want to pick a strike price that is high—maybe $50 or $55—because that will increase his chances of finishing out of the money—it will increase his chances of the stock price never reaching that high. If the stock price never reaches that high he won't be called out, he'll get to keep his shares, and of course he'll keep the credit he received for entering the deal in the first place."

> *If I want to finish out of the money—for example, because I want to keep my shares—I need to* start *out of the money.*

"I get it," said Shorty. "If I want to finish out of the money—for example, because I want to keep my shares—I need to *start* out of the money."

143

"Good. Now the second part of why we don't place strikes in the money is a function of the delta," said Aaron. "Remember, the delta is a mathematical relationship that identifies how much an option value will change as the stock value changes. For example, as we said earlier, a delta of 0.5 would mean that the option value would change $0.50 for every $1 change in the stock price. If the stock price goes up or down by $1, the option value will go up or down by $0.50.

"Now as we said earlier," Aaron continued, "this delta itself changes; it doesn't remain static. It might be 0.5 at one time and 0.55 at another and 0.35 at another. And what's critical to know is that this delta *doesn't change at a constant rate*; instead, it changes at different rates *depending on where the strike price is*. Specifically, the closer the strike price gets to being in the money, the faster the delta changes—the faster its rate of change. And interestingly, once the strike price goes in the money, the rate of change goes down dramatically. It doesn't change as fast anymore. The delta is higher, but its rate doesn't change as quickly. Of course, as with all rules there are some exceptions to this, but this is what happens the vast majority of the time."

"So think about it," said Nate. "Suppose Lon places a long call on 100 of his shares that are trading at $45. He wants the stock price to go higher than that—say, to $50 or $55. Because of his long call he can buy at $45 and turn around and sell at $50 or $55. So he wants his strike price to go in the money by having the stock price pass it up."

"Right," said Lon.

"Okay, fair enough," continued Nate. "But we want now to focus strictly on the value of the *option*. Remember, we're learning how to trade options themselves, whether we own any underlying stock or not. So, what's happening to the value of Lon's option while the stock price is moving up?"

"It's moving up, too," answered Shorty.

"*And when is it moving up the fastest?*" Nate asked with emphasis.

"Well, right before it goes in the money. It will go up slower after that," said Shorty.

"Oh, I get it!" exclaimed Lon suddenly. "That's why we place our strike price at least slightly out of the money: it's how we take advantage of the faster rate of return that we get *just before* it goes in the money—and then slows down."

"Exactly," said Nate. "If we placed trades like this in the money we would miss out on the faster rate of change—the faster increase—that occurs just before that. Not to mention that in-the-money options are also more expensive—as we've seen and as you two discovered on your own."

"Fair enough?" asked Aaron.

"Fair enough," Shorty and Lon both answered.

"But I have another question about strike prices," said Lon. "What determines *how* far out of the money we want to place them? Some of them are pretty far out, after all."

"That's true. Unfortunately, your question is so general that a complete answer to it is a bit complex. Too complex for where we are right now. The answer is different for each option instrument, for example, and it's also different depending on whether we own the underlying stock or not. It's even different depending on whether we *want* to own the underlying stock or not. So there are a lot of variables to consider."

"We *can* say this much, though," added Nate. "We always choose the strike price that gives us the best chance of making money while reducing risk, given our expectation of what the stock will do. Now, that's a lot to chew on ... which, after all, is why we're not going to stop and chew on it. Tomorrow night we'll talk about two basic option trades, and five spread trades, and we'll explain the choice of strike prices in those cases. That's the best way to learn, and doing so will then help you think about strike placement in other circumstances. I'm afraid that any other way of proceeding would just bog us down and you'd never learn to actually make a trade. Fair enough?"

"Okay. Fair enough."

"Good. Then let's do a review."

REVIEW

"If we want to _____ out of the money—for example, because we want to keep our shares—we need to _____ out of the money. That's one reason for placing our strike price _____.

"Option value moves up fastest _____ going _____. That's one reason we place our strike price at least _____."

"Okay, now let's talk about actually choosing stocks," said Nate.

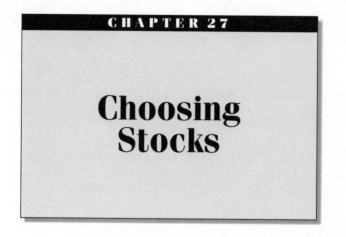

CHAPTER 27

Choosing Stocks

"**O**bviously, picking stocks is one of the first things you have to do when you begin trading seriously. Once you gain experience you will have more ways to think about how to choose stocks, but for now I just want to get a few fundamentals on the ground."

"The first principle," Aaron jumped in, "is to find companies that you believe are bullish long term. This isn't because you expect to buy shares and hold them forever. That's a different strategy altogether, and a risky one. No, you're going to be more active than that; you're going to be trading options on a regular basis."

"Right," added Nate. "Some people trade options frequently, others much less so. But we're never just buying and holding shares, hoping the stock goes up enough over the long haul to make money. As Aaron said, that strategy is risky. Every stock, no matter how bullish, goes through periods that are nonbullish, and a buy-and-hold strategy leaves us helpless during those times. Trading options, on the other hand, helps us make money even then."

"But none of this means that company quality doesn't matter." Aaron said it with emphasis. "The backbone of your trading activity should still be strong companies that will grow over time. That at least gives you long-term growth potential, *and* it allows you to predict how your companies will perform over time."

"Now as you look for companies, there's more than one way to evaluate their quality," added Nate, "but it's pretty common to focus on some key numbers that predict a company's *growth*. If we want a company that is bullish long term, we want a company that will grow. And the best measure of that is how it has grown in the past in some key areas."

> *The backbone of your trading activity should be strong companies that will grow over time.*

"You're an accountant, Shorty," he continued, "but we're going to share these ideas as if you weren't. We're going to keep it very simple."

"Fine by me."

FIVE KEY AREAS OF PERFORMANCE

"So what we want to do," said Aaron, "is to look at the history of a company in the key areas of performance that Nate's talking about. For example, we want to know if *sales* are growing. Is the company selling more this year than last ... and what about 5 or 10 years before that? If sales are up this year, is that a fluke, or is it something the company does routinely? Historical growth rates in sales provide an important indicator of the strength of a company and of whether it will *continue* to grow.

"Another key number is *earnings* growth. Each public company declares its *earnings per share* (EPS) every quarter, and this gives us a regular measure of the company's profitability: is profitability growing every year, or not? That's a key indicator of a company's overall strength and growth potential, and, again, it pays to look at this indicator over a five- or ten-year period; that's the only way to have any chance of predicting what the future holds."

"Another very important number," added Nate, "is called *return on invested capital* (ROIC). Each year companies invest cash in themselves; the question is, What return do they make on that investment? Obviously, the higher the return the better, and that's what we're looking for: companies that have a strong ROIC (say, 10 percent or so) year after year. It's an important sign of strength and of management competence.

"We also want to look at a company's ability to grow its *equity*. You might think of equity as the *liquidation value* of the company: it answers the question, How much cash would the company have left over if they closed their doors, sold everything, and paid off all their debts—in other words, if they completely liquidated? What we want to know, then, is whether a company is *growing* this liquidation value, this equity, year after year. A company that consistently increases its equity is fundamentally strong and will likely grow in market value over time. And that's what we're looking for."

> *There's a web site you can visit that will provide all these numbers for you. It's called* OptionsAnimal, *and it's easy.*

"Another factor to look at carefully," said Aaron, "is the *debt* position of the company. How much of the company's equity is lowered by the company's debt? Or, put another way, what is the *ratio* of debt to equity? And is that ratio growing over time, or is it decreasing? As you can imagine, we want a company's debt to be lower than its equity, so we want the debt-to-equity ratio to be less than 1.0. If it's over 1.0, that's a problem. And again, we'd like to see this low debt-to-equity ratio year after year."

INTRINSIC VALUE: IS THE COMPANY PRICED RIGHT?

"Okay, a final factor to look at is what's called the *intrinsic value* of a company," said Nate. "You might think about it this way. If we look at a company's current stock price, we can see how the market currently values that company. If Nextall is selling for $30 per share, for example, that means the market—as played out through countless negotiations expressing the forces of supply and demand—currently thinks Nextall is *worth* $30 per share."

"But that doesn't mean the market is *right*," added Aaron. "See, Nextall might be a strong, high-growth company, that should be selling for *more* than that—and the market just isn't noticing right now. Doing your own homework, you might determine that it's the best in its industry—that it has more potential for growth than any of its competitors, and that it has more growth potential than the market is recognizing. In that case, what you're saying is that the market as a whole is *under*valuing Nextall. It's worth more than it's currently selling for. In that case, you're making a judgment about its intrinsic value, rather than about its current market value. Make sense?"

"Sure."

"Okay. Well, there's a pretty good shorthand way to actually calculate this intrinsic value. The first step is to compare (1) what a stock is *earning* to (2) what the stock is *selling for*.

"Think back to the concept of 'earnings per share.' Remember, that tells us a lot about the profitability of a company—how much it's making per share. Now we simply want to divide *that* into the market price of the stock. See, the stock is *selling* for so much per share, and it's also *making* so much per share. So what's the relationship between the two?"

"Well," continued Nate, "let's say Nextall has earnings per share of $2, and it's selling on the market for $30 per share. Here's how we would show that:

$$\frac{\$30 \ (\text{Price: Market price of the stock})}{\$2 \ (\text{Earnings: EPS})}$$

"In this case, the stock is selling for 15 times as much as it's earning. That's called the P/E ratio, by the way: *price* (stock price) divided by *earnings* (EPS). So we would say that Nextall has a P/E of 15, which just means, again, that it's selling for 15 times as much as it's earning. That's why you will also see this referred to as a *multiple*. The market price is a 'multiple' of the earnings. In this case, a multiple of 15."

"Just a second," interrupted Lon. "I've never realized before that when I invested I was actually paying more for a stock than it was earning. But I guess everyone is doing the same thing. But why? Why are we all paying more—in this case, 15 times more than the stock is earning?"

"Good question," replied Aaron. "And the answer is because of expected *growth*. The market is judging—again, through countless negotiations expressing the forces of supply and demand—that the company will be worth more down the road than it is today. It's earning at a certain rate, and it's growing at a certain rate, and that predicts certain earnings and growth down the road. It's all based on expectation. Make sense? People paying $30 today are simply expecting to be able to sell for more at some point in the future. Well, because a lot of people have this expectation, the price just gets pushed up higher and higher. It's just a matter of demand naturally leading to higher prices."

"Incidentally," added Nate, "we should mention that a multiple of 15 isn't really very high. It's about average, in fact. Where expectations are *really* high for a stock, the demand will also be high, and then you can have multiples of 30 and 40 and higher. Well, you get the idea. Does it make sense?"

"Sure. The higher the expectations are for a stock, the more people will want it. The more people want it, the higher the price will get pushed. And the higher the price gets pushed, the higher the multiple will be."

"Good," said Aaron. "So the first step, then, in our shorthand calculation of intrinsic value is to determine this P/E ratio, this multiple. And the second step now is to compare our P/E of 15 to the *earnings growth rate* of Nextall ... an element we've already talked about. Let's say it's 25, for example, meaning that Nextall's earnings are growing at a rate of 25 percent per year. Now, generally speaking, a fair market price has a multiple that *matches* the earnings growth rate, which means that Nextall ought to have a multiple of 25, not 15. And if it *did* have a multiple of 25, then the stock should be selling for $50 rather than $30."

"Sorry," said Lon. "That was too fast. I need you to break that down for me."

"No problem. Here's the idea. If Nextall's growth rate is 25 percent per year, then all we're saying is that the multiple should *also* be 25. And if it were—and if Nextall's earnings were, as we've supposed, $2 per share—then a fair market price for Nextall would be $50 per share: $2 times 25. In other words, $50 per share is the *intrinsic* value of the stock—what it's really worth, whether the market realizes it or not."

"Another way to put this," said Nate, "is that the stock is simply under-priced. It's worth $50 per share, and it's selling for only $30. The intrinsic value of Nextall is higher than its current market price . . . and that makes it a good deal.

"Well, anyway, that's the concept of 'intrinsic value.' It's the relation-ship between the P/E and the earnings growth rate of the company. And you can calculate it easily to see how it compares to the market value of the company."

LET SOMEONE ELSE CRUNCH THE NUMBERS FOR YOU

"So there you have it," concluded Aaron. "In evaluating a company, we want to look at six major factors: sales growth rate, earnings growth rate, equity growth rate, ROIC, debt-to-equity ratio, and intrinsic value."

"Sounds simple," said Lon, "but actually that's quite a bit to take in. Even more than you think. I don't have a clue how to go about collecting these numbers. I've got to admit that since I've been in the market I've never been very good at this kind of thing. I've gone more or less by the seat of my pants, I guess."

"Well, you've got to stop that," replied Nate. "It really pays to under-stand the fundamentals of the companies you work with. You have to do your 'due diligence,' as we say, which simply means that you have to do your homework. You have to know if the company is worth putting your money into. You have to be wise."

"We've also got some good news for you," added Aaron. "There's a web site you can visit that will provide all these numbers for you. It's called *Op-tionsAnimal*, and it's easy. In fact, Lon, that was the web site you stumbled across and that led you to Nate in the first place. You just go to that web site, plug in the ticker symbol of the company you're thinking about, and it will calculate these numbers for you for the past 10 years—or whatever years are available up to 10."

"Right," said Nate, "and basically you're looking for these growth rates: *sales*, *earnings* (EPS), and *equity*. Ideally, you're looking for these growth rates to be consistently 10 percent or higher. In other words, you want sales, earnings per share, and equity all to be growing 10 percent per year *every* year. That's not a hard-and-fast rule, but you get the idea. The more a company is growing in these areas, and the more consistently it is growing in these areas, the better it is for you."

"Now when it comes to *return on invested capital* (ROIC)," said Aaron, "we're not really looking at growth rates. All we want is for the ROIC to be strong every year, and 10 percent isn't a bad number here, either. If you look at a 5- or 10-year history and the ROIC is 10 percent or higher every year, that's a strong indicator of a sound company. Obviously, anything higher than that is even better."

"The same goes for the debt-to-equity ratio," added Nate. "We're not looking for growth; we just want a good history of the ratio being under 1.0."

"In sum, as you look at companies, you can just go to the *OptionsAnimal* web site and find your basic information there. How does that sound?"

"Sounds great. It would be way too time consuming for me to figure all this out on my own." Lon was shaking his head. "This will be a huge help."

"Yeah, me too," said Shorty. "This will save a ton of work."

ADDITIONAL FACTORS IN CHOOSING STOCKS

"While we're on the subject of choosing stocks," said Aaron, "we should mention a few more matters. First, we're obviously looking for stocks that are what we call *optionable*. See, you can't actually trade options with every stock that's out there. You can with most of them, but not with all. So, obviously, you want to make sure you're looking at companies where you can actually trade options. To find this out all you do is go to *OptionsAnimal*, plug in a stock you're interested in, and click on the *Options* link. If the stock is optionable, option information will appear; if it's not, no option information will appear. Easy as that."

"Another matter," added Nate, "is that we're not looking to invest in a basketful of companies the way a mutual fund might do. No, we're looking for a *handful*. We want to watch 15 to 20 companies, and become familiar with them, but we want to invest in no more than 4 to 5 at any one time. At least not until we get a lot of experience."

"Why's that?"

"Well for one thing, we want to really know the companies we put money into, and you can know only a few companies really well. Not only do we want to know the kind of fundamentals we've been talking about; we also want to know how companies normally act in the marketplace. How are they typically affected by news events? By economic changes? By Fed announcements? By good and bad earnings reports? It pays to have a "feel" for a company, and you can only have that with so many.

> *It usually pays to focus on the* best *companies in a particular industry or sector of the market.*

"A second reason for only trading a few companies at a time," continued Nate, "is that it usually pays to focus on the *best* companies in a particular industry or sector of the market. Those companies give us the best chance to make money over time and, by definition, there will always be just a few of them. So if we focus on the best, we will necessarily limit the number of companies we put money into at any one time.

"Finally, focusing on a few companies at a time allows us to keep things simple—to have our eyes on only a few companies, *but to milk each investment for all it's worth.* You both said you invested in Plum, for example. Good; that's a strong company with good fundamentals. Still, over time Plum will go up, down, and sideways ... but that's not bad news for you, because *each* of those movements still gives you a chance to make money. When Plum starts to move down, for example, you don't just sell that stock and look for another company to invest in. No! You can stick with Plum and simply use the option instruments that make money in a downward trend. Then, when Plum moves up again, you simply use the option instruments that make money in an upward trend. You don't take your eye off Plum; you just change how you *trade* with Plum."

"That doesn't mean that you would never sell Plum shares," inserted Aaron. "You could do that at any time if doing so promised the best results. It only means that you have a lot more options than that. There are more ways to make money with Plum than just buying and selling it; you can buy and sell options *around* it. Using options with just a handful of companies makes life much simpler, and yet gives you a lot more ways to make money."

"I can see that."

"Me, too."

"Okay, a second matter you should pay attention to," said Nate, "is the volume of shares that are traded every day on a particular stock. Generally speaking, the more shares that are being traded, the more flexibility you have—the quicker you can get in and out when you want to. So a good rule of thumb is to look for a volume of at least a million shares per day.

"Related to that is another factor we call *institutional ownership*. See, most buyers and sellers in the market are actually professional investors who handle huge amounts of other people's money. Because they manage so much money, they buy and sell shares in enormous chunks. That's good news for us because it means that those professional investors examine companies very carefully. They generate estimates of companies' current soundness and of their anticipated growth. In other words, *they do some of our homework for us*. That's why it pays, at least generally speaking, to restrict ourselves to companies that have a significant institutional ownership; we know that professionals are examining them closely. For the most part, we want institutional ownership to be 50 percent or higher. That simply means that institutional investors own 50 percent or more of the company's shares. And you can find this out by simply going to *OptionsAnimal* and following the links. Couldn't be easier."

"Does all this make sense?"

"Yup."

"Good. Then let's do a quick review."

REVIEW

"We want to look at six fundamentals to examine the growth potential of a company: _____, _____, _____, _____, _____, and _____. We want the growth rates to be at least _____, we want the ROIC to be at least _____, and we want the debt/equity ratio to be _____. P/E refers to the _____ ratio. Another term for this is _____, which is determined by dividing the _____ per _____ by the _____ per _____. We determine the intrinsic value of a company by comparing its _____ rate to its _____ ratio. In trading options, we obviously want a stock that is _____. We also want the stock to trade at least _____ shares per day. Finally, we want institutional ownership to be _____ or higher."

"Okay," said Aaron, "the idea of trends has come up a couple of times. It's time to get more specific."

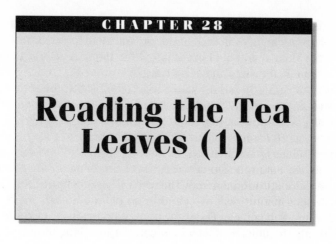

CHAPTER 28

Reading the Tea Leaves (1)

"We need at least to get a few fundamentals in place regarding trends," he said.

"All right," Lon and Shorty agreed.

"The whole idea is to know enough about trends to have some sense of what a stock might do. That prepares us to make the most money. No one can read the future perfectly, of course, but it's possible to make educated guesses and to be prepared. That's what we want to do."

THE OVERALL MARKET

"Before we talk more about watching the trend of a particular stock," said Nate, "there's something you need to know about stocks in general. It's that 80 percent of stocks simply follow the trend of the overall market. Now if you think about it, that's obvious, of course. In fact, it's almost redundant. After all, 80 percent of the market practically *is* the market, right? So to say that the market is in a certain trend is simply *to say* that a high percentage of stocks are in a certain trend. Right?"

"Sure," answered Shorty.

"But there's still an important point that follows from this," said Aaron. "It means that, at any point in time, any stock you pick is likely to be following the same general trend that most other stocks are following. You can always find exceptions, of course, and you can even find whole sectors of the market that will be exceptions. But finding those exceptions doesn't matter so much when you know how to use options. Here, you can just accept the general trend of the market and, working with the stocks you've picked, take advantage of that trend, whatever it happens to be. This is much easier than searching high and low for the exceptions and then trying to buy and sell them at the right time."

"With that point in mind," said Nate, "let's briefly cover the major indicators of an overall market trend. The first is the Dow Jones Industrial Average. As you know, it tracks 30 major companies that are thought to reflect the overall economic base of the United States."

Nate brought up a screen on his laptop. "Here's a $2\frac{1}{2}$ year look at the Dow Jones, for example. Don't worry about anything on the chart but the overall 'look' of it, as indicated by the arrows." (See Figure 28.1.)

"With such a long look, we can see an overall bullish trend from the end of 2005 until July 2007. Then a bearish trend begins in October 2007. Of course, there are smaller movements within these long-term trends; these would show up more clearly if we took, say, a six-month view—but you get the idea. The Dow Jones is a good overall indicator of the market, and thus helps us think about the specific stocks we're in."

"A second helpful indicator," said Aaron, "is the Standard & Poor's (S&P) 500—a 500-stock cross-section of the market. Figure 28.2 shows a $2\frac{1}{2}$ year look at this indicator. Again, just get the overall look of the chart."

"We see the same basic trend as the Dow Jones showed."

"And a third major indicator of the market," continued Aaron, "is the Nasdaq—an index made up primarily of technology companies. Here's a $2\frac{1}{2}$ year look at the Nasdaq." (See Figure 28.3.)

"This indicator has some differences, but speaking broadly it shows the same trend as the other two."

"Now all we've said so far," observed Nate, "is (1) that overall market trends give valuable information about our specific stocks, and (2) that there are three major indicators that most people look at to determine the market trend: the Dow Jones, the S&P, and the Nasdaq. What's nice is that there are a number of places you can go to find this information for free. One good place is stockcharts.com. Simply go to that site and enter the ticker symbol for the index you want to look at. For the Dow Jones you would enter $INDU; for the S&P, SPX; and for the Nasdaq, COMPQ. The data will then appear. You can also modify the chart in any number of ways, including modifying it to show different lengths of time."

READING MARKET SENTIMENT

"There are additional indicators that help us read the overall market as well," said Aaron. "Two of them help us read its 'mood' or 'sentiment.' One

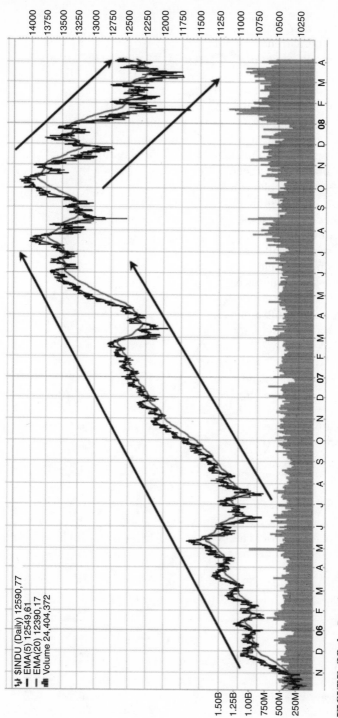

FIGURE 28.1 Dow Jones

Source: Chart courtesy of StockCharts.com.

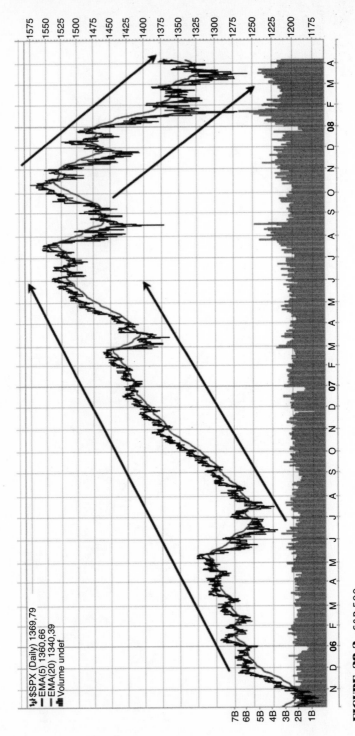

FIGURE 28.2 S&P 500

Source: Chart courtesy of StockCharts.com.

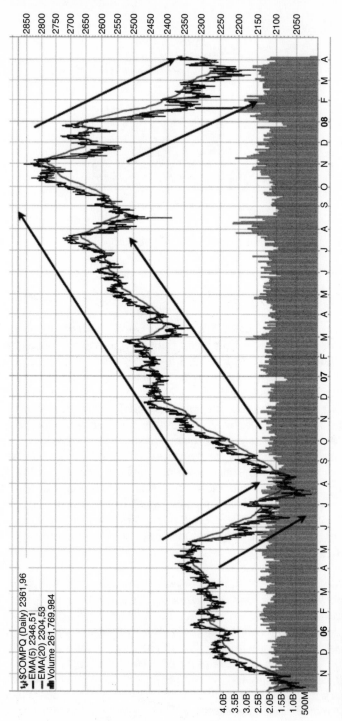

FIGURE 28.3 Nasdaq

Source: Chart courtesy of StockCharts.com.

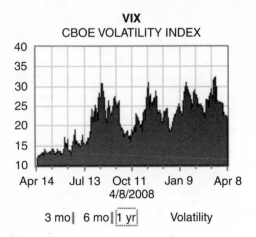

FIGURE 28.4   VIX

is called the *volatility index*, or VIX, for short, and it essentially measures the volatility of the S&P 500. You might think of it as a gauge of the fear in the market. Look at Figure 28.4, for example.

"This gives us a one-year view, from April to April, and notice that the scale of this chart ranges from 10 to 40. Now the range between 15 and 30 gives us only generalities about the market, even though they're useful. For example, the higher the VIX level, the greater the fear in the market, and the lower the VIX level, the greater the optimism."

"And that's good to know, as Aaron said," added Nate, "but the extremes tell us even more. In fairly normal times, for example, a VIX level over 30 tells us not only that there is fear in the market, but also that it's likely reached its bottom. The downward trend is probably played out, and a bullish move is likely. Similarly, a VIX level below 15 in fairly normal times tells us not only that the market is pretty bullish—even complacent—but also that the best may be over. In that case, a bearish move is likely."

"Now look, you guys," Aaron said with emphasis. "An indicator like this isn't *perfect*. There can be extreme times, for example—like late 2008—when the VIX level can go much higher, even to 80 or 90. In times like that, a level of 30 has little meaning. And even in fairly normal times, the VIX doesn't predict with precision. The VIX is only an *indicator*. Perfection in predicting isn't the point. The point is simply to find clues that will *help* us by alerting us to what's going on. So, while no indicator is perfect, every indicator is helpful, and this one can help us see when the mood of the market might be changing. That's good to know. It's also good to know that you can find this information in a number of places online for free. You might try cboe.com, for instance."

"Another indicator of market 'mood' or 'sentiment,'" added Nate, "is simply the ratio between puts and calls in the market. To see why this is so, let me ask you a couple of questions. First, when an investor places a long call, or in other words *buys* a call, what is he normally thinking?"

"He's thinking the stock is going up. A long call is basically a bullish move," Lon said confidently.

"So what does it mean if a lot of people in the market are placing long calls?"

"Well, they're pretty confident. They're bullish."

"Okay. Now what is an investor normally thinking when he places a long put or, in other words, *buys* a put?"

"He's thinking the stock might go down," answered Shorty. "It's a bear-ish move; he's protecting himself."

"So what if *a lot of people* in the market are placing long puts?"

"It means they're worried. They're all trying to protect themselves."

"Good. Then here's what you need to know. In general, people buy calls more than they buy puts. Most people only know how to make money when values are rising, so that's when they buy: when they think values are rising. That's why most of the action in options, most of the time, is in calls, and not in puts. In fact, normally there are about 80 percent as many puts being traded as calls. So we say that the 'put-to-call ratio' is 0.8. It just means that for every 100 calls being traded, only 80 puts are being traded at the same time. And that's the normal case."

"So what do you suppose it means if we have a put-to-call ratio that is lower than that—say, anywhere between 0.5 and 0.8?" asked Aaron.

Lon thought about it for a second. "It would mean that even *fewer* puts are being traded. And that would suggest that investors are pretty confi-dent: they're focusing on calls even more than usual. So a lower put/call ratio is an indicator of a bullish mood."

"Okay. Exactly right. So now what do you suppose happens when in-vestors are worried?" asked Nate.

"Well, I guess more people start buying puts. That's the way you protect yourself—which is what you do, I guess, if you're worried."

"Right. And then the ratio changes. You might see a put-to-call ratio of 0.95, for example, which means that for every 100 calls being traded, 95 puts are also being traded. That's a significant increase and means that the mood of the market is bearish. When the ratio gets even higher—between 0.95 and, say, 1.5—you could say that the market mood is downright fear-ful. People are looking to protect themselves."

"So do you get the idea?" asked Aaron. "Looking at the put-to-call ratio can tell us at a glance what option investors in general are feeling—whether they're confident or fearful. And that's important information for us to have. It tells us the current mood of the market."

> *We just want to be poised to take advantage of whatever the market gives us. The more information we have, the more poised we will be.*

"Now, as you might imagine," added Nate, "there are a number of ways to calculate this put-to-call ratio; for reasons we don't need to go into now, we just want to make clear that we're talking about the *total* put-to-call ratio. There are others, but we're only talking now about the total ratio."

"It's worth noting, too," added Nate, "that we can use this put-to-call ratio as a predictor, just as we use the VIX."

"What do you mean?" asked Shorty.

"Well, remember that with the VIX, extreme levels suggest that a change is likely. For the reasons that we mentioned, an extreme level at the high end of the VIX suggests that a bearish move might be coming, and an extreme level at the low end suggests that a bullish move might be coming. Well, the put-to-call ratio can give us the same kind of indication."

"You might think about it this way," said Aaron. "Remember that the put-to-call ratio is normally about 0.8. So if the ratio gets *very* low—say, around 0.3 or 0.4 or even 0.5—that might suggest that the market is *unreasonably* bullish, and that a downward adjustment is likely. At the same time, if the put-to-call ratio gets very high—say, around 1.25 or 1.50—that might suggest that the market is unreasonably *bearish*, and that an upward adjustment is likely."

"There's no hard-and-fast rule to this," added Nate. "It's just that when we see extremes we want to be very alert because those extremes may signal a change. We just want to be poised to take advantage of whatever the market gives us. The more information we have, the more poised we will be."

"Got it."

"Now, just as with the VIX, you can get this put-to-call ratio in a number of places online for free, including, again, cboe.com."

"Good," said Aaron. "Now just complete this review to make sure you've got these basics of looking at the market."

REVIEW

"We normally look at three overall indicators of market trends. They are the
_____, the _____, and the
_____. We also determine the 'mood' or 'sentiment' of the
market by looking at the _____, and at total _____ ratios.
In both cases, higher numbers tell us the market is basically _____,
and lower numbers tell us the market is basically _____.
At the extremes, both indicate that the market may be ready to
_____ its current direction."

"Okay, once you've identified the stocks you want to trade with, and once you have a feel for overall market trends," said Aaron, "now you want to know *when* to make trades in your stocks."

CHAPTER 29

Reading the Tea Leaves (2): Stock Trends

"**T**o do this," he continued, "you need to have a sense of the trends of those specific stocks. We mentioned earlier five trends you ought to have in mind: slightly bearish, bearish, stagnant, slightly bullish, and bullish. Look at the chart in Figure 29.1, for example—again, just pay attention to the overall look of the chart as indicated by the arrows.

"The first set of arrows identifies a steep bullish trend for this stock. The second set shows a more normal bullish movement, and the third set of arrows shows a bearish trend. And in the chart in Figure 29.2 we can see a stagnant trend (the first arrows) and also a slight trend—here, in a bearish direction (the second arrows)."

"So these charts give you a picture of what the trends look like, more or less," said Nate. "Now, why do you think this is important? Why does it help to be able to determine trends?"

"Well, because different option instruments optimize different trends," answered Lon.

"Okay . . . but again, in plain English."

"All right: different option instruments *take advantage of* different trends. We simply want to use whatever option instrument will make money for us, given the trend we're in. A long call, for instance, is good for bullish trends. As the stock goes up in value, the long call normally goes up, too. I can then sell that long call for a profit. The long call therefore makes the most of—or optimizes—this bullish trend."

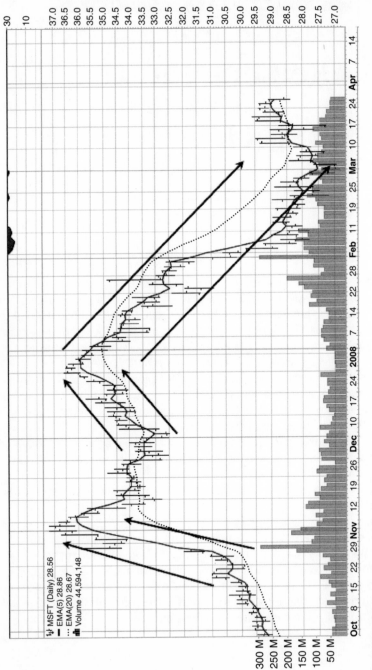

FIGURE 29.1 Bullish and Bearish Trends
Source: Chart courtesy of StockCharts.com.

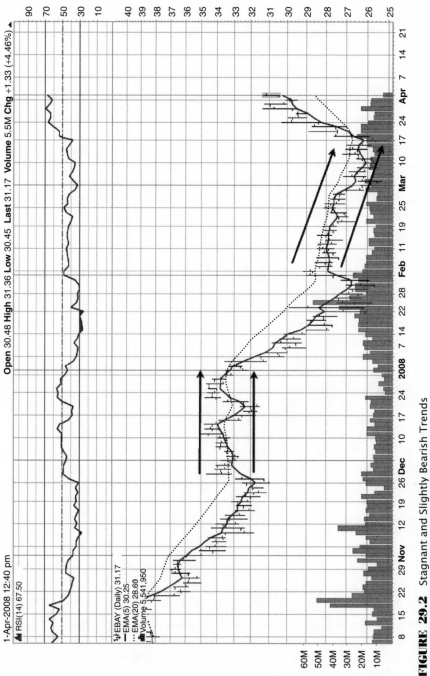

FIGURE 29.2 Stagnant and Slightly Bearish Trends

Source: Chart courtesy of StockCharts.com.

We simply want to use whatever option instrument will make money for us, given the trend we're in.

"Right," said Aaron, "and remember that that same long call is *bad* in a bearish or stagnant trend. In both of those cases, the value of the stock is not rising, so the value of the long call is not rising, either. Even worse, the long call will actually be dropping in value because of time decay. So while the long call is good in a bullish trend, I don't want to be stuck with it in stagnant or bearish trends."

"At the same time, of course," added Shorty, "a short call is *good* in a slightly bearish or stagnant trend. By selling the call I take in a credit. That credit is profit to me, and I get to keep that profit even though the stock is going down in value or just staying stagnant. I come out ahead either way. The short call makes the most of—or optimizes—a slightly bearish or stagnant trend."

"That's right, and you can do the same analysis for long puts and short puts," said Nate. "A long put is good in, or *optimizes*, bearish trends, because generally speaking it rises in value as the stock *goes down* in value. Again, that's just the nature of insurance. Thus, as the stock goes down in value, I can actually sell my long put for a profit."

"But," Lon jumped in, "that same long put is *bad* in a bullish or stagnant trend. In both of those cases, the value of the stock is not falling, so the value of the long put, the insurance, is not rising. In addition, the long put will actually be dropping in value because of time decay. So I don't want to be in a long put in a bullish or stagnant trend. Right?"

"That's right," answered Nate.

"And of course," added Shorty, "at the same time, a short put is *good* in more bullish and stagnant trends. By selling the put, I take in a credit, and that is profit to me. I get to keep it even though the stock is rising in value or just staying stagnant. I make and keep a profit either way. So the short put makes the most of a slightly bullish or stagnant trend. It *optimizes* these trends, so to speak."

"Okay, good. You've got all that."

TECHNICAL INDICATORS

"So now the question is, how do we recognize these trends *just as they are beginning*? Anyone can identify a trend once it's over, but that's no help at all. We want to be able to take advantage of a trend while it's happening."

"That's why," added Aaron, "we want to show you three signals we can look for that will help us identify trends. There are many more such signals that are available and that could be examined—they're called *technical indicators*, by the way—but these three lay the best foundation."

"We should also add," said Nate, "that it's possible to go into a lot of detail to explain exactly how these indicators work—the deep mathematics and assumptions that lie behind them—and if you two are interested in all that, there are places you can go to discover them. But, fortunately, that's not necessary. It's less important to know exactly *how* the indicators work than it is to know that they *do* work and that they are helpful in identifying trends. That's our focus."

"Okay then," continued Aaron, "let's have a look at these three technical indicators. It's easiest to explain them by looking at an actual chart. (See Figure 29.3.)

"Let's start at the top. This section is called the RSI (circled on the left) and stands for relative strength index. Notice that it has a range from 10 to 90. Now the key issue for us at this point is the '50' line. When the RSI line crosses this 50 line, going up, that is a bullish signal. So we would say that around March 17–18 the RSI gave us a bullish signal."

"Now move down the chart to the largest section," said Nate. "There are three measurements here that we want to look at. The first is a series of vertical bars going up and down across the page. These indicate actual daily stock prices and show where a stock opened on that day, what its high was, what its low was, and where it closed. These are therefore called 'OHLC' bars. Figure 29.4 shows what they look like on that same chart if we remove the other lines.

"Now if you go back to the original chart (Figure 29.3)," Nate continued, "you will notice that, in addition to these OHLC bars, there are two lines—one dotted and one solid—moving up and down across the page. Each is a measure of what is called the *EMA* or *exponential moving average*. Here's why: the solid line tells us the average value of the stock over the past 5 days, and the dotted line tells us the average value of the stock over the past 20 days. Now in both cases the most recent days are given more weight in determining the average; that's because the most recent activity is what matters most to us. That's also why these lines are referred to as *exponential* moving averages: they are exponential because the most recent days are given exponential weight."

"The details of this calculation don't matter," added Aaron. "What matters is the *relationship* between the two lines. When the 5-day EMA is higher than the 20-day EMA, it means that recent stock value is higher than previous stock value. That's bullish. What we want, then, is to find this trend at its beginning. And we do that by looking for the point at which the 5-day EMA *crosses over* the 20-day EMA, going up. We've drawn a square at that point on this chart. You can see that the 5-day crosses over the 20-day on March 17. That's an indicator of a beginning bullish trend."

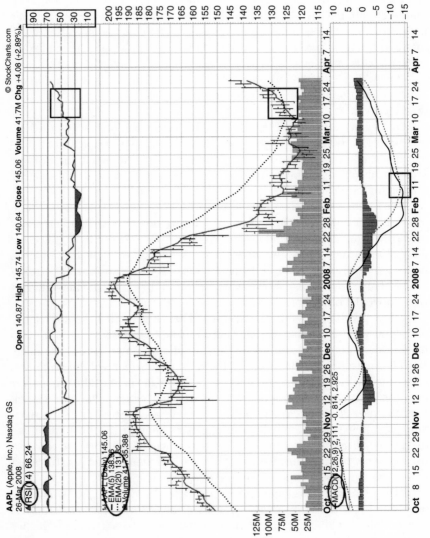

AAPL (Apple, Inc.) Nasdaq GS

26-Mar 2008

Open 140.87 High 145.74 Low 140.64 Close 145.06 Volume 41.7M Chg +4.08 (+2.89%)

© StockCharts.com

RSI(14) 66.24

AAPL (Daily) 145.06
EMA(5) 138.56
EMA(20) 131.92
Volume 41,735,388

MACD(12,26,9) 2.111, -0.814, 2.925

FIGURE 29.3 Three Technical Indicators

Source: Chart courtesy of StockCharts.com.

170

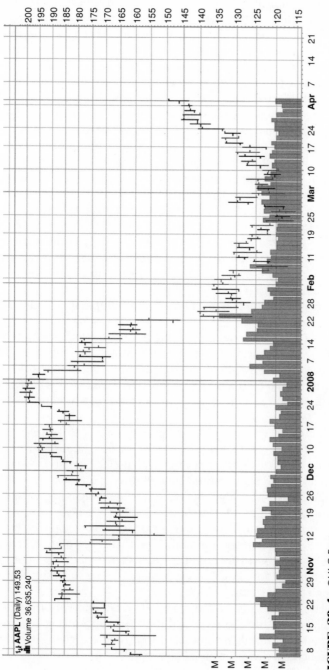

FIGURE 29.4 OHLC Bars

Source: Chart courtesy of StockCharts.com.

"And a third indicator is at the bottom of this chart," said Nate. "As you can see, circled on the left, this is called the moving average convergence/divergence, or *MACD*, which is normally pronounced 'mack-dee.' Putting all mathematical details aside, we're simply looking at the relationship between the two lines that appear there. Often, one of the lines is black and the other is red. In this figure, we've represented the "black" line with a solid line and the "red" one with a dotted line. The beginning of a new trend is indicated whenever the solid line crosses over the dotted line (in this case, going up), just as we've indicated here by the square."

"Now what we're always looking for," added Aaron, "is for *all three* indicators to give us the same signal. You'll notice, for example, that the MACD gives a bullish signal on February 11, but the RSI and the EMA don't give bullish signals until March 17. You'll also notice, in looking at the OHLC bars, that they don't start trending up until well after February 11, and very close to March 17. So by itself, the MACD was wrong … and that teaches a valuable lesson: you never rely on a crossover from a single indicator to make trading decisions. In fact, you never rely on just two. You wait until all three indicate a trend before taking any action. In this case that would be March 17."

"So the idea," said Shorty, "is that we would start making bullish trades on March 17, right?"

"Close, but not *quite* right. It's usually best to wait a day to see if the crossovers hold, because sometimes they will reverse immediately. But if they hold for a day, then yes, you start making bullish trades. The only exception would be if a major news event is what's driving the trend change; in that case you don't wait a day, but begin trading differently immediately."

"And, of course, we do the same type of thing with bearish trends," said Nate. "For example, Figure 29.5 shows a chart, on a different stock, that shows the three technical indicators signaling a bearish movement."

"In this case," said Nate, "notice that all three indicators—the RSI, the EMA, and the MACD—all give the same technical signal at virtually the same time, the beginning of March. They all give a bearish signal—the crossovers are *going down*—and that's exactly what happened with the stock price, as you can see in the OHLC bars. At that point, after waiting a day to see if the crossovers hold (again, if there's no major news event driving the change), you would want to start trading in a way that takes advantage of bearish trends."

"And," said Aaron, "just so that you will be familiar with the terminology, we usually say that the technical indicators are giving *buy signals* when they indicate a bullish trend, and that they are giving *sell signals* when they indicate a bearish trend. Make sense?"

"Yup," both Shorty and Lon answered.

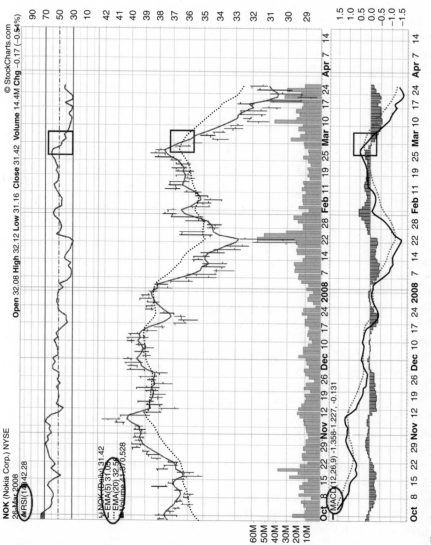

FIGURE 29.5 The Technical Indicators for a Bearish Movement

Source: Chart courtesy of StockCharts.com.

"Okay, now at this stage of your experience, it's easiest to see how you might use these technical signals with puts. Look at Figure 29.6, for example," said Aaron.

"Let's suppose you own this stock. Notice that it enjoys a nice bullish run from the end of November 2006 (see the first set of circles) to January 2007. Then about January 6 or 7 (see the squares), we get three sell signals; the RSI, the EMA, and the MACD all indicate a bearish trend. Now if we were just buying and selling stock, we might sell our stock at this point. But because we know how to use options, we don't have to do that. We can continue to hold our shares and simply place some long puts that will protect us in this downward trend."

> *Spotting the beginning of a trend, and using the right option instrument to make the most of it, gives us a way to make money even while everyone else is moaning and groaning. Unbelievable.*

"Right," added Nate. "And notice that this is a very significant downward trend. We don't know at the time how long it will last or how deep it will be; all we know is that our indicators are giving us bearish signals. So we add some long puts; because they will grow in value as the stock price drops, these long puts protect us against this bearish trend. And when you look at how this trend developed, you can see just how valuable this protection is. Anyone simply holding this stock saw a $65 drop in price from the time the sell signals appeared (at about $190) to the time the stock started moving back up again (at about $125). That's a drop of more than 30 percent, in $2^1/_2$ months. That's pretty serious."

"Right," said Aaron, "which is exactly why we never just hold stock and hope for the best. And we don't *have to* because we know how to use puts."

"So what do you suppose we do next?" asked Nate.

"Well," said Shorty, "we get one buy signal around February 11, but we don't get the other two until about March 17. If we look at the second set of circles, we see that the RSI, the EMA, and the MACD are all giving buy signals by then, indicating the beginning of a new bullish trend."

"Which means," Lon jumped in, "that we would probably *sell* our long puts at that point, right?"

"That's right. You bought them for protection, and you don't need this protection any longer because the stock isn't dropping any more. We say it has 'found bottom,' and is actually beginning a bullish movement. The long puts by now have grown in value by quite a bit, so you sell them for a good profit. And, if you want, you can take these profits and buy more of this stock, and do it at a low price."

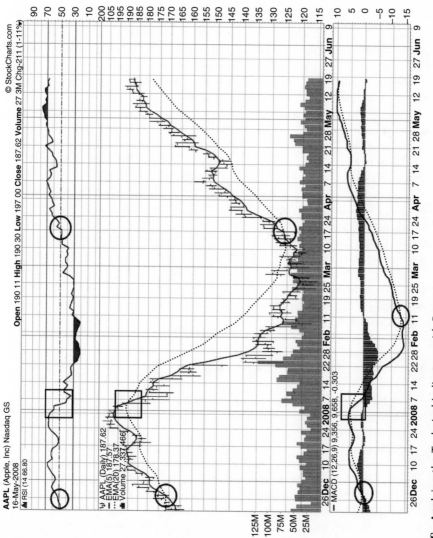

AAPL (Apple, Inc) Nasdaq GS
16-May-2008

Open 190 11 High 190 30 Low 197 00 Close 187.62 Volume 27 3M Chg-211 (1-11%)

© StockCharts.com

RSI (14 66.80

AAPL (Daily) 187.62
EMA(5) 187.57
EMA(20) 178.37
Volume 27,337,466

MACD (12,26,9) 9,356, 9,658, -0.303

FIGURE 29.6 Applying the Technical Indicators with Puts

Source: Chart courtesy of StockCharts.com.

"It's actually kind of incredible," said Aaron. "Everyone else who owns this stock is crying about the drop in price, but not you; you're actually *making* money from it. You're selling your puts for a profit, *and* you're picking up more shares of this stock at a low price. You're making money precisely *because* the stock price is falling. How can you beat that?"

"Yup," replied Shorty. "It is kind of amazing. Spotting the beginning of a trend, and using the right option instrument to make the most of it, gives us a way to make money even while everyone else is moaning and groaning. Unbelievable."

"That's right," agreed Nate. "Naturally, there's a ton more to learn about all this, but at least you have the basic idea. Good."

"Sorry, but I have another question before we move on." Lon leaned forward in his chair. "You've mentioned three technical indicators, but there must be others. Why stop with three?"

"You're right," replied Aaron, "there *are* others. But it's a question of practicality. We could look at a dozen indicators and still not have complete certainty about what will happen with a stock. In fact, if it's complete certainty we want, we'll *never* make a trade—ever—because complete certainty is impossible. We'll just sit there, paralyzed, in a trance, afraid to do anything. No, the most we can hope for is probability, so that's all we should expect. And that's what these indicators give us. In my experience, looking at these three indicators is the most practical way to get trend signals. Then we use option tools to make the most of the trend we expect, and then modify and adjust them when the trend changes. Make sense?"

"Yup. Got it."

SUPPORT AND RESISTANCE

"All right," said Aaron, "now that we have that concept in mind, there's one final set of concepts we should talk about regarding trends. To begin, have a look at Figure 29.7.

"From August 2006 through August 2007, this stock never fell below $14 per share. The bottom line makes it easy to see this. We might say that the market provided *support* for this stock at about $14; it just wouldn't trade below that amount. So we do in fact call this phenomenon *support*, the *support level* of the stock."

"And the top line helps us see the opposite phenomenon," added Nate. "We can see that for the same period, August '06 to August '07, the price of this stock never rose above about $19 per share. Whenever it even approached that level, the stock price would fall back down. We might say that the market *resisted* the stock ever getting above that price. So we call this phenomenon *resistance*, or the resistance level of the stock. Thus, the upper limit we call *resistance*, and the lower limit we call *support*. Make sense?"

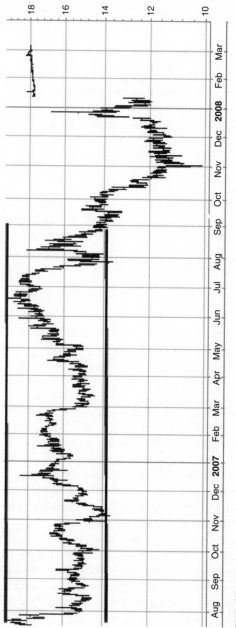

FIGURE 29.7 Support

Source: Chart courtesy of StockCharts.com.

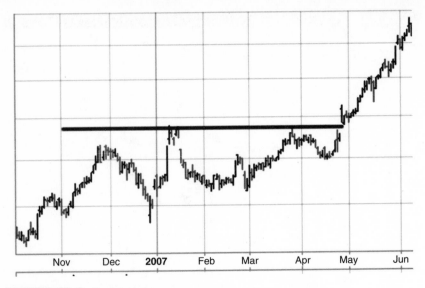

FIGURE 29.8 Resistance
Source: Chart courtesy of StockCharts.com.

"Sure," they both answered.

"These support and resistance levels have a number of implications," said Aaron, "but let me mention just one at this point. Notice, for example, what happened once the stock price fell below this $14 support level. (We call that *breaking support*, by the way.)"

"It looks to me like it didn't take long before it fell *way* below support," observed Lon.

"That's right. That's what often happens. When a stock has been trading at a certain level of support, once it breaks that support, it often signals a deeper drop. Psychologically, there's no longer a floor, and no one knows what price the stock might fall to before establishing a new support level. So whenever a stock breaks support, you have to pay close attention."

"Does the same thing happen with resistance levels?"

"Yes," replied Nate. "Look at this chart, for example." (See Figure 29.8)

"This stock had a resistance level between November 2006 and May 2007, but once it broke that resistance level, it took off. Psychologically, there was no longer a ceiling, and no one could know what price that stock would climb to before establishing a new resistance level. So just as with breaking support, you want to pay close attention when a stock breaks resistance. It could signal a strong bullish move. Make sense?"

"Got it," Shorty and Lon both replied.

"Good," said Aaron. "Then let's take this review to make sure you remember all we've talked about."

REVIEW

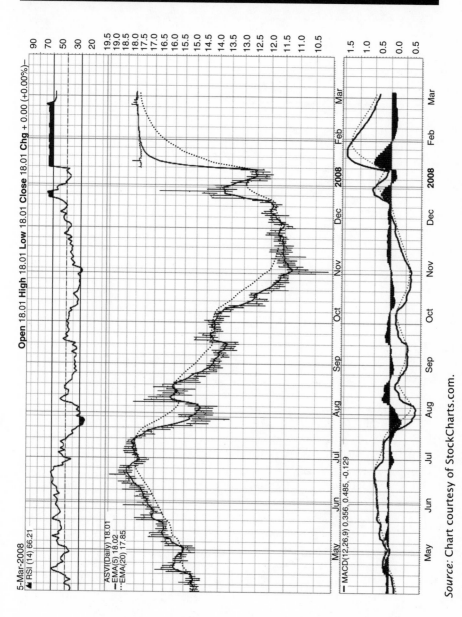

Source: Chart courtesy of StockCharts.com.

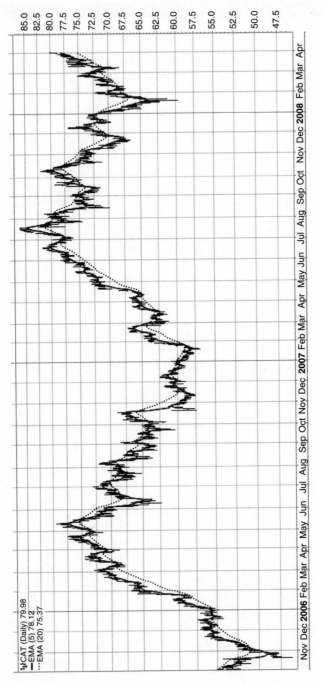

CAT (Daily) 79.98
—EMA (5) 78.12
···EMA (20) 75.37

85.0
82.5
80.0
77.5
75.0
72.5
70.0
67.5
65.0
62.5
60.0
57.5
55.0
52.5
50.0
47.5

Nov Dec **2006** Feb Mar Apr May Jun Jul Aug Sep Oct Nov Dec **2007** Feb Mar Apr May Jun Jul Aug Sep Oct Nov Dec **2008** Feb Mar Apr

Review

Source: Chart courtesy of StockCharts.com.

Regarding the chart on page 179:

1. How would you describe the trend between April and mid-June 2007 for this stock?

2. How would you describe the trend between July and November 2007?

3. How would you describe the trend for November 2007?

4. When does the first bullish crossover occur for the RSI on this chart?

5. When does the first bullish crossover occur for the EMA?

6. What does the MACD show at this time?

7. When does the first bearish crossover occur for the RSI on this chart?

8. When does the first bearish crossover occur for the MACD in 2008?

9. When does the first bullish crossover occur for the RSI in 2008?

10. In 2008, when did the first bullish crossover occur for the EMA?

11. Suppose you had had long puts in place the last quarter of 2007. When would you have sold them?

Regarding the chart on page 180:

12. Between late October 2006 and the end of January 2007, what would you say was the support level for this stock?

13. What would you say was the resistance level during the same period?

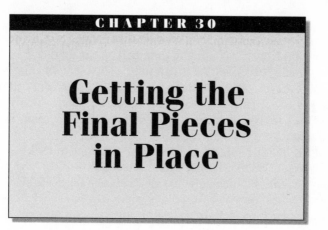

CHAPTER 30

Getting the Final Pieces in Place

"**O**kay, let's review a few things." Nate stood to write on the white board that hung in Lon's office.

"If we're going to be successful, there are some fundamentals we have to have in place. Remember, first, that we're looking for stocks that are optionable (that should be obvious!), that trade at a good volume every day, and that are largely owned by institutional investors. Then we have to do *due diligence* on the stocks we're considering. To do this we want to look at a number of factors: sales growth rate, earnings growth rate, equity growth rate, ROIC, debt/equity ratio, and the intrinsic value of the company. As we said earlier, these numbers inform us about a company's strength: they tell us if it's growing and if it's likely to continue to grow. And *that* tells us whether the market is likely to find this stock attractive. After all, if the market likes this stock, its price will grow simply because there will be demand for it. Now, none of these numbers guarantee that the market will like a stock and that its price will grow, but they do tell us what the market *ought to* like and therefore what stocks we ought to keep our eye on."

"Right," added Aaron. "Just because there are no guarantees doesn't mean that we just guess and jump into the stock market willy-nilly. No, we always bring our brains with us. And, as we saw, another way to bring our brains with us is to look at the trends in the overall market. That's important background information as we consider what to do with individual stocks. That's why we look at the Dow Jones, the S&P, and the Nasdaq: they give us the overall view we need."

"And," said Nate, "we also look at the volatility index and the total put-to-call ratio to give us an indication of what the market *might* do. They give us a sense of the overall sentiment or 'mood' of the market."

"And, finally, we look *very* carefully at what individual stocks are doing," said Aaron. "For one thing we want to know what trend they're in—whether they're slightly bearish, bearish, stagnant, slightly bullish, or bullish. All of this is important for picking the best option strategy for making money."

"And for another thing," added Nate, "we want to look for signs of a change in trend. That's why we look at the RSI, the EMA, and the MACD. A change in trend is indicated when all three give the same sign, and when that change holds for a day. And that's when we change what we're doing: we shift whatever strategy we've been using to a new strategy designed to make money in the new trend."

As Nate stepped back from the white board, everyone could see what he had written.

Things to Know		
Company Factors	**Market Direction**	**Stock Direction**
Optionable	Trends	Current trend
Good volume	• DJIA	• Slightly bearish,
Institutional ownership	• S&P 500	bearish, stagnant,
Strength	• Nasdaq	slightly bullish, bullish
• Sales growth rate	Mood	Trend change signals
• Earnings growth rate	• VIX	• RSI
• Equity growth rate	• Put-to-call ratio	• EMA
• ROIC		• MACD
• Debt-to-equity ratio		
• Intrinsic value		

"Having reviewed that, it's now time to teach you a little bit more about how option trading works and the kind of terminology that's used. We've been a bit loose up until now, so it's time to tighten up."

SOME MECHANICS AND TERMINOLOGY IN OPTION TRADING

"To begin," said Aaron, "remember that there's a whole industry out there. Lots of Lons and Shortys trading with each other. So, just as there are stock exchanges that facilitate the buying and selling of stocks (the New York Stock Exchange is the one you two know best), so there are *option exchanges* that facilitate the buying and selling of options. That's why there are standard option chains, for example, with all the strike prices, bid/ask amounts, deltas, and so on built in. All of that structure and detail simply provide a platform for all these Lons and Shortys to be able to trade with each other. The calls and puts are just 'out there,' so to speak, with all this elaborate structure, and the Lons and Shortys of the world simply trade them with each other according to this structure."

"I suppose there are brokerage houses that specialize in option trading as well," said Shorty. "Is that right?"

"Yes, that's right. The typical brokerage house for buying and selling stocks is not equipped to handle option trading very well—certainly not any kind of complicated trades. In fact, most of them won't even permit such trades. It's understandable: option trading just isn't their business. So, yes, you find a broker that specializes in option trading, and there are a number of them to choose from."

"Now here's basically how option trading works," said Nate. "Let's say, Lon, that you like the idea of a long call on the stock in this option chain. You're bullish." (See Figure 30.1.)

"Let's say you decide to place a long call, at close to three months out, at a strike price of $32. The ask amount—the debit you will pay—is $1. Now this is obviously a debit trade for you—you are wanting to buy—so you're looking for someone who is willing to *sell*: sell at this same strike price, with this same time frame, and at the option chain's bid price of $0.90. So we say you are *buying to open* a contract. The common abbreviation for this is BTO. You're trying to open a contract with someone and you're doing it by buying."

Jul 08 Calls								Jul 08 Puts					
		(80 days to expiration)				NOK@30.08							
NAYGD	9.20	0	9.80	10.20		1.00	20.00	NAYSD	0.15	0	0.05	0.10	48.1	-.03
NAYGX	7.20	+0.50	7.30	7.70		1.00	22.50	NAYSX	0.20	-0.03	0.15	0.25	44.7	-.07
NAYGE	4.80	-0.05	5.00	5.20		1.00	25.00	NAYSE	0.50	-0.10	0.50	0.55	43.3	-.15
NAYGC	2.25	+0.25	2.20	2.30	28.2	.65	29.00	NAYSC	1.90	-0.10	1.65	1.75	40.9	-.38
NAYGF	1.70	+0.10	1.70	1.80	29.0	.55	30.00	NAYSF	2.15	-0.40	2.15	2.25	41.1	-.45
NAYGW	1.25	0	1.25	1.35	29.0	.45	31.00	NAYSW	2.80	-0.40	2.75	2.85	42.0	-.51
NAYGS	0.90	+0.05	0.90	1.00	29.0	.36	32.00	NAYSS	3.80	0	3.40	3.50	42.6	-.57
NAYGT	0.60	0	0.65	0.70	29.0	.28	33.00	NAYST	4.30	-0.80	4.10	4.30	43.9	-.63
NAYGV	0.50	+0.15	0.45	0.50	29.1	.22	34.00	NAYSV	5.40	0	4.90	5.10	45.5	-.67

FIGURE 30.1 Option Chain
Source: Screenshot courtesy of optionsXpress, Inc. © 2008.

"And," said Aaron, picking up the thread, "let's say that you, Shorty, happen to want to *sell* a call on this stock. In that case you are *selling to open*. When you see the abbreviation STO, that's what it means: you are opening a contract by selling, and for you it's a credit trade. And further, let's suppose that your conditions match Lon's: you want to sell a call on this stock at a $32 strike price, with this expiration date, and with a bid amount of $0.90."

"Now the next thing you have to know, as you both look to open contracts, is that when we're working with options, stock shares come in 'clumps' of 100. That means this: Lon, if you want this trade to apply to 100 shares of stock, you open only one contract. The cost of that—your debit—will be $1 per share, or $100 total. If you want more shares involved, then you can buy two contracts; that will mean 200 shares—still with a $1-per-share debit, but for a total cost of $200."

"And the same for you, Shorty," said Aaron. "If you want to sell a contract that covers 100 shares of this stock, you open only one contract. You take in a credit of $0.90 per share, or $90 total. If you want more shares involved, then you can sell two contracts; that will mean 200 shares—still with a $0.90 per share credit, but for a total credit of $180. And so on. For both of you, the minimum for a contract is 100 shares, and every increment above that is 100 more. Does that make sense?"

"Yeah, I get it," answered Shorty. "If I'm buying stock, I can buy one share at a time. I can buy a single share of Plum, for example."

"Right," added Lon, "but if I want to trade Plum *options*, then I have to do it in clumps of 100: one option contract for every 100 shares I want to involve."

"Good, which brings up a point of terminology," said Nate. "You will sometimes hear people talk of an option contract 'controlling' 100 shares. And that's right. Each option contract determines what can happen to 100 shares of stock, and in that sense the contract 'controls' those shares. So you could say that we enter a contract for every 100 shares that we want to *control*."

"Okay. That makes sense."

"So here we are, then," said Aaron. "Lon, you want to place a long call on this stock, with this expiration date, at an ask price of $1. Shorty, you want to place a short call on this stock, with this expiration date, at a bid price of $0.90. Now notice something about the option chain that we haven't mentioned yet: each option has its own unique symbol. See, you're both dealing with a call that has a $32 strike price and an expiration date of July 2008. The only difference is that one of you is buying that call and one of you is selling it. But it's the same *call option*. And it has its own symbol, displayed at the far left: NAYGS. And you can see that all of the other strike prices also have their own symbols. That's how everything is tracked."

"I see that that includes the puts, too," observed Lon. "They also have their own symbols, at the far left of the put section."

"That's right. Again, that's how everything gets tracked. So now you both simply enter your orders with your brokerage firms, the brokerage firms pass them on to the exchange, and the exchange "matches' you, so to speak. You have an option contract around this specific call, designated by its own symbol."

"Now none of this happens for free, of course," said Nate. "Remember what we mentioned briefly last night: there's a fee for matching you. As you see in this example: Lon, you pay $1 in buying this call, but Shorty, you receive only $0.90 for selling it. That's because the difference, the $0.10, goes to the exchange. That's their fee. Now there are nuances to how this works, but this is the foundation. It's all you need to know to get started."

"And, of course, your brokerage firm will also charge a commission for their services," added Aaron. "Normally, if you place your order over the phone the fee is higher than if you place it online, but there's always a fee, and it's something you need to know."

"Here's another point of terminology, too," added Nate. "Shorty, because you're selling this option, it's common to refer to you as the *writer*. See, in many business transactions, it's the seller who creates the contract that buyers then sign; the sellers are the ones who 'write' it. Even though the situation isn't completely the same with options, the terminology is. The person in the short position is referred to as the option *writer*.

"While we're on the subject of terminology, let me point out the kinds of expressions that are used in the option industry." Aaron wrote on the white board:

Place a short call
Open a short call position
Open a short call
Sell a call
Short a call

"All of these mean the same thing: I'm selling, and what I'm selling is a *call*. As you two figured out long ago, that means that, for me, this is a credit trade—I'm receiving money—and that I'm incurring the obligation to sell shares of stock if they're called out from me.

"From time to time," he continued, "you will even encounter the expression *short sell a call*. Technically, of course, that's redundant because the terms *short* and *sell* mean the same thing; so to use them both in one expression is a bit repetitious. Still, it's not an uncommon way to talk and you should be aware of it. Don't let the grammatical oddity of it get in your way."

"And the terminology works the same for puts." Nate now wrote on the board:

Place a short put
Open a short put position
Open a short put
Sell a put
Short a put

"These are equivalent expressions: I'm still selling, but what I'm selling is a *put*. And again, as you two figured out long ago, that means that this is a credit trade for me, and that I'm incurring the obligation to *buy* shares of stock if they're put to me."

"And, of course, you might run into the expression *short sell a put*. Technically, it sounds a little weird—this phrase is redundant, too—but big deal. Lots of expressions break grammatical rules; you just get used to them."

"And the expressions are pretty similar for when we're long." Aaron wrote:

Place a long call
Open a long call position
Open a long call
Buy a call

"It's also pretty common to say *buy a long call*. That's another example of redundancy, but you'll hear it fairly often. And all of these expressions simply mean that I'm buying, and that I'm buying a call. As you know, this means that, for me, this is a debit trade—I'm *paying* money—and that I'm buying rights: for example, the right to buy shares at my chosen strike price anytime within the expiration period."

"And for puts, the expressions are the same."

Place a long put
Open a long put position
Open a long put
Buy a put

"Okay," interrupted Lon, "and I'll bet it's common to say something like 'buy a long put,' right?"

"Right. Again, I'll admit it's redundant because *buy* and *long* mean the same thing, but it's a common expression, and besides, you should be used to grammatical oddities by now, anyway," laughed Nate. "And, of course," he continued, "all these phrases mean the same thing: I'm still buying, but what I'm buying is a *put*. So I'm still entering a debit trade, and I'm still buying rights. But this time I'm buying the right (to name only one) to *sell* shares at my chosen strike price anytime within the expiration period. Got it?" he asked.

"Sure," answered Shorty, "but I've got another question about language. I notice that we say things like 'short a call' and 'short a put,' but we don't say 'long a call' or 'long a put.' We don't use the word *long* as a verb, but we do use the word *short* that way. Why the difference?"

"There's no real reason," replied Nate. "It's just the convention that's developed over the years. It's like a lot of expressions; you can't really identify where they came from, you just know how people use them. Even *bullish* and *bearish* are that way. Sorry. That's just how it is."

"Okay. It's just kind of tough to figure everything out and to use the right language."

"I know. But you'll get used to it. You just need a little time and experience."

"Now while we're at it, I want to mention one more convention," said Aaron. "It's that we rarely, if ever, use the dollar sign when talking of strike prices. We will normally say something like 'a strike of 35,' and not 'a strike of 35 dollars.' And that shows up in writing, too. We don't normally write 'a strike of $35,' but instead 'a strike of 35.' For the most part, the only time we'll do it differently is when we're performing a calculation using the strike price. Then we're emphasizing the dollar amount, and so we'll show the dollar sign. Otherwise, we won't. Okay? Up to now, it seemed easier for you to learn the concept if we used the typical convention for talking about dollars. But you're past that now. So from now on we won't use it—except, again, in calculations."

"Fair enough."

"I should add that it's also common to use all of the following expressions to mean the same thing: *strike, strike price, striking price*. You'll run into all these expressions, and they're identical in meaning."

ASSIGNMENT

"But now let's get back to the big picture," said Nate. "We're talking about this deal between you two, and I said that the exchange matches you two up. One of you wants to buy and one of you wants to sell the very same call (which, again, has its own unique option symbol). You match up, so that's how you enter a contract. Now that's a simple conceptual version, but it's actually a little more dynamic than that. In the real world, all that really gets matched up is the total number of buy and sell *contracts* for a particular option. Remember, there are lots of option traders out there, some wanting to buy and some wanting to sell—including some wanting to buy and some wanting to sell *the same option,* just like you two. All the exchange has to do is make sure that the long and short *contracts* match . . . that there's an equal number of both."

"Now that means this," said Aaron. "Let's suppose Lon decides to exercise his option. Remember: as the buyer—being long—Lon has the right to call out 100 shares of this stock anytime within the expiration period. That's what it means for him to 'exercise' his option. And let's say he does that. Well, there are lots of sellers on the other side of this contract—more than just Shorty, right? They *all* entered a contract to sell their shares of this specific option if called out. So the exchange now randomly assigns one of these sellers to fulfill that obligation. It's called *assignment,* and it's simply a random process. It could fall to Shorty, but it could also fall to anyone else in Shorty's shoes. Make sense?"

"Sure. Anyone holding the same contract that I hold runs the same chance of being assigned that I run. The selection is random."

SIX WAYS THE DEAL COULD END

"Good," replied Nate. "That's all clear. Now let's push our understanding a little further by thinking of all the ways this trade could end. For simplicity's sake, let's assume that Lon doesn't own any of the stock, but just wants to place a long call to control 100 shares. So he buys one contract with an ask price of $1—so he's shelled out a total of $100—and has a strike price of 32."

"Okay, so one way for this to end," said Aaron, "is for the strike to go in the money before the option expires—for the market price to pass up the 32 strike. Say it goes to $33. That means Lon could exercise his option: call out 100 shares for $32 per share (the strike price) and turn around and sell them for $33. That's a $100 profit. But remember, he already paid $100 to buy the call in the first place, so if he does this he only breaks even. And that means he probably won't exercise his option unless it gets *over* this breakeven point. So let's suppose it does, and that it goes all the way to $36 before the expiration date. In that case, let's suppose Lon exercises his option to buy 100 shares at $32 (again, the strike price), and turns around and sells them for $36. That gives him $400—$4 profit on 100 shares—and when we subtract the $100 debit he paid to make the deal in the first place, he ends up with a $300 net profit."

"And all this means, of course," inserted Nate, "that someone on the other end of the deal was *assigned* to sell Lon these 100 shares. Let's say it was Shorty. Shorty gets to keep the $100 credit he received, but he sells his shares for $32. That's not necessarily bad; that's just what happens. The point here is that all this happens *before* the expiration date arrives, so we call it *early assignment*. Anytime you're in Shorty's position, and the strike goes in the money before expiration, someone like Lon—on the long side—might exercise his option. And that means that you could get assigned to fulfill that contract . . . and all before the expiration date."

"But something else can happen, too," said Nate. "Let's suppose, for example, that the stock price never passes the strike of 32 during the whole expiration period: it never goes in the money. Then, as you two figured out on your own, Lon won't exercise his option. It'll simply expire when the expiration period ends. That means that no one gets assigned: all the people like Shorty get to keep their shares *and*, obviously, they keep the credit they received in selling the contract in the first place. In this case we say that the option 'expires worthless.'"

"There's also a third alternative. Suppose the stock never passes the strike price—the strike never goes in the money—but it rises enough that the value of the option also rises. Suppose it goes from $1 to $1.10. And suppose Lon decides that the 32 strike will never go in the money and that he ought to at least salvage what he can from the current increased value of the call—before time decay erodes it. So he sells his long call to someone else, and makes 10 percent on it: he bought it for $1 and sells it for $1.10. Not much in the way of dollars, but it's a good percentage ROI."

"In this case, too," continued Aaron, "Shorty and others like him don't get assigned. They're not involved in the deal at all. The only way they're at risk for assignment is if the *new* owner of the option decides to exercise it. And in that case, we're simply back to the first scenario."

"So notice what's happened," said Nate. "Lon was in this contract, and now, by selling it to someone else, he's out of it. For him the contract is now 'closed.' He opened this contract in the first place by buying, and he now closes it by selling it to someone else. So the terminology in a long position like this is *buy to open* and *sell to close*, and that's the terminology we would use in telling our broker what we want to do. We would say 'sell to close,' and then we would identify the option we were talking about. Also, when you see the expression *STC*, it simply means 'sell to close.'"

"And again," reminded Aaron, "Shorty and others in his short position are not affected by this. Their contracts are still in place, only now with a different person on the other end. Make sense?"

"Yeah. Got it."

"Now, fourth," said Nate, "we should mention the possibility of the strike going in the money at the very end of the expiration period. If that happens, all the people on the buy side, like Lon, will have their options exercised *for them*, automatically. They receive the shares that their contracts call for, and they receive them at the strike price. And this means that everyone on the sell side, like Shorty, is automatically *assigned*; all have their shares called out and sold at the strike price. Some brokerage firms won't do this if the day ends exactly at the strike price, but only if it's a nickel or more over. But you get the idea. If the expiration period ends with the strike in the money, then, if you're Lon, your option will be exercised for you, and, if you're Shorty, you will automatically be assigned."

"Fifth," added Aaron, "the same thing occurs if the option goes in the money sometime during the expiration period, but Lon just never exercises it for some reason. If it's still in the money at expiration, Lon doesn't need to exercise his option: it will be exercised for him in the manner Nate just described. The general rule is: any option that's in the money at expiration gets exercised—by the brokerage firm, if not by the contract buyer, like Lon, himself. And that means that everyone on the sell side of the option is automatically assigned."

"And these last two possibilities lead to a final way this deal could end," said Nate. "Suppose, for example, that Shorty sees the strike going in the money, or at least heading in that direction, and decides that he doesn't want to get assigned. He wants to keep his shares rather than have them called out and have to sell them. In that case, *he* closes the contract. Now remember, Shorty opened this contract in the first place by selling and taking in a credit of $0.90. So how does he close it? Well, he simply *buys it back*. He sold in the first place at the bid price on the option chain, and he now buys it back at whatever the *ask* price is on the option chain. That releases Shorty from any obligation to sell his shares; he's *bought* himself out of the contract."

"Now Shorty's buying himself out of this contract doesn't leave the short position empty," said Aaron. "Whoever sold this call to Shorty simply replaces him in the contract, and this new person now has the obligation to sell the shares if called out. He took in a credit by selling to Shorty and he assumes the contractual obligations that Shorty had."

"Now look," said Nate, "in the real world, again, it's more dynamic than that. All that really gets matched up are contracts, not specific people. There's even a separate organization that *insures* a balance in contracts. All we're trying to do is make sure you get the basic idea: Shorty buys himself out of his obligations, true, but only because someone else picks them up. Lon is not affected."

"So what Shorty does here, then," continued Aaron, "is 'buy to close.' The price he pays to buy back his option is simply the price required to cancel the contract he's in—to let someone else become the seller to Lon. So the terminology in a short position like this is *sell to open* and *buy to close*, and that's the terminology we would use in telling our broker what we want to do. We would say 'buy to close,' and then we would identify the specific option we were talking about. And when you see the expression *BTC*, that's what it means: 'buy to close.'"

"Okay, I think I get all that," said Lon. "The deal could end in one of six ways:

1. The strike goes in the money and becomes profitable to Lon before the expiration date. So he exercises his option, and someone on the 'short' side is assigned to fulfill the call by selling their shares. That's called *early assignment.*

2. The strike never goes in the money, and Lon never exercises his option. The option expires worthless and no one is assigned.

3. Lon sells his call option to someone else. No one on the short side is involved at all; no one will be assigned unless the *new* owner exercises the option, in which case we're back to (1).

4. The option goes in the money at the very end of the expiration period; everyone on the short side gets assigned automatically, and everyone on the 'long' side receives the appropriate number of shares automatically.

5. The option goes in the money sometime before expiration, but the buyer never exercises his option. The option is still in the money at expiration. In that case we're just like (4): everything gets handled automatically.

6. Shorty decides to close the contract himself by buying it back. Then if it's in the money at expiration, someone else gets assigned, and that person then fulfills the obligation to sell the appropriate shares.

EXPIRATION

"But now I want to ask about expiration dates," he continued. "Shorty and I always just picked a date that was one month, six months, or whatever, away from the date we made the deal. How does it work for everyone else?"

"Well, for everyone else expiration dates are very specific, definite, and unchanging. Each month has an expiration date, and, to be specific, it's always the Saturday following the third Friday of the month. For practical purposes, you keep your eye on Friday. Options are either assigned or not, based on stock prices at the close of trading on that Friday."

"So that must be why you never see specific expiration dates listed on option chains," said Lon. "They give you the month and the year, but not the specific date. It's because the date is based on a formula everyone already knows."

"That's correct. Good," said Aaron.

OPTION HIEROGLYPHICS

"Now I must say," Nate interjected, "that you've learned a lot in the last little while. It's almost like learning a new language. In fact, you have. You've learned new concepts and you've learned the language that captures them. For example, if I give you this string of expressions, I'll bet you can translate it for me. It's fictional, but it still has meaning. So see if you can translate it."

He wrote on the board:

BTO 5 GOOG Oct 520 Calls (GOFEJ) @ 25

"Sorry, but it reminds me of Egyptian hieroglyphics. It's all in 'code,'" said Lon.

"Yes. But the good news is, *you two know the code.* Just think about it."

"Okay, here goes," said Shorty eagerly. "I'll take the terms one at a time and then try to figure out the overall meaning.

"Now of course, *BTO* means 'buy to open,' but I have no clue what the *5* means. I'll come back to that one. Okay, *GOOG* is the ticker symbol for Google, so that must mean Google. *Oct* must mean that the expiration date is in October. But the expression *520* is tough again. I don't know, but I'm going to guess. I don't see a strike price anywhere else, and we know that a dollar sign won't appear with the strike price, so that's probably what it is; 520 seems awfully high, but that must be what it means: a strike price of 520. *Calls* obviously means that this is a call option, not a put, and the letters *GOFEJ* must be the unique symbol for this call option. And @ *25* must refer to the ask amount on the option chain. That's the debit for this call. That just leaves the *5*." Shorty was stumped. "I don't see it," he said finally.

"Well, try this. Translate as much of this whole line as you can, and then see if you can figure out what the *5* means."

"Well, this is a command or a request. It's saying that I ought to buy Google calls with an October expiration date, at the 520 strike price, paying $25 per share as a debit. So this is a long call. And the symbol 'GOFEJ' just gives me—well, the symbol for this call." Shorty paused for a moment, looking back at that 5. Finally, he exclaimed, "Of course! I get it now. The '5' just tells me *how many* contracts to buy: 5 of them. So the idea here is to buy 5 contracts of calls for Google (which means I control

500 shares), with an October expiration, at a strike price of 520, and an ask price of $25. Right?"

"That's right. Good job. So now let's make sure you remember everything we've covered in the last bit. Here's a review."

REVIEW

Sep 08 Calls		(132 days to expiration)				NFLX@30.72					Sep 08 Puts	
QNQID	20.20	0	10.70	11.00		1.00	20.00	QNQUD	0.70	0	0.65	0.75	67.0	-.10
QNQIX	8.30	0	8.60	8.90	42.7	.91	22.50	QNQUX	1.27	0	1.05	1.25	64.1	-.15
QNQIE	6.70	0	6.60	6.90	43.2	.83	25.00	QNQUE	1.75	0	1.75	1.90	62.3	-.22
QNQIY	4.90	0	5.00	5.30	45.0	.72	27.50	QNQUY	2.93	0	2.55	2.80	60.2	-.31
QNQIF	3.50	0	3.70	3.90	45.4	.60	30.00	QNQUF	3.80	0	3.70	4.00	59.6	-.39
QNQIT	2.54	0	2.60	2.80	45.1	.48	32.50	QNQUT	5.57	0	5.10	5.40	59.1	-.48
QNQIG	1.75	0	1.80	2.00	45.2	.38	35.00	QNQUG	7.30	0	6.80	7.10	59.9	-.56
QNQIZ	1.23	0	1.20	1.40	45.0	.29	37.50	QNQUZ	9.44	0	8.70	9.00	61.1	-.63
QNQIH	0.70	0	0.80	0.95	45.0	.21	40.00	QNQUH	11.51	0	10.70	11.00	61.9	-.69

Source: Screenshot courtesy of optionsXpress, Inc. © 2008.

1. If you wanted to buy a put at a strike of 30, what would you pay?
2. What is the symbol for that put?
3. How much would you pay if you wanted 10 contracts?
4. What are some other expressions for buying a put?
5. If you wanted to sell a put at a strike of 30, what would you receive?
6. What is the symbol for this put?
7. How much would you receive if you sold 5 contracts?
8. What are some other expressions for selling a put?
9. What is another name for the person selling an option?
10. When does the expiration date always occur?
11. Let's suppose Lon buys 2 call contracts at a strike of 35, and Shorty shorts 2 calls at a strike of 35. We would say that Lon is _____ to open, and Shorty is _____ to open.
12. How much does Lon pay for his call? How much does he pay in total?
13. How much does Shorty receive for his call? How much does he receive in total?
14. *Scenario 1.* The option goes in the money, and Lon exercises his option before expiration at a market price of $40. Shorty is assigned to sell his shares. This is called _____ for Shorty.

15. How many shares does Lon receive?

16. How much does Lon pay for them?

17. How much does Lon make per share?

18. How much does Lon make in total?

19. By being assigned, Shorty sells 200 shares. Suppose he had paid $30 for them initially. How much does he receive for them by being assigned?

20. How much did he receive in shorting this call in the first place?

21. So how much does Shorty make per share on this deal?

22. How much does Shorty make in total?

23. *Scenario 2.* The option never goes in the money, and Lon never exercises his option. In that case we say that the option expires _____. Shorty keeps the _____ of $1.80, and he keeps his _____. Lon forfeits the $2 _____ he paid.

24. *Scenario 3.* Lon sells his call to someone else, and the option never goes in the money by expiration. We say that Lon sold to _____ his option, and he has sold at the _____ price on the option chain. Shorty never gets _____.

25. *Scenario 4.* The option goes in the money right as the expiration period ends. Lon does not exercise his option. In that case, Shorty will be _____ automatically, and Lon will _____ shares automatically.

26. *Scenario 5.* The option goes in the money before expiration, but Lon never exercises his option. In that case, at expiration Shorty will be _____ automatically, and Lon will _____ shares automatically. As a general rule, every option in the money at expiration gets _____ automatically.

27. *Scenario 6.* Shorty decides to cancel the contract. He does so by _____ the contract back. We say that Shorty has bought _____ his option, and he has bought at the _____ price on the option chain.

28. Suppose Lon wrote the following note to himself. What does it mean? STC 10 NXL 45 Dec Calls (NUFLQ) @ 10.75 In other words, he already _____ these _____options, and he is now closing the contracts by _____.

29. What does the following string of expressions mean? STO 5 PLUM 32.50 Jun Puts (PEMLZ) @ 6.50?

"Okay, with all these pieces in place, the fun begins," announced Aaron.

CHAPTER 31

Fun, Fun, Fun!

" **N** ow you begin *practicing*."

"Right," added Nate. "See, there's a way for you to trade options—to use all these instruments we've talked about—without using any real money. You just go to the web site *OptionsAnimal*, click on 'virtual trading,' and follow the instructions. You can create a portfolio of $10,000 ... or $1 million. Whatever suits your fancy. Just have fun."

"Because you're not using real money," explained Aaron, "this is called *paper trading* or *virtual trading*. You get all the value of trading experience without risking any actual money along the way."

TRACKING THE PERFORMANCE OF CALLS

"However," said Nate, "before you actually begin paper trading—before you begin buying and selling on this web site—we suggest you do a little preparation first. Here's what you do: using this web site, pick one stock you want to work with, and then track the performance of *calls* with that stock over the course of a month."

"A whole month?" asked Shorty. "A whole month of tracking before we begin trading?"

"Yes, and even that may be too short. But at least a month for our purposes here."

"Now the best way to do this," said Nate, "is to choose two different strike prices to follow—one near the money and one three strikes out of the money, but both with the same expiration date. That will give us a chance to see how calls play out for different strikes in the same time period."

"Right," said Aaron. "And then we pick a single strike price to follow, but in two different *time frames*—one about one month out and one about six months out. That will give us a chance to see how the same strike plays out in different time periods."

"So we're going to create two tables for calls," explained Nate, "using the same stock as a platform. One table helps us track the effects of where we place the strike price, and one helps us track the effects of where we place expiration. Figure 31.1 shows the first chart."

TRACKING STRIKE PLACEMENT FOR CALLS		
Stock: _____ Expiration date: _____		

DATE	STOCK PRICE	STRIKE PRICE DATA
		Delta Bid Ask NTM _____ OTM _____
		Delta Bid Ask NTM _____ OTM _____
		Delta Bid Ask NTM _____ OTM _____
		Delta Bid Ask NTM _____ OTM _____
		Delta Bid Ask NTM _____ OTM _____
		Delta Bid Ask NTM _____ OTM _____

FIGURE 31.1 Tracking Strike Placement for Calls

TRACKING TIME FRAMES FOR CALLS		
Stock: _____ Strike Price: _____		

DATE	STOCK PRICE	TIME FRAME DATA		
			Delta	Bid	Ask
		ONE _____			
		SIX _____			
			Delta	Bid	Ask
		ONE _____			
		SIX _____			
			Delta	Bid	Ask
		ONE _____			
		SIX _____			
			Delta	Bid	Ask
		ONE _____			
		SIX _____			
			Delta	Bid	Ask
		ONE _____			
		SIX _____			
			Delta	Bid	Ask
		ONE _____			
		SIX _____			

FIGURE 31.2 Tracking Time Frames for Calls

"Make the chart long enough to track this data for a month, and then fill in each box every day. Now at the same time, as I said, we also have a chart for tracking the effects of different time frames. Again, we choose an expiration date about one month out and one about six months out. It might look like Figure 31.2."

"Again, make the chart long enough to accommodate a month's worth of data and then fill in each box every day."

"Now once you get going and get a few days filled in," said Aaron, "put on your 'long call' hat and look at the data specifically from the standpoint of a long call. Look at the first chart, and imagine that you had placed two long calls on the first day, one at the near-the-money strike and one at a price that is three strikes out of the money. Now look for patterns. Ask yourself:

- What's happened to the stock price? What trend is it following?
- What's happened to my NTM strike price?
- What's happened to my OTM strike price?
- How are their deltas behaving?
- How are the bid/ask amounts behaving?
- How comfortable do I feel with my NTM strike price?
- How comfortable do I feel with my OTM strike price?

"Once you've done that," he continued, "and noticed the patterns that are occurring, then put on your 'short call' hat and look at the data specifically from the standpoint of a short call. Look at the first chart, and imagine that you had placed two *short calls* on the first day. Based on the patterns you've already identified, ask: How comfortable do I feel with my NTM strike price? How comfortable do I feel with my OTM strike price?"

"Then look carefully at the second chart from the standpoint of a long call. Ask yourself:

- What's happened to the one-month delta?
- What's happened to the one-month bid and ask prices?
- What's happened to the six-month delta?
- What's happened to the six-month bid and ask prices?
- How comfortable do I feel with my one-month expiration period?
- How comfortable do I feel with my six-month expiration period?

"And, finally, look at this chart from the standpoint of a short call. Based on the patterns you've already identified, ask: How comfortable do I feel with my one-month expiration period? How comfortable do I feel with my six-month expiration period?"

"You get the idea," said Nate. "The best way to develop a feel for how options operate is to chart this information daily and watch the patterns that develop. This is extremely important and can save you a world of hurt."

"What do you mean by that?" Lon sat forward in his chair.

"Well," replied Nate, "let me give you an example. Most beginning option traders find long calls appealing. After all, we just find a bullish stock, buy some calls (that's cheaper than buying the stock, after all), and then just watch the money roll in as the calls increase in value ... right? Well, not necessarily. Remember that time decay eats away at the value of those calls we bought; so the stock itself may be stagnant, or even slightly bullish, but as we get closer to expiration the calls will be *losing* value just due to the passage of time. So we're *losing* money even though the stock itself is doing fine."

"So," said Aaron," in a very bullish market, long calls are deceiving. We do make money pretty easily with them. But they're actually like Delilah; they set us up to fail. They make us think we're geniuses when *we're not*. We're just lucky. And then, when the market turns on us—and it will—we'll be stuck and not know what to do. We'll be left *hoping* that the trend turns around. But when it comes to the stock market, believe me, *hope* is a four-letter word. It's a profanity. We never allow ourselves even to think it. The whole idea of option trading, as we do it, is to trade without fear. So if we're relying on hope, we've simply failed. We've let greed get the better of us and put ourselves in a fearful situation, with hope as our only alternative. Well, that's the wrong way to invest and the wrong way to live."

"Of course, the good news," said Nate, "is that we can find all this out for ourselves without losing any money. That's one of the purposes of charting like this and, for that matter, of paper trading. We can get the greed kicked out of us—learn firsthand to 'beware of Delilah,' so to speak—without having to lose anything while it's happening. We don't *have* to be knuckleheads."

"Right," added Aaron. "And we can also get a feel for how options operate. More than just memorizing what happens, we can actually see it happen. And that's the best way to learn. Think about it. Do you remember how long it took you to learn the rules of baseball when you were a kid? Someone could *tell* you the rules while you were sitting at a kitchen table, maybe, but you could never really understand them until you actually watched a game. Or played one. Well, this is like that."

TRACKING THE PERFORMANCE OF PUTS

"That's right," added Nate. "That's why all this is important. So, just like with charting calls, we want to do the same thing with puts. We pick a stock and choose two different strike prices to follow—one near the money and one three strikes out of the money, but both with the same expiration date. That will give us a chance to see how puts play out for different strikes in the same time period."

"And then we pick a single strike price to follow," added Aaron, "but in two different *time frames*—one about one month out and one about six months out. That will give us a chance to see how the same strike plays out in different time periods."

"So we're going to create two tables for puts, just like we did for calls," explained Nate. "We'll look at the same stock for both charts. One table

		TRACKING STRIKE PLACEMENT FOR PUTS			
		Stock: _____ Expiration date: _____			
DATE	STOCK PRICE	STRIKE PRICE DATA			
			Delta	Bid	Ask
		NTM _____			
		OTM _____			
			Delta	Bid	Ask
		NTM _____			
		OTM _____			
			Delta	Bid	Ask
		NTM _____			
		OTM _____			
			Delta	Bid	Ask
		NTM _____			
		OTM _____			
			Delta	Bid	Ask
		NTM _____			
		OTM _____			
			Delta	Bid	Ask
		NTM _____			
		OTM _____			

FIGURE 31.3 Tracking Strike Placement for Puts

helps us track the effects of where we place the strike price, and the other helps us track the effects of where we place expiration. Figure 31.3 shows the first chart."

"As before, make the chart long enough to track this data for a month, and fill in each box every day. Now at the same time, we also have a chart for tracking the effects of different time frames. We pick one expiration date about a month out and another about six months out." (See Figure 31.4.)

"Again, make the chart long enough to accommodate a month's worth of data and then fill in each box every day."

		TRACKING TIME FRAMES FOR PUTS		

Stock: _____ Strike Price: _____

DATE	STOCK PRICE	TIME FRAME DATA		
			Delta	Bid	Ask
		ONE _____ SIX _____			
			Delta	Bid	Ask
		ONE _____ SIX _____			
			Delta	Bid	Ask
		ONE _____ SIX _____			
			Delta	Bid	Ask
		ONE _____ SIX _____			
			Delta	Bid	Ask
		ONE _____ SIX _____			
			Delta	Bid	Ask
		ONE _____ SIX _____			

FIGURE 31.4 Tracking Time Frames for Puts

"Now once you get going and get a few days filled in," said Aaron, "you do the same kind of thing you did with calls. Put on your 'long put' hat and look at the data specifically from the standpoint of a long put. Look at the first chart, and imagine that you had placed two long puts on the first day, one at the near-the-money strike and one at a price that is three strikes out of the money. Now look for patterns. Ask yourself:

- What's happened to the stock price? What trend is it following?
- What's happened to my NTM strike price?
- What's happened to my OTM strike price?
- How are their deltas behaving?

- How are the bid/ask amounts behaving?
- How comfortable do I feel with my NTM strike price?
- How comfortable do I feel with my OTM strike price?

"Once you've done that," he continued, "and noticed the patterns that are occurring, then put on your 'short put' hat and look at the data specifically from the standpoint of a short put. Look at the first chart, and imagine that you had placed two *short puts* on the first day. Based on the patterns you've already identified, ask: How comfortable do I feel with my NTM strike price? How comfortable do I feel with my OTM strike price?"

"Then you look carefully at the second chart from the standpoint of a long put. Ask yourself:

- What's happened to the one-month delta?
- What's happened to the one-month bid and ask prices?
- What's happened to the six-month delta?
- What's happened to the six-month bid and ask prices?
- How comfortable do I feel with my one-month expiration period?
- How comfortable do I feel with my six-month expiration period?

"And, finally, you look at this chart from the standpoint of a short put. Based on the patterns you've already identified, ask: How comfortable do I feel with my one-month expiration period? How comfortable do I feel with my six-month expiration period?"

"Just as we said before," explained Nate, "you begin to develop a feel for how options operate by charting this information and watching the patterns that develop. You will see why you're careful with short puts, and you will see the kind of strategy that works best with long puts. At that point the option instruments will start to make sense to you, rather than just being strategies you've memorized. Make sense?"

"Sure. But I have a question," said Shorty. "Should we do a month for calls and *then* a month for puts? Or can we do both simultaneously—have all four charts going at the same time?"

"It all depends," replied Nate, "on how much you can absorb at one time. It might depend on how busy you are. For some, it will be easier to do the charts in sequence; others will prefer to do them simultaneously. But even if you do them simultaneously, you want to *look* at the charts separately. You really want to focus in on each instrument by itself. That's the only way to get away from rote memorization, and to get a 'sense'—to *understand*—how each instrument behaves in different circumstances. In fact, it would be best for you to do this for a number of months . . . until the instruments truly become second nature to you."

"Well, you get the idea," said Aaron. "It's important to have a systematic way to follow options and to see how the pieces move with each other. These charts are one way to do this. Then you're in a position to actually buy and sell options using the virtual trading system. Again, choose a portfolio of any amount you want, and then place *informed* trades. Watch what happens and have fun. It's a learning experience and it doesn't cost you a dime—even if you lose a million dollars!"

"And," added Nate, "a good way to do this is to pick one particular strategy, master it, and then add another. Build your competence as you go. For example, you might decide to master short calls first. Once you manage several trades this way and get familiar with the properties and nuances of selling calls, then maybe you focus on long calls. Once you feel comfortable and know your way around the block with these, then maybe you go to short puts and so on. You get the idea. Master one strategy, and then build on it. You will probably learn faster that way than by just diving in without any plan at all."

"That's my recommendation, too," said Aaron. "Master the option instruments, one at a time. I believe you'll learn them much faster that way. So go to the web site, and also start charting immediately. Then, following the instructions, begin actually trading. You will want to trade on this virtual system for quite a while—until you get proficient enough to succeed in at least 7 out of every 10 trades you place—but you'll have fun the whole time."

"Okay, good," said Nate. "We've accomplished a lot. Let's break now and get together again tomorrow night. We'll focus on two basic option trades and five spread trades. You'll want to paper trade them, too, until you get proficient, but you're now in a position to really focus on them. These seven trades will lay the foundation for your entire future in spread trading."

"Great. See you tomorrow night."

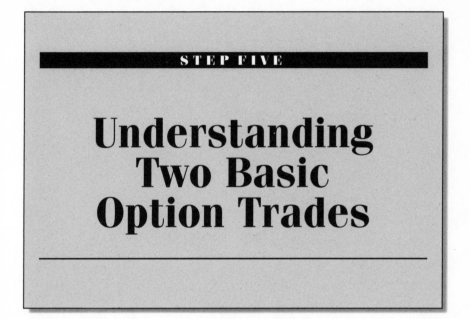

Understanding Two Basic Option Trades

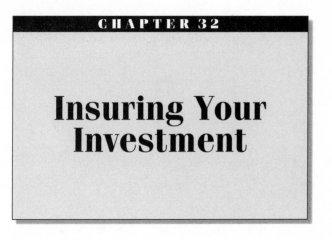

CHAPTER 32

Insuring Your Investment

The group gathered again in Lon's study for their third and final night together.

Aaron began. "Remember that what we're doing here is laying a foundation. It's taken us years to learn all we know and we can't share it all in just three evenings. That would be impossible. But still this is a great foundation for you."

"In fact," added Nate, "before we're finished tonight, you'll know the structure for the two most basic trades in options, as well as five *spread* trades ... and that's a lot more than most investors know. So you've really come a long way."

The first trade we'll talk about is the protective put.

"It sure feels that way," said Shorty, "but I'm anxious to learn more."

"So let's get started," replied Nate. "To begin with, I want to emphasize that in all option trades we're trying to find the best combination for (1) making money, and (2) reducing risk. Trying to make money without reducing risk is just gambling, and there's no reason to do that. It's always possible to significantly reduce risk, so it's just irresponsible not to do it. In fact, we can lower the risk so much that we can literally trade without fear."

"At the same time," added Aaron, "there's no sense in trading if we're not going to make money: we want to rely on ourselves for our financial security; we don't want to rely on others. That's why we're trading. So all

Long Call	Short Call
Right to Buy	May have to Sell
Long Put	Short Put
Right to Sell	May have to Buy

FIGURE 32.1   The Protective Put

we want to do, in any given circumstance, is find the best combination for both reducing risk *and* making money. That's how we take charge of our future without being fearful all along the way."

"Now in the spirit of all this, the first trade we'll talk about is one you already have some experience with. It's called the *protective put*. In this trade, as you know, we own stock and we add a long put to it. That's the combination, and the long put is the option instrument we use. As Lon discovered on his own, this long put protects us if the stock goes down. It's like insurance." (See Figure 32.1.)

"Now notice that in this trade we own the underlying stock *by defini-tion*," Nate added. "If we aren't long in the stock, then by definition it isn't a protective put. In fact, the reason it's called a protective put in the first place is that the long put protects the stock we own."

"Got it."

"Okay, so now the first thing we do in building our protective put is to choose a strike price," said Aaron, "based on the degree of insurance we want and how much it will cost us. Usually we will want pretty full pro-tection. If the stock is trading at $42, for example, we'll probably want to protect that full amount so we will choose a *near-the-money* strike price. If that seems too expensive, we could protect less of the price and place the long put at a lower strike price and thus pay a smaller debit to make the trade. Usually, however, we want to stay with near-the-money strike prices."

"Then," said Nate, "we want to pick a time frame that puts time on our side. If an earnings event is coming up, for example, we want to have enough time in the trade to get past the earnings event. So we look at the option chain that is *at least* 30 to 90 days out and pick our strike price from there. Figure 32.2 shows a chain we can look at to illustrate."

"The stock is selling at $34.25, and we want to protect it pretty fully, so we pick a strike of $32.50. That means we'll be able to sell this stock at

Jan 08 Calls			(39 days to expiration)			NVDA@34.25						Jan 08 Puts	
UVAAE	8.60	0	9.30	9.60	51.3	.98	25.00	UVAME	0.10	0	0.05	0.15	56.8 -.04
UVAAY	7.16	-0.04	7.00	7.20	49.3	.93	27.50	UVAMY	0.25	-0.40	0.20	0.25	51.4 -.08
UVAAF	4.90	+0.30	4.80	5.00	45.9	.84	30.00	UVAMF	0.45	-0.15	0.45	0.55	46.7 -.17
UVAAZ	3.00	+0.15	2.95	3.10	43.3	.68	32.50	UVAMZ	1.15	-0.15	1.10	1.20	44.8 -.32
UVAAG	1.70	+0.05	1.60	1.70	42.0	.48	35.00	UVAMG	2.25	-0.25	2.25	2.30	43.7 -.52
UVAAU	0.83	-0.07	0.75	0.85	41.4	.29	37.50	UVAMU	4.00	-0.10	3.80	4.00	43.0 -.70
UVAAH	0.40	+0.05	0.35	0.40	42.3	.16	40.00	UVAMH	6.00	-0.40	5.90	6.10	45.9 -.82
UVAAV	0.20	0	0.15	0.25	44.8	.09	42.50	UVAMV	8.60	0	8.20	8.50	51.7 -.87
UVAAI	0.10	0	0.05	0.15	46.3	.05	45.00	UVAMI	15.20	0	10.70	10.90	59.4 -.90
Mar 08 Calls			(102 days to expiration)			NVDA@34.25						**Mar 08 Puts**	
UVACE	9.80	0	10.10	10.30	56.1	.90	25.00	UVAOE	0.65	-0.10	0.60	0.70	58.2 -.11
UVACY	8.00	+0.10	8.10	8.30	54.7	.83	27.50	UVAOY	1.10	-0.25	1.05	1.15	55.9 -.17
UVACF	6.30	+0.10	6.30	6.40	52.2	.75	30.00	UVAOF	2.00	0	1.70	1.80	53.8 -.26
UVACZ	4.70	0	4.70	4.90	51.1	.65	32.50	UVAOZ	2.70	-0.20	2.60	(2.75)	52.7 -.35
UVACG	3.40	-0.10	3.50	3.60	50.5	.54	35.00	UVAOG	3.90	-0.30	3.80	1.00	52.1 -.45
UVACU	2.55	+0.15	2.45	2.55	49.1	.44	37.50	UVAOU	5.40	-0.60	5.30	5.40	51.3 -.56
UVACH	1.65	-0.25	1.70	1.75	48.3	.34	40.00	UVAOH	7.50	0	7.00	7.20	51.5 -.65
UVACV	1.25	0	1.10	1.25	47.9	.25	42.50	UVAOV	11.00	0	9.00	9.10	52.1 -.72
UVACI	0.90	-0.05	0.75	0.85	48.0	.19	45.00	UVAOI	12.00	0	11.10	11.30	54.0 -.78

FIGURE 32.2 Applying the Protective Put
Source: Screenshot courtesy of optionsXpress, Inc. © 2008.

$32.50 no matter what happens. We also want a little longer than 38 days to expiration, so we choose a later month that gives us 102 days."

"Then," he continued, "using our online broker, we simply buy our put. As we learned yesterday, this is called *buying to open* (BTO). And obviously, because we're buying, this is a debit trade."

"Now the reason we create a protective put in the first place," added Aaron, "is because (1) we think the stock is bullish long term—that's why we own the stock in the first place—and (2) we want to protect ourselves against bearish potential in the near term. Suppose, for example, that this company will be reporting earnings in a few days. You never know what the report will say and you never know how the market will respond to it. The stock could really take a dive. The natural thing to do, then, is to place this long put that will protect us against this possibility. We don't have to sell the stock out of fear (after all, what if the stock goes *up*?); we only have to insure it. So do you get it? We're trying to optimize bullish and bearish trends simultaneously."

"Now remember," said Nate, "that we have the right to sell this option to someone else. In fact, that's the best way to close out this contract. It's what we call the *primary exit*. It's one of those times we 'sell to close,' as we discussed last night. And essentially we sell the long put when we don't need it any more. For example, suppose the stock price does go down—say, to $26. Well then, remember that our protective put will be worth more at that point. We've paid $2.75 for it, and now let's suppose it's worth $5. And suppose the stock price is turning back up and, because of our technical signals from the RSI, EMA, and MACD, we have reason to expect that trend to continue. That means we can sell our long put to someone else for $5, pocket the profit of $3.25 ($5 – $2.75), and, if we want, turn around and buy more shares of our stock at this lower price of $26. Pretty good deal."

"Sure is," agreed Shorty and Lon.

"Now be sure to notice something we haven't emphasized yet," said Aaron. "Remember that we bought this long put at the *ask* price. But when it comes time to sell, we will sell it at the *bid* price. Remember? We buy at the ask price and sell at the bid price. So when we sell to close this option, we look at the *bid* price to determine how much we'll be selling it for."

> *Usually, we want pretty full protection. And, essentially, we sell the long put when we don't need it anymore.*

"And remember that the purpose of this option is to give us protection. We don't sell it until we don't need the protection any more," added Nate. "Got it?"

"Got it," they both said.

"Now look, if we were buying a long put *without* owning the underlying stock, then our advice would be different," said Aaron. "In that case, we wouldn't be buying the put as protection; it would be an investment tool on its own. And in that case, we would just be looking for the put to increase 20 to 25 percent in value and selling for it for a profit."

"Right," agreed Nate. "But remember that here we're talking about a protective put. By definition we own the stock, and we're adding the long put as protection. Again, that's why it's called a *protective* put."

COST BASIS

"Now it's always important to be absolutely clear about the cost basis of any trade: how much money we have invested in it. So what's our cost basis for this protective put we've been talking about?" asked Aaron.

"Well," answered Lon, "the cost basis would be the price we initially paid for the stock—in this case $34.25—plus the debit we paid to open this protective put—in this case $2.75. So $34.25 plus $2.75 is $37. That's how much we have invested in this trade; that's our cost basis."

REWARD

"Good. And what's our maximum potential reward in this protective put?" asked Nate.

"Well, look," responded Lon, "there's a sense in which it's theoretically unlimited. After all, we own stock in this protective put, and the stock could go up dramatically. Right? Well, in that case, our potential reward is whatever this top is—and it's really infinity—minus the debit we paid to buy the put. So it's theoretically unlimited, just by virtue of owning the stock."

"That's true. Whenever we own stock along with an option, we could say that our maximum potential reward is unlimited, and for just the reason you mentioned. But remember—as you also said—that potential is only *theoretical*. It's not going to happen in the real world."

> *Sometimes we make a profit on the put and sometimes we don't, but at least it offered us protection while we had it.*

"Right," agreed Lon, "and that's why I think a better way to look at a protective put is in terms of what it's *designed* for, and it's designed to protect us. So the question is, what's the maximum potential reward from the standpoint of *protection*? At least, that's the conclusion Cass and I came to when we first talked about this months ago."

"Good," said Aaron, "I think that's right. So if we look at it that way we need to think in terms of what would happen if the stock went to zero. Again, we're buying this insurance in the first place because we own stock and we think the stock could go down in the near term. So if we want to talk about maximum *potential*, we have to consider the worst case that might happen in order to see just how valuable our protection is. So we paid $34.25 for the stock, and chose a near-the-money strike price of $32.50. Then if the stock went to zero, we would still be able to sell *our* shares for $32.50. Looked at that way, our reward potential is $32.50: it's the difference between our strike price—what we can sell the shares for—and zero—the lowest the stock price might go to. Of course, we can't forget that we paid a $2.75 debit for this insurance—for this protective put—so we don't make a full $32.50; we make the $32.50 *minus* the debit of $2.75 we paid to buy the insurance in the first place—in other words, $29.75 ($32.50 – $2.75). That's our maximum potential reward, at least in this way of looking at it."

"So in this way of looking at it, the quickest way to determine our maximum potential reward," added Shorty, "is simply to make this calculation: *strike price (what we are able to sell our shares for) minus the debit (the total expense of the trade)*. In this case that's $32.50 – $2.75, which equals $29.75."

"That's good," said Aaron. "It makes sense to determine 'maximum potential reward' by that formula: the strike price of the long put minus the debit. But remember that stocks don't often go to zero any more than they go to infinity. Either way of looking at it, we're rarely getting anything called *maximum potential reward.* In the normal case, we buy a protective put to protect us in the short term, and then we turn around and sell the put to someone else when we don't need it any longer. Sometimes we make a profit on the put and sometimes we don't, but at least it offered us protection while we had it."

"It's also helpful to me," added Shorty, "to remember that I can never make more with this protective put than I set the strike price at. If I choose a strike price of $32.50, I'm guaranteed to be able to sell my shares at $32.50, but I'm not going to get any price higher than that. With regard to this protective put, I'm capped at $32.50."

"I guess it's also worth mentioning," said Nate, "that again we're talking specifically about a protective put. We would think differently about our reward potential if we were just placing a long put, without owning any stock. So, again, keep in mind that we are assuming ownership of stock in this trade strategy."

"Sure. Got it."

RISK

"So now let me ask you what the risk is in a protective put. How much could you lose?" asked Nate.

"Well, let's see," answered Shorty. "I have a total cost basis of $37: $34.25 for the stock and $2.75 for the debit I paid to buy the protective put. But I have insurance for $32.50 of that: that's where I set the strike price for my long put, so I'm guaranteed to be able to sell shares at $32.50 no matter what happens. So all I stand to lose is the amount of my cost basis that *isn't* protected. And in this case that's $4.50 ($37 – $32.50). The calculation is simply this: *cost basis (my total expense in the trade) minus the strike price of the long put (how much of my investment is protected).*" That tells me how much of my investment *isn't* protected, and that's my risk. In this case, it's $4.50."

"That went too fast for me," said Lon. "You're an accountant, but I'm not. Can you give it to me again?"

"Sure. When you think about insurance, the risk—how much you have to lose—is just a matter of the total you have invested minus how much of that total is protected; that difference is your risk. Here's an example. Let's say, to use round numbers, that you own a $25,000 car and you pay $1,000 per year for insurance. That's a $26,000 investment, or cost basis, for this car. Now let's suppose your deductible is $500. That means that $24,500 of the value of your car is insured; that's how much you can't lose, no matter what happens. So you're spending a total of $26,000, but $24,500 (all of the car's value—$25,000— minus the deductible—$500) of that is protected. Now let's suppose you total your car; its value would drop to zero, but obviously you wouldn't lose all of that value because $24,500 of it is protected. So all you're out is the $500 deductible and the $1,000 you paid for the insurance in the first place. So you would be out a total of $1,500: the difference between your $26,000 investment, or cost basis, and how much you have protected, which is $24,500. The difference, what you *don't have* protected, is your risk. And that's all that's happening with a protective put. Our risk is the total amount we can be 'out;' it's the difference between our cost basis—the total amount we have invested—and how much of that investment is protected. Again, *cost basis (the total expense in the trade) minus the strike price of the long put (how much of the investment is protected)*. Make sense?"

"I think I've got it. All I have to know is how much my total investment is, and how much of that investment is protected. The difference between the two is how much I have to lose."

WHEN TO USE A PROTECTIVE PUT

"Good. Now let's make explicit exactly when we're interested in a protective put. There are only two situations: (1) prior to a quarterly earnings report, and (2) whenever we get bearish signals from our technical indicators: the RSI, the EMA, and the MACD."

"Right," said Aaron. "The first is a situation of uncertainty: we don't know how the market will react to an earnings report, so we have to protect ourselves in case the stock goes bearish on us. That's why we buy puts. The second case is one where we can *see* that the stock is turning bearish on us; that's what the indicators mean. So, obviously, we use a protective put: the option makes money while the stock is losing money, and it also guarantees that we can sell our stock at a certain price if we want to."

"So that means," observed Shorty, "that we have to know when the companies we're in will be reporting earnings, and we also have to watch the technical indicators."

"That's right," said Nate, "but both are easy to do. We're in only a handful of companies at a time, so it's easy to check when quarterly earnings reports are due. Again, you can just go to *OptionsAnimal* to find this information. And it's also easy to go to StockCharts.com to keep up on the technical signals. Both are very important, and they only take a few minutes at most. And this is all the information we need to determine when to place a protective put."

PRIMARY EXIT

"That's right," said Nate. "And, finally, I want to remind you of what we said earlier about closing a protective put. Essentially, we close the put when we don't need it anymore. We still keep the stock; we just close the long put."

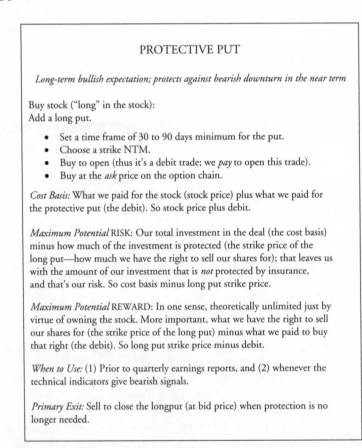

> PROTECTIVE PUT
>
> *Long-term bullish expectation; protects against bearish downturn in the near term*
>
> Buy stock ("long" in the stock):
> Add a long put.
>
> - Set a time frame of 30 to 90 days minimum for the put.
> - Choose a strike NTM.
> - Buy to open (thus it's a debit trade; we *pay* to open this trade).
> - Buy at the *ask* price on the option chain.
>
> *Cost Basis:* What we paid for the stock (stock price) plus what we paid for the protective put (the debit). So stock price plus debit.
>
> *Maximum Potential* RISK: Our total investment in the deal (the cost basis) minus how much of the investment is protected (the strike price of the long put—how much we have the right to sell our shares for); that leaves us with the amount of our investment that is *not* protected by insurance, and that's our risk. So cost basis minus long put strike price.
>
> *Maximum Potential* REWARD: In one sense, theoretically unlimited just by virtue of owning the stock. More important, what we have the right to sell our shares for (the strike price of the long put) minus what we paid to buy that right (the debit). So long put strike price minus debit.
>
> *When to Use:* (1) Prior to quarterly earnings reports, and (2) whenever the technical indicators give bearish signals.
>
> *Primary Exit:* Sell to close the longput (at bid price) when protection is no longer needed.

FIGURE 32.3 The Protective Put Summary

"And we do that," Lon jumped in, "basically when all the technical indicators give us bullish signals on the stock for at least a day. The RSI, the EMA, and the MACD. And since we bought this put in the first place to open it, we *sell* it to close it. And we sell at the bid price. Have I got all this right?"

"You've got it. Good. So now all you have to keep in mind is that once you close this long put, you no longer have protection on your stock. It's no longer a protective put, and your risk is now greater: that's okay, of course, since you've made a calculated decision to sell the put and you're keeping your eye on the stock. Just remember that your risk position is changed and you *have* to keep a close eye on it."

"Okay. So let's summarize the protective put this way," said Nate. (See Figure 32.3)

"And now you begin paper trading protective puts, just as you paper trade the individual instruments. Pick a couple of stocks, choose all the other elements of a protective put (strike prices and time frames), and then follow the results. Get good enough to succeed 7 times out of 10 before even thinking of using real money.

"And now for a review. Just answer the questions based on the following two option chains."

REVIEW

Jan 08 Calls		(43 days to expiration)				BA@91.91							Jan 08 Puts
BAAQ	8.40	+0.60	8.20	8.50	28.0	.82	85.00	BAMQ	1.05	-0.23	1.00	1.10	29.7	-.19
BAAR	4.70	+0.80	4.60	4.80	26.4	.63	90.00	BAMR	2.35	-0.48	2.30	2.40	27.5	-.37
BAAS	2.13	+0.33	2.10	2.20	25.2	.40	95.00	BAMS	4.60	-0.90	4.70	4.90	26.5	-.60
BAAT	0.80	+0.05	0.75	0.85	24.6	.19	100.00	BAMT	8.90	0	8.40	8.70	27.8	-.78

Feb 08 Calls		(71 days to expiration)				BA@91.91							Feb 08 Puts
BABQ	8.80	0	9.20	9.50	28.3	.78	85.00	BANQ	2.25	0	1.90	2.00	31.4	-.24
BABR	5.30	0	5.80	6.00	27.1	.63	90.00	BANR	3.60	-0.40	3.40	3.60	29.9	-.38
BABS	3.30	+0.45	3.30	3.50	26.6	.45	95.00	BANS	6.00	0	5.90	6.10	29.6	-.54
BABT	1.65	+0.20	1.65	1.75	25.7	.28	100.00	BANT	9.90	+0.60	9.20	9.50	29.9	-.69

May 08 Calls		(162 days to expiration)				BA@91.91							May 08 Puts
BAEQ	11.60	+0.10	11.60	11.80	27.0	.74	85.00	BAQQ	4.00	0	3.60	3.80	31.3	-.28
BAER	8.50	+0.60	8.30	8.60	26.1	.63	90.00	BAQR	5.50	-0.20	5.40	5.60	30.6	-.37
BAES	5.80	+0.30	5.80	6.00	25.7	.51	95.00	BAQS	8.00	-0.20	7.70	8.00	30.1	-.48
BAET	3.70	+0.20	3.80	4.00	25.3	.39	100.00	BAQT	11.10	0	10.80	11.00	30.4	-.58

Source: Screenshot courtesy of optionsXpress, Inc. © 2008.
Review

1. What is the current market price of this stock? (See the option chain on page 217.)

2. If you bought a protective put with an expiration period between 45 and 90 days, what would you pay for a 90 strike price?

3. What is the cost basis for this trade—your total investment?

4. What is the maximum potential risk in this trade?

5. What is the maximum potential reward in this trade (from the standpoint of protection)?

Jan 08 Calls					(43 days to expiration)		VLO@64.74					Jan 08 Puts	
VLOAK	9.95	-0.35	10.50	10.70	41.7	.89	55.00	VLOMK	0.40	-0.05	0.35	0.40	38.2	-.09
VLOAY	7.70	0	8.30	8.50	39.1	.84	57.50	VLOMY	0.60	-0.10	0.60	0.65	35.9	-.14
VLOAL	5.90	-0.20	6.20	6.40	35.9	.77	60.00	VLOML	1.15	0	1.00	1.10	34.0	-.22
VLOAZ	4.00	-0.08	4.40	4.60	34.2	.66	62.50	VLOMZ	1.85	-0.35	1.70	1.75	32.5	-.34
VLOAM	2.50	-0.30	2.90	3.10	32.6	.53	65.00	VLOMM	2.90	-0.05	2.65	2.75	30.9	-.47
ZPYAR	1.55	-0.30	1.85	1.90	31.7	.39	67.50	ZPYMR	5.00	0	4.00	4.20	30.5	-.61
ZPYAN	1.05	-0.01	1.05	1.10	30.8	.27	70.00	ZPYMN	5.50	-0.50	5.80	6.10	31.5	-.73
ZPYAV	0.60	0	0.60	0.65	31.1	.17	72.50	ZPYMN	8.25	0	7.80	8.00	30.6	-.83
ZPYAO	0.35	0	0.35	0.40	32.0	.11	75.00	ZPYMO	9.93	-1.07	10.10	10.30	32.9	-.88
Mar 08 Calls					(106 days to expiration)		VLO@64.74					**Mar 08 Puts**	
VLOCK	11.90	+0.50	11.60	11.80	36.0	.84	55.00	VLOOK	1.25	-0.14	1.25	1.30	37.8	-.16
VLOCL	7.40	0	7.90	8.10	34.7	.72	60.00	VLOOL	2.65	-0.08	2.45	2.55	36.0	-.29
VLOCZ	6.30	0	6.30	6.50	34.0	.64	62.50	VLOOZ	3.40	-0.10	3.30	3.50	35.5	-.36
VLOCM	4.94	+0.24	4.90	5.10	33.3	.56	65.00	VLOOM	4.80	+0.05	4.40	4.50	34.6	-.44
ZPYCR	3.80	+0.10	3.80	4.00	33.3	.48	67.50	ZPYOR	6.00	-0.20	5.70	5.90	34.6	-.52
ZPYCN	2.65	-0.30	2.85	2.95	32.6	.39	70.00	ZPYON	8.10	0	7.20	7.50	34.5	-.60
ZPYCV	2.00	+0.05	2.05	2.20	32.2	.32	72.50	ZPYOV	9.40	0	9.00	9.20	34.7	-.67
ZPYCO	1.60	+0.05	1.50	1.60	32.1	.25	75.00	ZPYOO	11.50	0	10.90	11.10	35.0	-.73
Jun 08 Calls					(197 days to expiration)		VLO@64.74					**Jun 08 Puts**	
VLOFK	12.80	0	13.20	13.40	35.1	.81	55.00	VLORK	2.56	0	2.35	2.50	38.2	-.21
VLOFL	9.35	0	9.80	10.00	34.2	.71	60.00	VLORL	4.00	0	3.90	4.00	37.1	-.30
VLOFZ	9.11	0	8.30	8.50	33.7	.65	62.50	VLORZ	5.00	0	4.80	5.00	36.5	-.36
VLOFM	6.60	-0.10	7.00	7.20	33.5	.59	65.00	VLORM	6.35	0	6.00	6.10	36.3	-.41
ZPYFR	5.60	0	5.80	6.00	33.1	.53	67.50	ZPYRR	7.20	0	7.20	7.40	35.9	-.47
ZPYFN	4.60	+0.20	4.70	5.00	32.7	.47	70.00	ZPYRN	9.10	0	8.70	8.90	36.2	-.52
ZPYFV	3.70	+0.10	3.90	4.10	32.6	.41	72.50	ZPYRV	10.94	0	10.30	10.50	36.3	-.57
ZPYFO	3.08	0	3.10	3.30	32.1	.35	75.00	ZPYRO	12.20	0	12.00	12.30	36.6	-.62

Source: Screenshot courtesy of optionsXpress, Inc. © 2008.
Review

6. What is the current market price of this stock? (See the option chain on page 218.)

7. If you bought a protective put with no more than a 90-day expiration period, what would you pay for a $62.50 strike price?

8. What is the cost basis for this trade—your total investment?

9. What is the maximum potential risk in this trade?

10. What is the maximum potential reward in this trade (from the standpoint of protection)?

11. On this same stock, if you bought a protective put with a 90- to 120-day expiration period, what would you pay for a $62.50 strike price?

12. What is the cost basis for this trade—your total investment?

13. What is the maximum potential risk in this trade?

14. What is the maximum potential reward in this trade (from the standpoint of protection)?

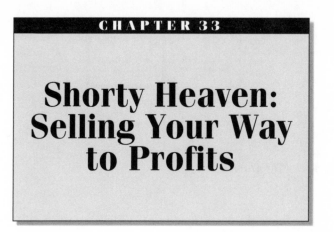

CHAPTER 33

Shorty Heaven: Selling Your Way to Profits

"**O**kay, now let's turn our attention to the covered call," said Aaron. "In this trade, I own stock and I add a short call to it. That's the combination. I add the short call because it allows me to take in a credit—I can make money on my stock without doing anything. This is what Shorty discovered on his own about short calls." (See Figure 33.1.)

"This is referred to as a *covered call*," he continued, "because we own the stock, and we can think of the stock we own as 'covering' the short call we're placing. As we mentioned earlier, if we *didn't* own the stock, then—through our short call—we would be entering an obligation to sell shares we don't own *precisely when the cost of the stock is higher than our strike price*—meaning, again, that we would have to go out on the market to buy shares at the higher market price so we could turn around and meet our obligation to sell them at the lower strike price we agreed to. That *guarantees* a loss."

> *I add the short call because it allows me to take in a credit—I can make money on my stock without doing anything.*

"Right," added Nate, "which is precisely why we never do such naked calls. In fact, unless you meet certain conditions, your broker won't let you. But still, that's what it's called—a naked call—and what we're going

Long Call	Short Call
Right to Buy	May have to Sell
Long Put	Short Put
Right to Sell	May have to Buy

FIGURE 33.1 The Covered Call

to talk about is called a *covered call* to distinguish it from this dangerous version."

"Now to be a bit simplistic, basically two things can happen in a covered call," continued Nate. "First, if the stock is bullish and goes in the money—if it goes higher than the strike price I chose—then, at least by the expiration date, I will be assigned and have to sell my shares. But notice what that means: it means that my stock value has increased, I am able to sell it for the strike price at some level of profit, and I still get to keep the credit I received in the first place. So this is one of the 'exits' for a covered call.

"But let's suppose," he continued, "that the stock is more or less stagnant, or even goes down, and never goes in the money—it never goes higher than the strike price I chose. Then the option will expire worthless: I won't be assigned, I won't sell my shares, and I still get to keep the credit I received. Much of the time, this is the desired outcome, and thus letting the option expire worthless is also one of the 'exits' for a covered call."

"So you can see how important the strike price is," said Aaron. "If we *want* to go in the money and get assigned, we choose a *near-the-money* strike price, or maybe even an *in-the-money* strike price. If we're not bullish on the stock long term, that's probably what we want to do: just take the credit and have the stock go away. If we want to hang onto our shares, however, we choose an *out-of-the-money* strike price; in fact, we probably choose one that is 1 to 2 strikes out of the money to increase our chances of *finishing* out of the money. In sum, the strike price we choose depends pretty much on how bullish we are about the stock. If we're bullish, we do one thing; if we're not, we do another. "

"Now in picking a time frame," added Nate, "we normally want to go 3 to 12 months out. Remember that the further out we go, the higher the bid/ask prices will be. So if we go a few months out, we can take in a higher credit. This credit has an advantage we haven't talked about yet, too. Notice, for example, that every time we take in a credit on a stock we own, we lower the cost basis of our stock: we lower the amount of our investment, the amount we're 'out.' Think about it. If I paid $40 per share for 100 shares of stock, and if I then take in a credit of $5 on those shares, my cost basis in those shares is automatically reduced to $35. So the credit is important.

"But," he continued, "you also have to consider that the longer the time frame, the better the chances that the strike will go in the money and that you'll be assigned—forcing you to sell your shares. So, Shorty, just as you discovered on your own, you're always balancing credit amount with time frame in choosing a strike price and a time frame."

"Okay, now with all that in mind, let's look at an example," said Aaron. (See Figure 33.2.)

"In this case, we're paying $23.49 for the stock, and we're placing a covered call at an out-of-the-money strike of 27.50 at a bid price of $2.20. That means we're taking in, in a credit, $2.20 per share."

Mar 08 Calls			(102 days to expiration)			NFLX@23.49					Mar 08 Puts		
QNQCS	11.20	0	11.00	11.20		1.00	12.50	QNQOS	0.80	0	0.15	0.25	79.9	-.04
QNQCC	10.10	0	8.70	9.00	55.7	.96	15.00	QNQOC	0.45	0	0.35	0.45	72.8	-.08
QNQCW	7.00	0	6.60	6.90	57.8	.88	17.50	QNQOW	0.87	0	0.75	0.85	68.6	-.15
QNQCD	5.30	0	4.80	5.00	56.6	.77	20.00	QNQOD	1.40	-0.15	1.40	1.50	65.2	-.25
QNQCX	3.50	0	3.30	3.50	55.8	.63	22.50	QNQOX	2.42	-0.13	2.35	2.45	62.6	-.37
QNQCE	2.15	-0.15	2.10	2.25	53.3	.49	25.00	QNQOE	3.81	0	3.60	3.80	61.0	-.49
QNQCY	1.35	-0.16	1.25	1.35	51.2	.35	27.50	QNQOY	5.20	0	5.20	5.40	59.6	-.62
QNQCF	0.87	0	0.75	0.80	50.8	.24	30.00	QNQOF	7.00	0	7.10	7.30	59.6	-.72
QNQCT	0.45	-0.05	0.35	0.45	48.8	.14	32.50	QNQOT	8.70	0	9.30	9.40	61.6	-.78
Jun 08 Calls			(193 days to expiration)			NFLX@23.49					Jun 08 Puts		
QNQFC	0	0	9.00	9.30	47.6	.94	15.00	QNQRC	0.75	0	0.70	0.80	66.3	-.11
QNQFW	7.10	0	7.20	7.40	52.1	.85	17.50	QNQRW	1.35	0	1.30	1.40	64.4	-.18
QNQFD	5.80	0	5.60	5.80	53.2	.75	20.00	QNQRD	2.20	0	2.15	2.25	63.0	-.26
QNQFX	4.30	0	4.20	4.40	52.4	.65	22.50	QNQRX	3.30	0	3.20	3.40	62.0	-.35
QNQFE	3.20	0	3.40	3.30	52.0	.54	25.00	QNQRE	4.49	0	4.50	4.70	60.6	-.44
QNQFY	2.25	0	(2.20)	2.35	50.7	.43	27.50	QNQRY	6.30	0	6.10	6.30	60.6	-.53
QNQFF	1.65	0	1.30	1.65	49.4	.34	30.00	QNQRF	8.10	0	7.90	8.00	60.1	-.61
QNQFT	1.15	0	1.00	1.10	48.2	.25	32.50	QNQRT	9.80	0	9.80	10.00	60.7	-.67

FIGURE 33.2 Applying the Covered Call
Source: Screenshot courtesy of optionsXpress, Inc. © 2008.

"And that means our cost basis," said Shorty, "is $21.29. What we paid for the stock—$23.49—is lowered by our $2.20 credit ($23.49 − $2.20 = $21.29)."

COST BASIS AND RISK

"So what is our risk?" asked Nate.

"Well, look," answered Shorty, "we own the stock at $23.49 and there's the *theoretical* possibility that the stock price will go to zero. If that happens, we've lost $23.49—the whole thing. On that part of the deal, our risk is ... well, $23.49. On the other side, however, we have taken in a credit of $2.20. And because we've actually taken in $2.20, we can't really lose $23.49. Even if the stock price goes to zero, the most we can lose is $21.29 ($23.49 − $2.20). The formula for this theoretical risk is simple: *stock price (what we paid out) minus the credit (what we took in).*

"So in a covered call," said Lon, "cost basis and risk are the same. My risk is losing everything I have invested in the trade, which is simply my cost basis. I have a net investment of $21.29, and if the stock goes to zero, I will lose the total $21.29. That's a large risk ... much different than a protective put."

"That's right," answered Nate. "That's the accepted and formal way of calculating risk in a covered call, and in that sense the risk is large. We'll be able to say a lot more about reducing this risk a little later, but for now, just keep two things in mind. First, this risk comes from owning the stock itself, not from the short call we add to it. The short call itself doesn't create the risk, or even increase it. In fact, as we've just seen, it actually reduces the risk somewhat because it lowers the cost basis of owning the stock. It *is* important to remember, though, that this isn't a defensive strategy like the protective put is, so the risk *is* much greater. If the stock price plummets rapidly—or if it drops more gradually and we're just not paying attention—then we stand to lose a lot."

"But that brings us to the second thing to keep in mind," said Aaron. "In the more normal case—where we're keeping our eye on things and the stock isn't plummeting overnight—remember that we face no risk of losing the $2.20 credit we received to make the deal in the first place. In this typical case, our risk is that the stock price moves higher and we get assigned. If that happens we lose our shares, it is true, but we also reap the profit we've made on them *and* we get to keep the $2.20 credit. If the stock price doesn't do that, however, and our strike stays *out* of the money, then we don't get assigned, we get to keep our shares, *and* we get to keep the $2.20 credit."

"Right," added Nate. "And note that in that case we're the ones who determine the risk we face—whether we're likely to lose our shares or not—because we're the ones who choose the strike price and the expiration date in the first place. We actually exercise a lot of control."

REWARD

"Yes," agreed Aaron, "and as Nate said, we'll be able to say more about reducing risk a little later, when we talk about spread trades. But for now let's turn our attention to the matter of reward. What do you suppose is the maximum potential *reward* on a covered call?"

"Let me think about this," said Lon. "I think the main factor here must be my obligation to sell my shares at the strike price I chose. For example, I chose an out-of-the-money strike price of 27.50. In this case, even if the stock price goes to $60 or $70 or even $1,000, I'm still obligated to sell my shares *for the $27.50 I agreed to*. I can't make more than that, no matter how high the stock goes. When I choose the strike price, I choose the highest amount I'll be able to sell for."

"And then of course," added Shorty," there's the cost basis of the trade—what we've already invested in the deal. In this case that's a net cost of $21.29: remember that we spent $23.49 on the stock itself and took in a credit of $2.20, which leaves us with this net cost of $21.29. So even with a strike price of 27.50 we obviously don't *make* $27.50; we have to subtract our costs. So in this case we subtract $21.29, for a profit of $6.21 ($27.50 – $21.29). That means no matter how high the stock price goes—even to $1,000—if I have a strike price of 27.50 and a cost basis of $21.29, my maximum reward is $6.21."

"So in a covered call," Lon jumped in, "my maximum potential reward is a function of the strike price and the cost basis, whatever they are. The potential reward will always be figured this way: *strike price (the maximum I can sell the stock for) minus cost basis (my total investment in the trade)*. Right?"

"That's right," assured Aaron. "You've got it."

WHEN TO USE A COVERED CALL

"So what general rule do we follow in using covered calls?" Shorty asked.

"The basic rule," replied Aaron, "is that we *always* look to use covered calls. Whenever we own stock we look to place a covered call on it. Think about it. A covered call allows us to take in cash no matter what the stock itself is doing, and it doesn't cost us anything. That's pretty attractive. It's true, of course, that in strong bullish or bearish trends other instruments are better—they take better advantage of those trends—but a covered call is never *wrong*, per se. At least not if we are managing the risk by placing our strike price and expiration date appropriately, and if we're not taking our eye off the stock itself."

"Really," added Nate, "the only time we're not looking to use a covered call is when an earnings report is coming out. We don't know what the report will say, and we don't know how the market will react to it: the price could go down, but it could also jump up. One problem with a covered call is that it limits the upside potential. If the stock jumps up and our option goes in the money, we face the possibility of early assignment and of having to sell our shares prematurely—while the stock is still headed up. That's why, just prior to an earnings report, we close our covered call and let a few days go by to see how the market is reacting. That way, if the stock price does jump up, we're able to take advantage of it. We're not assigned prematurely. Make sense?"

"Sure," answered Lon. "The covered call always brings in cash, at no cost, but it also limits our upside potential. So we use these factors to our advantage by (1) always looking to use covered calls, except (2) during earnings. Right?"

"Right."

PRIMARY EXITS

"So now let me review the two basic ways this covered call could end," said Nate. "On one hand, the strike price might never go in the money—the stock price stays lower than the 27.50 strike—and I'm never assigned. In that case I get to keep my shares, and I have the $2.20 credit I received to make the deal in the first place."

"The other main way it could end," said Nate, "is for the strike price to go in the money. The stock price goes higher than the 27.50 strike price, and I get assigned. In that case, I sell my shares at $27.50, plus I still have the $2.20 credit I received to make the deal in the first place. So I essentially sell my shares for $29.70."

"Both of these exits are fine," added Aaron. "We come out ahead either way, and that's why we consider both of them 'primary exits.' There are other possibilities for what we might do with a covered call—you might recall that we talked briefly before about 'adjustments'—but these

---

COVERED CALL

Best for stagnant or slightly bearish trend; okay, but not as good, for bullish trend

Buy stock ("long" in the stock).
Add a short call.

- Set a time frame of 3 to 12 months for the call.
- Choose a strike price, either NTM (if we want to be assigned and sell our shares), or 1 to 2 strikes OTM (if we don't want to be assigned and sell our shares).
- Sell to open (thus it's a credit trade; we are *paid* to open this trade).
- Sell at the *bid* price on the option chain.

Cost Basis: What we paid for the stock (the stock price) minus what we took in (the credit). So: stock price minus credit.

Maximum Potential RISK: Theoretically (imagining the stock to go to zero), the amount we have invested (the stock price) minus how much we took in (the credit). So: stock price minus credit. However, there is no risk of losing the credit.

Maximum Potential REWARD: What we're guaranteed to sell the shares for (the strike price of our short call) minus our total investment to make the trade (our cost basis). So: short call strike price minus cost basis.

When to Use: All the time. The only time not to use a covered call is during earnings.

Exit: Option goes in the money and we are assigned: we sell our shares for a profit, at the strike price, and keep the credit we received.

Exit: Option stays out of the money and expires worthless: we keep our shares, plus the credit we received.

FIGURE 33.3 Covered Call Summary

are the two primary exits. They're the ones you should know about at this point."

"So let's summarize the covered call this way." (See Figure 33.3.)

"So now you paper trade, just as you paper trade protective puts. You will want to be successful 7 times out of 10 before you think of using real money.

"But now for a review. Just answer the questions based on the following option chain."

REVIEW

Apr 08 Calls				(134 days to expiration)		NOK@38.47					Apr 08 Puts	
NAYDF	9.60	-0.50	9.70	9.90	44.3	.87	30.00	NAYPF	0.80	+0.05	0.80	0.90	46.2 -.14
NAYDG	6.10	-0.20	5.90	6.10	40.3	.72	35.00	NAYPG	2.00	+0.10	1.95	2.05	42.1 -.28
NAYDH	3.20	-0.20	3.10	3.30	37.9	.51	40.00	NAYPH	4.10	+0.10	4.10	4.30	40.5 -.48
NAYDI	1.55	-0.10	1.50	1.60	37.2	.31	45.00	NAYPI	6.70	0	7.40	7.60	40.6 -.67

Jul 08 Calls				(225 days to expiration)		NOK@38.47					Jul 08 Puts	
NAYGF	10.10	-0.40	10.00	10.20	34.0	.88	30.00	NAYSF	1.30	-0.05	1.30	1.40	44.0 -.16
NAYGG	7.10	0	6.50	6.70	34.3	.73	35.00	NAYSG	2.60	0	2.75	2.85	42.0 -.29
NAYGH	4.00	-0.10	3.90	4.00	33.7	.54	40.00	NAYSH	5.10	+0.10	5.10	5.20	41.6 -.44
NAYGI	2.40	-0.10	2.15	2.25	33.3	.37	45.00	NAYSI	7.80	0	8.30	8.50	42.8 -.58

Jan 09 Calls				(407 days to expiration)		NOK@38.47					Jan 09 Puts	
VOKAF	11.40	-0.60	11.10	11.30	31.2	.86	30.00	VOKMF	2.10	0	2.05	2.25	42.5 -.18
VOKAG	8.30	-0.10	8.00	8.20	32.6	.73	35.00	VOKMG	3.80	0	3.70	4.00	41.6 -.28
VOKAH	5.70	0	5.60	5.70	32.9	.59	40.00	VOKMH	6.90	0	6.20	6.40	41.8 -.40
VOKAI	4.00	0	3.60	3.90	32.5	.45	45.00	VOKMI	8.90	0	9.20	9.40	42.3 -.50

Source: Screenshot courtesy of optionsXpress, Inc. © 2008.
Review

Suppose you bought this stock today and wanted to place a covered call, with a 6- to 7-month expiration period, and you eventually wanted to be assigned.

1. What month would you choose?
2. What strike price would you choose?
3. What would be the cost basis for this trade?
4. What is your maximum potential risk?
5. What is your maximum potential reward?
6. What is the primary exit for this trade?

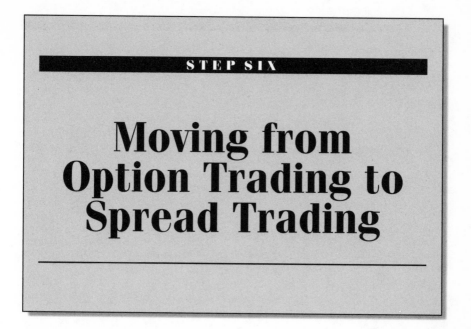

Moving from Option Trading to Spread Trading

CHAPTER 34

Trading in Surround Sound: The Fundamental Spread Trade

"With these two option trades under our belts," said Nate, "we're now ready to make a quantum leap in our effectiveness with options."

"That's right," said Aaron. "Remember how we told you earlier that we can actually combine option instruments in one trade?"

"Sure."

"Well, that's what we're prepared to do now. We're going to combine the covered call and the protective put into one deal. It's called a collar trade. So now there are three elements: buying the stock, buying a put, and shorting a call: long stock, long put, short call. The long put and the short call are the option instruments we use." (See Figure 34.1.)

"Look what this does for us," he continued. "The stock itself helps optimize a bullish trend. We bought it in the first place because we're expecting the stock to increase in value. The short call brings a credit into our account up front, and the long put then protects us if the stock happens to trend bearish."

"Now because we're using two option instruments in this trade," said Nate, "we distinguish between them in this way: we say that the short call is the *primary* option instrument in this case, because it's the one we're using to make money—because of the credit we receive in selling it. We say that the long put is the *limiting* instrument in this case because it's the one we're using to limit our risk—it's what offers us protection."

Long Call	Short Call
Right to Buy	May have to Sell
Long Put	Short Put
Right to Sell	May have to Buy

FIGURE 34.1   The Collar Trade

One of the most effective trades we can make is to combine the covered call and the protective put into one deal. It's called a collar trade.

"To see how it works," said Aaron, "let's look at the option chain." (See Figure 34.2.)

"Here's how it works," he continued. "We buy this stock at $33.43. We place the *long put* strike at the money or near the money—here, at 32.50—because that kind of strike price gives us pretty full protection: it allows us to be able to sell our shares at $32.50—less than $1 from the actual stock price—even if the value goes below that (even to zero, as we've learned). Now we look at a time frame of a minimum of 45 days for this long put because we need protection for a reasonable length of time. We might even want a time frame of 3 to 5 months ... but in any case, at least 45 days. Here we've chosen a time frame of 106 days, or just over three months. And we're able to buy this put at an ask price of $3.30. Remember, when we open a long put we're buying, and we buy at the ask price."

"So to this point our cost basis is $36.73, right?" asked Lon. "The $33.43 cost of the stock, plus $3.30 to buy this put."

"That's right."

"Okay, the next piece of the puzzle," said Nate, picking up the explanation, "is the short call. And you'll be able to execute this short call at the same time you execute the long put; whether you do it by phone or online, your broker will be able to place them simultaneously.

"Now usually when we're combining a short call with a protective put we want to go out anywhere from 3 to 12 months in time for the short call, and we want to pick a strike price that is higher than the strike of the long put—one that is 1 to 2 strikes out of the money. These two factors help us get a higher credit amount—to be able sell a call at a higher bid price.

Mar 08 Calls			(106 days to expiration) NVDA@33.43											Mar 08 Puts
UVACX	10.50	0	11.60	11.80	59.8	.92	22.50	UVAOX	0.70	0	0.45	0.55	62.7	-.08
UVACE	9.80	0	9.50	9.70	58.2	.87	25.00	UVAOE	0.85	0	0.80	0.90	59.8	-.13
UVACY	8.00	0	7.60	7.80	56.8	.80	27.50	UVAOY	1.35	0	1.35	1.45	57.8	-.20
UVACF	6.21	0	5.90	6.10	55.2	.71	30.00	UVAOF	2.20	-0.05	2.10	2.20	55.9	-.29
UVACZ	4.90	+0.	Long Put				32.50	UVAOZ	3.20	-0.10	3.10	(3.30)	55.0	-.38
UVACG	3.40	-0.12	3.30	3.50	53.3	.52	35.00	UVAOG	4.60	+0.30	4.40	4.60	54.2	-.48
UVACU	2.45	-0.10	2.40	2.50	52.3	.42	37.50	UVAOU	6.10	+0.37	6.00	6.10	53.7	-.58
UVACH	1.70	-0.15	1.70	1.75	51.4	.33	40.00	UVAOH	7.50	0	7.80	7.90	53.9	-.66
UVACV	1.30	0	1.15	1.25	50.9	.25	42.50	UVAOV	11.00	0	9.70	9.90	54.0	-.73

Jun 08 Calls			(197 days to expiration) NVDA@33.43											Jun 08 Puts
UVAFX	11.00	0	12.50	12.70	59.6	.88	22.50	UVARX	1.70	0	1.05	1.15	60.9	-.12
UVAFE	9.60	0	10.60	10.80	57.7	.83	25.00	UVARE	1.65	0	1.60	1.70	59.1	-.17
UVAFY	9.07	0	8.80	9.10	55.8	.77	27.50	UVARY	2.30	0	2.30	2.45	57.6	-.23
UVAFF	6.20	0	7.30	7.50	54.5	.71	30.00	UVARF	3.10	-0.50	3.20	3.40	56.6	-.30
UVAFZ	6.40	+0.10	6.00	6.20	54.0	.63	32.50	UVARZ	4.50	0	4.30	4.50	55.6	-.37
UVAFG	4.90	+0.30	(4.90)	5.00	53.2	.56	35.00	Short Call					54.9	-.44
UVAFU	4.00	-0.20	3.80	4.00	51.7	.49	37.50	UVARU	7.00	0	7.10	7.30	54.6	-.51
UVAFH	3.11	0	3.00	3.10	50.6	.41	40.00	UVARH	8.70	-0.10	8.80	8.90	54.3	-.57
UVAFV	2.60	0	2.35	2.45	50.1	.35	42.50	UVARV	12.00	0	10.60	10.80	54.7	-.63

Jan 09 Calls			(407 days to expiration) NVDA@33.43											Jan 09 Puts
OLIAX	12.50	0	14.10	14.40	57.0	.85	22.50	OLIMX	2.90	0	2.20	2.40	60.2	-.15
OLIAE	12.99	0	12.40	12.60	54.5	.81	25.00	OLIME	3.80	0	3.00	3.20	59.3	-.19
OLIAF	9.80	+0.10	9.50	9.80	52.8	.72	30.00	OLIMF	5.30	0	4.90	5.10	56.9	-.28
OLIAG	7.40	0	7.20	7.40	51.2	.62	35.00	OLIMG	9.40	0	7.40	7.70	56.2	-.37
OLIAH	5.20	0	5.40	5.60	50.3	.52	40.00	OLIMH	11.20	0	10.40	10.70	55.7	-.46

FIGURE 34.2 Applying the Collar Trade
Source: Screenshot courtesy of optionsXpress, Inc. © 2008.

Remember, when we open a short call, we are selling, and we sell at the bid price. So let's say we open this short call at a strike of 35 and receive a credit of $4.90.

> *Amazing. It's like buying insurance with someone else's money. It didn't cost us anything.*

"Notice what this means," he continued. "We've spent $3.30 to buy our long put, but we've taken in a $4.90 credit for the short call: in essence, the short call *pays for* the long put; it pays for our insurance."

"Amazing," said Shorty. "It's like buying insurance with someone else's money! It didn't cost us anything."

"That's one of the advantages of this kind of trade," said Aaron. "One part, or 'leg,' of the trade pays for the other leg of the trade. It's one of the main purposes of a short call. That's the reason, in this case, for going further out in time and picking an out-of-the-money strike price for the call: it helps pay for the protective put we're combining it with. We always want to do that."

"Now notice something about this kind of trade," Nate added. "We're long in the stock—we own it—because we expect it to increase in value over time. Owning the stock will optimize the bullish trend we expect. But we also have a protective put (our long put), which optimizes a bearish trend. It gives us protection if the stock price goes down, and the put itself *increases* in value, other things equal, as the stock price goes down. On top of all that, we have a short call that keeps our position positive if the stock goes stagnant or slightly bearish: the credit we received helps offset those movements in the stock price."

"That's why this is called a *collar trade*," said Aaron. "We've got the stock surrounded. No matter what trend the stock goes through, the collar trade will be able to make something out of it. It's a phenomenal way to make profit while reducing risk."

"That's right," added Nate. "In this trade we limit our risk by having the protective put, and we generate profit by owning the stock and by placing the short call."

"I guess this is what you meant when you said earlier that there was more to say about reducing the risk of a covered call. Right?" asked Lon. "In other words, the most effective way of reducing the risk of a covered call is simply to combine it with a protective put. Then we have a whole collar."

"That's exactly right."

"Okay, now because all of these elements—the stock, the long put, and the short call—are involved in the trade," said Aaron, "we have to look at all of them in determining our total cost basis, our risk, and our reward."

> *We've got the stock surrounded. No matter what trend the stock goes through, the collar trade will be able to make something out of it. It's a phenomenal way to make profit while reducing risk.*

COST BASIS

"So look at the cost basis," said Nate. "You already noticed that we paid $33.43 for the stock and $3.30 in debit for the put, giving us a cost basis, *at that point*, of $36.73. But as I just pointed out, we *took in* a credit of $4.90 on the short call, so that has to be subtracted from the $36.73 to give us our actual cost basis in the trade. So $36.73 – $4.90 gives us a total cost basis of $31.83."

"So we figure our cost basis this way, right?" asked Shorty. "*The stock price (what we pay to buy shares), plus the debit (what we pay for the long put), minus the credit (what we take in for the short call).* That's our cost basis."

"That's right."

RISK

"Now our risk," said Aaron, "obviously depends a lot on this cost basis. It's what we have invested. But our risk also depends on the strike price we've chosen for the long put. This protective put is how we're limiting our risk, so the strike price we choose for it will largely determine just how much risk we face. This is because the strike price determines how much of our investment is protected. In this case we chose an out-of-the-money strike price of 32.50—again, less than $1 from the stock price—and that means we are insured to that amount: we are guaranteed to be able to sell our shares for $32.50 no matter what happens. So that's how much of our investment is protected."

"Wow," interrupted Shorty. "That means this trade has no risk at all. Look. Our net investment—our cost basis—is $31.83 (again, including the price of the stock, the debit we paid for the put, minus the credit we received for the short call), but this total cost is *protected* up to $32.50—that's how much we're *guaranteed* to be able to sell our shares for: $32.50. So to know our risk, all we have to know is how much of this total cost we *don't* have protected. But in this case that's zero; *all* of it is protected. In fact, in this case we can't do worse than *make* $0.67. So that's our maximum risk: we don't make *any more* than $0.67."

"Right," agreed Nate. "So the formula for determining risk in a collar trade is simply: *the cost basis (our total investment in the trade) minus the strike price of the* LONG PUT *(how much of our investment we have protected).* And in this case, it's actually no risk at all.

"Now, of course, all that is true," he continued, "only as long as the long put is still in place. Remember, we placed the long put time frame at 106 days, but we placed the short call time frame at 197 days. And that means that the long put will expire long before the short call expires. In that interim, we're simply left with a covered call, which includes the risk of a covered call."

"Of course," said Aaron, "there are ways to handle this trade other than to simply let it transition to a covered call, but that's over your heads right now. And for now it doesn't matter much anyway because you know how to handle covered calls."

REWARD

"Now let's turn to figuring our maximum potential reward," said Nate. "Obviously, our total cost basis is important again because it's what we have invested; it represents our total expense. But now our *short call* strike price is what's important. This is our primary option instrument for getting profit, so it will determine our potential reward. That, of course, is why we always place it higher than the strike of the long put: the most we can *make* (which is determined by the short call strike) should obviously be higher than the most we can *lose* (which is determined by the strike of the long put)."

"In this case, we have a short call strike price of 35," said Aaron. "And let's suppose that the stock price goes to $50 or $60 or even $1,000. We still have an obligation to sell our shares at $35, because that's the strike price we agreed to. If we get assigned—and we will—that's the maximum we can sell them for. But we also have to account for our costs in the trade—our cost basis. And that's $31.83. So how much we make over and above our costs—up to a max of $35—is our potential reward. In this case it's $3.17: $35 (our short call strike price) – $31.83 (our cost basis), and that comes to $3.17.

"So the formula for determining the potential reward in a collar trade is simply this," said Nate: "*the strike price of the* SHORT CALL *(which is the maximum we can sell the shares for if we are assigned) minus the cost basis (our investment in the trade).*"

"Now notice," added Aaron, "that these calculations of risk and reward allow us to go into this trade already knowing our maximum risk and our maximum reward. We know from the start that we can't do worse than make $0.67 and that we can't do better than make $3.17. We limit our reward, it's true, *but we also limit our risk*. And we can do the same thing over and over again. And this allows us to trade literally without fear. It's a phenomenal way to make profits without drowning in anxiety."

"Not only that," said Nate, "but a collar trade like this also requires less time to manage. Think about it. You go into this trade already knowing the best and the worst that can happen, *and you have time frames that last for weeks, even months*. How much time do you think you have to spend every day looking at a trade like this? It's sweet. You're not obsessing about daily stock movements, and you don't have to react on a dime. All you do is set the trade up well in the first place, and then you can watch it almost casually."

"SPREAD" TRADE

"And notice something else," continued Nate. "All of this is a function of the *spread* between the two strike prices. The difference between these strikes—along with the difference that follows in their bid/ask amounts—is what determines how much we can make and how much we can lose. This spread determines everything."

"That's why," said Nate, "we can refer to the collar trade as one kind of 'spread' trade. It's a way of combining option instruments that allows us to determine for ourselves the best and the worst that can happen to us in the deal."

"Think how amazing that is," added Aaron. "Most people invest in the stock market hoping (1) that good things will happen and (2) that bad things won't. But they don't *control* anything. All they can do is hope . . . and try to time everything so that their hopes are realized."

"And that's why they can't sleep at night," said Nate. "Imagine investing thousands of dollars—even tens of thousands of dollars—and relying on *hope* that things will turn out. Well, the flip side of hope is fear . . . fear that things won't turn out as we hope. And that's what we're saddled with whenever we just 'hope': the fear that we might be wrong and that we might lose our investment instead of growing it. Well, that's not for me. And it's not even necessary. Think about it. With a spread trade like this specific collar we're talking about, we go to bed every night knowing that the *worst* that can happen to us is that we will make $0.67 per share. Not much to worry about there!"

"And that's the magic of spread trading," said Aaron. "We don't rely on 'hope' that things will turn out. We actually *control* how things will turn out. We simply structure a deal in the first place that has a risk we can live with and a reward we can live with. By simply managing the spread, *we get* to decide what will happen. That's what allows us to make money without fear. And that's what allows us to sleep at night."

"It's amazing to me," added Nate. "It's the best deal on the planet, and virtually no one knows about it. Oh sure, compared to the two of you there are a lot of people trading options. As we've shown you, there's a whole industry devoted to it. But compared to the whole investment community—not to mention the vast numbers of people around the world who ought to be investing, but aren't—virtually no one is doing it. Only a tiny percentage of people invest on their own at all; only a small percentage of *them* trade options; and only a percentage of option traders are *spread* traders. And it really is the best deal on the planet. Unbelievable."

BALANCE OF RISK AND REWARD

"But enough," he continued. "Let's get back to this specific collar trade we're talking about. Now as we think about how to set the trade up in the first place, remember that our short call strike price drives our profit potential. In choosing a strike price of 35, for example, we are choosing to sell for no higher than that. No matter how high the stock price might go—to $40 or $50 or even $1000—at expiration we will be assigned and sell our shares for $35. That short call strike automatically caps our potential."

"So if we want to be able to make more profit than that," said Aaron, "we simply need to choose a higher strike price—one that's further out of the money. Let's suppose we chose the 40 strike, for example, rather than the 35. In that case, our reward potential would still be capped, but it would be capped $5 higher simply because the strike price is $5 higher. And this means that our reward potential would be $8.17 instead of $3.17. Again, the formula is simply the strike price of the short call ($40 in this case) minus the cost basis ($31.83), which comes to $8.17. Again, our reward potential is the maximum we can make over and above our costs, and that's determined by our short call strike price. So our reward potential automatically goes up as our strike price goes up."

"So then why don't we always pick higher strike prices—the ones more out of the money?" asked Lon.

"That's a great question," answered Nate. "We're always looking to make more money, aren't we? The problem is, whenever we choose a higher strike price to try to increase our reward, we simultaneously increase our risk. Look at the option chain again at that 40 strike. Notice that the credit we bring in for a short call at that price is $3, which is $1.90 less than the $4.90 credit we're getting at the 35 strike price."

"And that gives us more risk," said Aaron. "See, our risk is driven largely by our cost basis—the amount of money we have invested. That's one reason we place a short call in the first place: the credit we bring in reduces our cost basis. But that means if we bring in a smaller credit, we reduce our cost basis *less*. And that means our risk automatically goes up. So think about it. With a 35 strike and a $4.90 credit, we had a cost basis of $31.83; and our risk was that we might make no more than $0.67. But with a 40 strike, we get only a $3 credit—$1.90 less. So our cost basis is now $33.43 (stock price) plus $3.30 (debit for the long put) minus only $3 (credit for the short call). That comes to $33.73, which is exactly $1.90 higher than the $31.83 we had before. Our cost has gone up by $1.90."

"And that means our risk is automatically $1.90 higher. Right?"

"That's right. Before, we couldn't do worse than make $0.67, but now we could actually lose $1.23 ($0.67 − $1.90 = − $1.23). Our risk swings one way or the other, based on the credit we bring in."

"So that lets us see a general principle," said Nate. "Our risk increases exactly as much as our credit *decreases*. So it's easy to figure out. Whenever we reduce the credit we take in, we increase our risk by exactly that much.

"So, get the point?" he continued. "There's always this trade-off between risk and reward in the collar trade. By choosing a higher short call strike price, it's true that we increase our reward potential, but we automatically increase our risk at the same time.

"That's why we want to pick a strike price for the short call that's 1 to 2 strikes out of the money, but not more. When we go further out of the money, the risk can get too high, and then it's not worth it. It's a personal decision, of course, and you can always decide to take more risk if you're comfortable with it. But the main idea of trading options, at least the 'spread' way we do it, is to make money *while reducing risk*. That's the magic: make money *and* sleep at night."

"There truly are a million deals out there," added Aaron emphatically. "It's simply foolish to act as if there aren't and to try to make a lot of money on any one deal. And why be foolish? Make sense?"

"Yup. Got it."

WHEN TO USE A COLLAR TRADE

"So when do we use collar trades?" asked Shorty. "What's the rule of thumb here?"

"I'm glad you asked," replied Aaron. "To see the answer, let's review for a minute. Let's start with the protective put. When do we use that?"

"Well," answered Shorty, "whenever an earnings report is coming up and whenever we get bearish signals from the technical indicators: the RSI, the EMA, and the MACD."

"Good. So in other words, we're always alert to the possibility of a protective put, right? Even when we aren't using it, we're always looking at the *possibility* of using it. Right?"

"Right. It's something we're always considering. It's never out of our minds, so to speak."

"Okay, and what about a covered call. When do we use that?"

"Well, you said that we *always* use it. Basically, the only time we don't is when we're going through an earnings period and we don't want a covered call to limit our upside potential. Other than that, we're always looking for the right strike price and expiration period for a covered call."

"Good. So now let me ask you: exactly what makes up a collar trade?"

"Owning stock, for one thing. But it's also having both a protective put and a covered call. Together, they make up the 'collar.'"

"Good. But now do you see what this means?" asked Nate. "A collar trade *just is* both a protective put and a covered call . . . and we're always at least *looking* to do both."

Lon thought hard. Finally, he spoke. "I think I see what you're driving at. This means, in a sense, that we're *always* working collar trades. It's the way we look at everything."

"That's exactly right," answered Aaron. "Very good. See, you might think of the collar trade as a *philosophy* of trading more than anything else. The idea is that we're always looking to surround our stock so that it will make money . . . and make it in any trend. Thus, we almost always have a covered call, and we're always considering whether to add a put. At any given time, the only question is whether we actually have a long put in place or not. But it's something we're always considering."

"So," said Nate, "we should look at a collar trade as something dynamic. At any given time, we may not have a covered call in place, and for a longer period of time, we may not have a protective put in place. But both of these are just temporary conditions. Over any reasonable period of time we're sure to have both. The pieces of the trade may be in flux—that's why I said it's dynamic—but the philosophy of the trade is unchanging."

"In other words, you're saying that a collar trade is really a state of mind." Shorty smiled wryly.

"Yes, that's exactly what we're saying," answered Aaron. "That's what I mean by calling it a *philosophy*. The collar trade is the overall approach we take to the market. We own stock, and we try to make money with it in every trend. And that just means that we surround the stock with these covered calls and protective puts. The exact pieces come and go as the market dictates, but the philosophy never changes: 'Use these instruments to make money while reducing risk.'"

"I see," said Lon. "In a sense, the protective put, the covered call, and the collar trade are three different trades. We can think of them as separate strategies, each one bringing something different to the table. But the bigger picture is that they mesh together into one overall *way* ... a single, distinctive approach to the market. In a sense, the strategies are all one."

"Sounds like Zen," muttered Shorty.

"Look, I don't mean it mystically," insisted Lon. "But why try to explain. You know what I mean. You're just being cynical."

"You're right. Sorry. And I do get the idea. On one hand, the collar trade is a specific strategy, and we say we have a collar trade in place when we have these specific elements: the stock, a protective put, and a covered call. But on the other hand, there's a more important sense in which we're always working a collar trade—it's the very *way* we approach the market. I get it and it makes sense."

PRIMARY EXIT

"Good," said Nate. "Now let's think about exiting the collar trade, supposing the concrete case where we have all three elements in place at one time. In that case the short call helps define our primary exit, which is for the stock to trend bullish so that we go in the money. Simply put, to go back to our example, if we set our short call strike price at 35, and if the stock price moves above that and stays there, we will be assigned at expiration (if not before) and have to sell our shares at $35 ... and we'll simply pocket our $3.17 profit. That's the end of it.

"Again, there are actually other ways to handle a collar trade, because it's always possible to make adjustments. But this is the basic way for a collar trade to end, and that's enough for now. You've already got plenty under your belts."

"So let's summarize a collar trade this way," said Nate. (See Figure 34.3.)

"All right. And now you paper trade collars just as you paper trade protective puts and covered calls. Give yourself plenty of practice, and make sure you're successful at least 7 times out of 10 before you ever use real money."

"But before you do anything, complete this review." (See pages 243–244.)

COLLAR TRADE

Works in all trends, but best for bullish

Buy stock ("long in stock").

Add a long put:
- Set a minimum time frame of 45 days.
- Choose a strike price NTM.
- Buy to open.
- Buy at the *ask* price on the option chain.

Add a short call:
- Set a time frame of 3–12 months
- Choose a strike price 1 to 2 strikes OTM.
- Receive a credit large enough to pay for the long put.
- Sell to open.
- Sell at the *bid* price on the option chain.

Cost Basis: Our investment in the trade (the stock price, plus the debit we paid for the long put) minus the amount we took in (the credit we received for the short call). So stock price plus debit, minus credit.

Maximum Potential RISK: The total we have invested (our cost basis) minus how much we have protected (the strike price of the *long put*). So cost basis minus long put strike price. (True as long as the long put is in place; when it expires, the trade becomes a covered call with the risk of a covered call.)

Maximum Potential REWARD: The maximum we can sell our shares for (the strike price of the *short call*) minus the total we have invested (our cost basis). So short call strike price minus cost basis.

When to Use: Best thought of as a dynamic strategy that we use all the time; the pieces may come and go as the market dictates, but the collar *approach* guides all our decisions.

Primary Exit: The short call goes in the money and we get assigned. We pocket the profit on the shares, plus the credit we received in opening the short call.

FIGURE 34.3 Collar Trade Summary

REVIEW

Mar 08 Calls		(106 days to expiration) RIMM@104.00									Mar 08 Puts			
RULCX	22.00	+1.80	21.55	21.80	70.8	.70	93.375	RULOX	9.98	-1.47	9.85	10.00	72.4	-.30
RULCY	19.75	+1.20	19.85	20.05	70.8	.66	96.625	RULOY	12.40	+1.35	11.35	11.50	72.4	-.34
RULCT	18.25	+1.06	18.20	18.30	70.5	.63	100.00	RULOT	13.00	-1.95	13.00	13.10	72.1	-.37
RULCZ	16.50	+0.80	16.50	16.75	70.2	.60	103.375	RULOZ	15.90	-1.25	14.70	14.85	71.8	-.40
RULCA	15.45	+0.95	15.10	15.30	69.9	.57	106.625	RULOA	16.60	-2.19	16.50	16.65	71.7	-.43
RULCB	13.95	+0.90	13.75	13.95	69.8	.53	110.00	RULOB	20.20	-0.50	18.50	18.65	71.6	-.46
RULCC	12.90	+1.15	12.45	12.65	69.5	.50	113.375	RULOC	20.70	-0.30	20.55	20.70	71.4	-.50
RULCU	11.90	+0.55	11.95	12.10	69.7	.49	115.00	RULOU	22.40	-1.56	21.60	21.75	71.5	-.51
Jun 08 Calls		**(197 days to expiration) RIMM@104.00**									**Jun 08 Puts**			
RULFS	24.45	-0.10	25.80	26.10	68.6	.69	95.00	RULRS	16.15	+1.14	14.85	15.05	71.1	-.31
RULFT	24.00	+1.85	23.50	23.75	68.5	.65	100.00	RULRT	17.55	-1.50	17.40	17.60	71.0	-.35
RULFL	21.65	+1.60	21.30	21.55	68.2	.61	105.00	RULRL	21.40	-1.10	20.15	20.35	70.9	-.38
RULFB	19.20	+0.70	19.35	19.60	68.2	.58	110.00	RULRB	25.00	+0.70	23.10	23.30	70.9	-.42
RULFU	17.50	+1.00	17.50	17.75	67.9	.54	115.00	RULRU	27.90	0	26.20	26.45	70.9	-.45
Jan 09 Calls		**(407 days to expiration) RIMM@104.00**									**Jan 09 Puts**			
VHOAX	36.65	0	34.55	34.95	65.6	.72	93.375	VHOMX	20.31	0	20.35	20.60	70.2	-.28
VHOAY	33.20	+0.70	33.05	33.45	65.3	.70	96.625	VHOMY	18.00	0	22.15	22.35	70.3	-.25
VHOAT	31.50	+1.30	31.65	32.05	65.2	.69	100.00	VHOMT	24.15	-0.25	23.85	24.15	70.0	-.31
VHOAZ	29.15	-0.20	30.30	30.65	65.1	.67	103.375	VHOMZ	26.65	+0.55	25.85	26.10	70.1	-.32
VHOAA	28.25	0	29.05	29.40	64.9	.65	106.625	VHOMA	28.30	-1.20	27.75	28.00	70.1	-.34
VHOAB	28.00	+1.40	27.75	28.10	64.7	.64	110.00	VHOMB	32.00	+0.50	29.60	29.95	69.8	-.35
VHOAC	27.40	0	26.55	26.85	64.5	.62	113.375	VHOMC	28.45	0	31.85	32.05	70.1	-.37

Source: Screenshot courtesy of optionsXpress, Inc. © 2008.
Review

Suppose we bought this stock today and wanted to add both a long put and a covered call immediately.

1. If we placed the long put in March at a strike of 103.375, what would we pay for it?
2. If we placed the short call in June at a strike of 110, what would we take in?
3. What would be the cost basis for this trade?
4. What is our maximum potential risk while the long put is in place?
5. What is our maximum potential reward?
6. What is the primary exit for this trade?

Apr 08 Calls									Apr 08 Puts			
			(134 days to expiration) AAPL@189.23									
APVDP	28.80	+2.05	28.90	29.00	49.9	.65	180.00	APVPP	16.97	-1.63	16.75	16.90	51.2	-.35
APVDQ	26.30	+1.80	26.30	26.45	49.7	.61	185.00	APVPQ	19.90	-1.10	19.15	19.30	51.2	-.39
APVDR	24.00	+1.80	23.90	24.00	49.5	.58	190.00	APVPR	22.37	-1.48	21.65	21.80	51.0	-.42
APVDS	21.65	+1.65	21.60	21.80	49.3	.55	195.00	APVPS	25.10	-1.70	24.40	24.55	51.0	-.45
APVDT	19.46	+1.41	19.55	19.70	49.2	.51	200.00	APVPT	28.00	-1.90	27.25	27.40	50.9	-.48

Jul 08 Calls									Jul 08 Puts			
			(134 days to expiration) AAPL@189.23									
APVGP	35.05	+1.30	35.85	36.20	49.2	.66	180.00	APVSP	22.35	-1.80	22.20	22.35	51.5	-.34
APVGQ	33.58	+2.58	33.45	33.65	49.1	.63	185.00	APVSQ	24.85	-1.85	24.65	24.80	51.4	-.37
APVGR	31.00	+2.65	31.10	31.35	49.0	.61	190.00	APVSR	29.85	0	27.20	27.40	51.4	-.39
APVGS	28.90	+2.20	28.90	29.10	48.8	.58	195.00	APVSS	36.75	0	29.90	30.10	51.3	-.42
APVGT	26.88	+2.33	26.85	27.05	48.7	.55	200.00	APVST	33.05	-2.55	32.80	33.00	51.4	-.44

Jul 08 Calls									Jul 08 Puts			
			(134 days to expiration) AAPL@189.23									
OBRAP	47.35	+2.30	47.30	47.80	49.5	.68	180.00	OBRMP	31.50	-2.00	30.85	31.30	53.7	-.32
OBRAR	42.45	+1.75	42.70	43.15	49.1	.64	190.00	OBRMR	36.70	-1.73	36.15	36.45	53.7	-.35
OBRAT	38.95	+2.05	38.65	39.00	48.9	.60	200.00	OBRMT	47.65	0	41.45	41.80	53.4	-.39

Source: Screenshot courtesy of optionsXpress, Inc. © 2008.
Review

Suppose we bought this stock today and wanted to add a long put and a covered call immediately.

7. If we placed the long put in April at a 185 strike, what would we pay?
8. If we placed the short call in July at a 195 strike, what would we take in?
9. What would be the cost basis for this trade?
10. What is our maximum potential risk while the long put is in place?
11. What is our maximum potential reward?
12. What is the primary exit for this trade?

"But I have a question," said Shorty.
"Yes?"
"Well, you said that the collar trade was one kind of spread trade. That implies that there are others. In fact, last night you said we would learn a total of five spread trades."

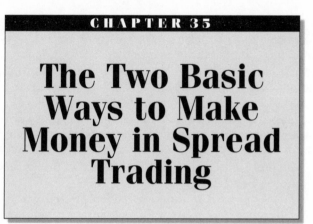

CHAPTER 35

The Two Basic Ways to Make Money in Spread Trading

66 **T** hat's true. And we will," said Nate. "We just need to review one matter, and then we'll get to them: four basic spread trades in addition to the collar."

"And what we need to review," said Aaron, "are the two basic strategies for making money with spread trades. We've already seen these two basic strategies with options in general, but now we need to be more explicit about them."

"One strategy," said Nate, "is basically to be in the selling position. In this kind of trade our main concern is to sell an option and receive a credit for it. That credit becomes our profit, and typically all we're trying to do is protect it. In this kind of trade, we just want everything to expire worthless so that we can keep the credit without dealing with shares—without being forced either to buy or to sell them."

> *One strategy is basically to be in the* selling *position. The other is basically to be in the* buying *position.*

"That's what I was always trying to do," said Shorty.

"That's right," answered Aaron, "but now there's a difference. In spread trading, we don't *only* sell an option; we also buy one. That's our combination: we do both. We take in a credit for the option we sell, and pay out a debit for the option we buy. And we manage the spread between these options in a way that will allow us to make money while reducing our risk."

245

"And," said Nate, "whenever this combination puts us in a *net credit* situation—whenever we've taken in (in our credit) more than we've paid out (in our debit)—we call this a *credit trade*. It's what Aaron said above: we're basically in a selling position, because we've taken in more than we've paid out, and again, typically, all we're trying to do is protect the profit we've built into our trade—our net credit position."

"And I guess that's why we want the options to expire worthless," said Lon. "We keep the net credit without being forced to either buy or sell any shares."

"And I suppose that goal will affect the strike prices and the time frames we choose," said Shorty.

"That's right, and we'll get into all that," answered Aaron. "But now let's mention the other basic strategy for making money with spread trades. It's basically to be in the *buying* position. This is the type of strategy Lon has always favored. The difference is that now we will both buy *and* sell options; it's still a buying strategy, however, because we will pay out more for what we buy than we take in for what we sell. Here we want our long option—the one we buy—to increase in value over time; and we primarily want our short option—the one we sell—to provide us with a credit that will help offset the cost of the long option."

"So in this type of trade," said Nate, "we don't simply want options to expire worthless; we want our long option to increase in value. When our total trade reaches an acceptable profit level—say, 20 to 25 percent—we close the trade and pocket our 20 to 25 percent gain."

"Now it's important to understand," added Aaron, "that this type of spread trade starts out in the hole. We call this a *debit trade* because we start out with a 'net debit': we spend more in our debit than we take in in our credit. So as I said, our *net* position is in the hole. So what we want in this trade is to make up that net debit and provide 20 to 25 percent *more*."

"And this goal will no doubt affect how we approach time frames and strike prices," said Shorty.

> *In both cases, we are combining options in order to give ourselves a chance to make money while reducing risk. Both option instruments are critical to our trade. One is the way we make money; the other is the way we reduce risk.*

"That's right," replied Nate, "and again we'll get into all that."
"So, have you got it?" asked Aaron.

"Sure," answered Shorty. "There are two basic types of spread trades. One type is a credit trade, where we buy and sell options that will give us a net credit to start with. That net credit is our profit, and we simply want the options to expire worthless. That way we simply keep the credit without being forced to either buy or sell shares—which is what we would have to do if the options were exercised."

"And the other type," added Lon, "is a debit trade, where we buy and sell options that will give us a net debit to start with. In this case, we specifically want the value of our long option—the one we bought—to increase in value so that we can close our deal for a 20 to 25 percent profit."

"And don't forget," said Aaron, "in both cases we are combining options in order to give ourselves a chance to make money *while reducing risk*. Both option instruments are critical to our trade. One is the way we make money; the other is the way we reduce risk. We simply manage the spread between them. Got *that*?"

"Got it," Shorty and Lon said in unison.

"Now," said Nate, "we could organize our discussion of spread trades into these two categories: credit trades and debit trades. But we could also divide the trades into the types of instruments we use. Remember, there are four option instruments, and we've shown them to you over and over." (See Figure 35.1.)

"So," he continued, "we can think of spread trades as falling into these two basic categories as well: those that use call options and those that use put options, because often in the basic spread trades that's what we're doing: using a combination of long and short calls to make a trade, or a combination of long and a short puts to make a trade. Thus, *call trades* and *put trades*. Make sense?"

"Sure," replied Shorty. "Although we've already seen that the collar trade uses both a put *and* a call. So that's an exception already."

"Right. That's why, all things considered, we think the best way to organize spread trades is by *trend*. Which spread strategies optimize a *bullish*

Long Call	*Short Call*
Right to Buy	May have to Sell
Long Put	*Short Put*
Right to Sell	May have to Buy

FIGURE 35.1 Option Instruments

direction, and which ones optimize a *bearish* direction? So we're going to show you both a debit trade and a credit trade for bullish trends, and also a debit trade and a credit trade for bearish trends. That will at least give you a feel for the kinds of things that can be done."

THE RELATIONSHIP BETWEEN THE COLLAR AND OTHER SPREAD TRADES

"But that brings up a couple of questions for me," said Lon.

"Shoot."

"Well, how do these trades we're going to learn about relate to the collar trade? You said the collar is the fundamental spread trade, so how are these different? And, for that matter, how are they the same?"

"Good questions," answered Aaron. "It's true that the collar is the fundamental spread trade. As we said earlier, it's really a philosophy of trading and that philosophy guides everything we do. In fact, it's the *main* thing we do: own stock and then work with protective puts and covered calls around that stock. But that doesn't mean we can't be creative and take advantage of other opportunities that the market offers. And that's where these other spread strategies come in."

"Right," said Nate. "It's like a pitcher with a strong arm. He might throw fastballs 90 percent of the time, but he mixes in sliders and change-ups to his advantage as well. That's what these other spread strategies do for us. Think of them as short-term and temporary supplements to the collar trade. When we use them, we don't own the stock, for example; we simply work with the options themselves, and we move in and out of them more quickly. They're far from the mainstay of our trading activity, but they're very helpful tools to have, and the more such tools we have the better off we'll be. Make sense?"

"Sure."

"Good. So let's take a second and make sure we're clear about the term *spread*," said Aaron. "It's really used to refer to two things. In a general sense, it refers to the difference, or spread, between the strike prices of the options we're using; we talk about the spread between them. But we also use the term in a more specific sense to talk about the difference between the *values* of the strike prices—the spread between the bid/ask amounts that they carry. Managing this spread is how we make money in spread trading."

"And that's what we're going to learn next, right?"

"Yes, right after you finish this review. Then we're on to the bull trades."

REVIEW

There are _____ basic types of trades. One is a _____ trade, where we buy and sell options that will give us a _____ to start with. That _____ is our _____, and we simply want the options to expire _____. That way, we simply _____ the _____ without being forced to either _____ or _____ shares—which is what we would have to do if the options were _____.

Another type of trade is a _____ trade, where we buy and sell options that will give us a _____ to start with. In this case, we specifically want the value of our _____—the one we _____—to increase in value so that we can close our deal for a _____ profit."

In both cases, we are _____ options in order to give ourselves a chance to _____ money while _____ risk. Both options are critical to our trade. One is the way we make _____; the other is the way we limit _____. We simply manage the _____ between them.

Understanding Bullish Spread Trades

CHAPTER 36

The Bull Call

66 "In the first trade we'll learn," said Nate, "we're going to follow a *debit* strategy to optimize a bullish trend, using the two call instruments. We're going to place a long call and a short call at the same time. And remember that we're not going to buy the stock. We're going to create this trade using option instruments only." (See Figure 36.1.)

"Now if this is a debit strategy, what do we know about these two options we're using?" asked Aaron.

"Well, we know we're going to spend more on the long call than we take in on the short call," answered Shorty. "We're going to start out in the hole. That's why it's called a debit trade."

"Right," answered Aaron, "so what does that mean about our strike prices?"

"Well, for one thing" said Lon, "we know that the further a strike price is out of the money, the less expensive it is."

"Right," said Aaron, "just as we see in this chain. For every expiration month, the further a strike price is away from being in the money, the less expensive it is." (See Figure 36.2.)

"So that means," continued Lon, "that we're going to place our short call further out of the money than our long call. Because we're using a debit strategy, we'll spend more on our long call than we take in on the short call. So the short call has to be further out of the money."

Long Call	Short Call
Right to Buy	May have to Sell
Long Put	**Short Put**
Right to Sell	May have to Buy

FIGURE 36.1 The Bull Call

Mar 08 Calls (106 days to expiration) RIMM@104.00 **Mar 08 Puts**

							Strike							
RULCX	22.00	+1.80	21.55	21.80	70.8	.70	93..375	RULOX	9.98	-1.47	9.85	10.00	72.4	-.30
RULCY	19.75	+1.20	19.85	20.05	70.8	.66	96.625	RULOY	12.40	+1.35	11.35	11.50	72.4	-.34
RULCT	18.25	+1.06	18.20	18.30	70.5	.63	100.00	RULOT	13.00	-1.95	13.00	13.10	72.1	-.37
RULCZ	16.50	+0.80	16.50	16.75	70.2	.60	103.375	RULOZ	15.90	-1.25	14.70	14.85	71.8	-.40
RULCA	15.45	+0.95	15.10	15.30	69.9	.57	106.625	RULOA	16.60	-2.19	16.50	16.65	71.7	-.43
RULCB	13.95	+0.90	13.75	13.95	69.8	.53	110.00	RULOB	20.20	-0.50	18.50	18.65	71.6	-.46
RULCC	12.90	+1.15	12.45	12.65	69.5	.50	113.375	RULOC	20.70	-0.30	20.55	20.70	71.4	-.50
RULCU	11.90	+0.55	11.95	12.10	69.7	.49	115.00	RULOU	22.40	-1.56	21.60	21.75	71.5	-.51

Jun 08 Calls (197 days to expiration) RIMM@104.00 **Jun 08 Puts**

							Strike							
RULFS	24.45	-0.10	25.80	26.10	68.6	.69	95.00	RULRS	16.15	+1.14	14.85	15.05	71.1	-.31
RULFT	24.00	+1.85	23.50	23.75	68.5	.65	100.00	RULRT	17.55	-1.50	17.40	17.60	71.0	-.35
RULFL	21.65	+1.60	21.30	21.55	68.2	.61	105.00	RULRL	21.40	-1.10	20.15	20.35	70.9	-.38
RULFB	19.20	+0.70	19.35	19.60	68.2	.58	110.00	RULRB	25.00	+0.70	23.10	23.30	70.9	-.42
RULFU	17.50	+1.00	17.50	17.75	67.9	.54	115.00	RULRU	27.90	0	26.20	26.45	70.9	-.45

Jan 09 Calls (407 days to expiration) RIMM@104.00 **Jan 09 Puts**

							Strike							
VHOAX	36.65	0	34.95	34.95	65.6	.72	93.375	VHOMX	20.31	0	20.35	20.60	70.2	-.28
VHOAY	33.20	+0.70	33.05	33.45	65.3	.70	96.625	VHOMY	18.00	0	22.15	22.35	70.3	-.29
VHOAT	31.50	+1.30	31.65	32.05	65.2	.69	100.00	VHOMT	24.15	-1.25	23.85	24.15	70.0	-.31
VHOAZ	29.15	-0.20	30.30	30.65	65.1	.67	103.375	VHOMZ	26.65	+0.55	25.85	26.10	70.1	-.32
VHOAA	28.25	0	29.05	29.40	64.9	.65	106.625	VHOMA	28.30	-1.20	27.75	28.00	70.1	-.34
VHOAB	28.00	+1.40	27.75	28.10	64.7	.64	110.00	VHOMB	32.00	+0.50	29.60	29.95	69.8	-.35
VHOAC	27.40	0	26.55	26.85	64.5	.62	113.375	VHOMC	28.45	0	31.85	32.05	70.1	-.37

FIGURE 36.2 Relationship between Strike Price and Debit/Credit Amounts
Source: Screenshot courtesy of optionsXpress, Inc. © 2008.

Jan 08 Calls					(41 days to expiration)	NOK@39.49						Jan 08 Puts
NAYAF	9.79	0	9.50	9.70		1.00	30.00	NAYMF	0.08	0	0.05	0.10	45.8 -.03
NAYAG	5.00	0	4.90	5.10	34.2	.87	35.00	NAYMG	0.40	0	0.35	0.40	36.9 -.14
NAYAH	1.52	0	1.50	1.60	31.3	.50	40.00	NAYMH	1.85	0	1.90	1.95	33.3 -.50
NAYAI	0.25	0	0.25	0.30	31.7	.13	45.00	NAYMI	6.10	0	5.60	5.80	37.5 -.82

Apr 08 Calls					(132 days to expiration)	NOK@39.49						Apr 08 Puts
NAYDF	10.40	0	10.50	10.70	42.5	.90	30.00	NAYPF	0.80	0	0.65	0.75	46.0 -.12
NAYDG	6.70	0	6.50	6.70	38.6	.76	35.00	NAYPG	4.65	0	4.65	1.75	42.0 -.25
NAYDH	3.70	0	3.60	3.70	37.2	.56	40.00	**Long Call**					39.9 -.44
NAYDI	1.75	0	1.75	1.85	36.5	.35	45.00	**Short Call**					40.4 -.63
NAYDJ	0.85	0	0.80	0.90	36.9	.19	50.00	NAYPJ	10.80	0	10.80	11.00	43.7 -.75

Jul 08 Calls					(223 days to expiration)	NOK@39.49						Jul 08 Puts
NAYGF	10.90	0	10.70	11.00	31.2	.92	30.00	NAYSF	1.10	0	1.10	1.20	43.6 -.14
NAYGG	7.10	0	7.00	7.30	32.3	.77	35.00	NAYSG	2.45	0	2.35	2.50	41.3 -.26
NAYGH	4.30	0	4.20	4.50	32.5	.58	40.00	NAYSH	4.60	0	4.50	4.60	40.4 -.41
NAYGI	2.50	0	2.35	2.50	32.1	.40	45.00	NAYSI	7.60	0	7.50	7.70	41.1 -.56
NAYGJ	1.22	0	1.20	1.30	31.7	.24	50.00	NAYSJ	12.30	0	11.30	11.50	43.2 -.67

FIGURE 36.3 Applying the Bull Call
Source: Screenshot courtesy of optionsXpress, Inc. © 2008.

"Right," added Shorty, "and with a debit strategy we must want time on our side, right? We want the long call to have time to grow in value, so we're going to place this trade further out in time."

"That's all correct," said Nate. "So let's look at the chain." (See Figure 36.3.)

"The stock is selling for $39.49, and we've placed the long call at the 40 strike price—which is near the money, but still out—and we've placed the short call at the 45 strike price—which is *further* out of the money. We take in a $1.75 credit for the short call, but we pay out a debit of $3.70 for the long call."

"Right," said Shorty, "we're in the hole. It's a debit trade."

"That's right," said Aaron, "so what we want is for the stock price to go up past $40 so that this strike price is in the money and increases in value. That's how we make money in this trade: the long call increases in value and we sell it to someone else for a profit. That's why we place the strike as near the money as we can."

"And yet we keep it out of the money, at least slightly," added Nate, "to make sure we take advantage of the accelerated delta change that occurs just before a strike goes in the money. So, out of the money but as close to the money as possible."

"Got it," said Lon.

"Me, too," agreed Shorty.

"So we call this long call," added Nate, "our *primary* instrument in the trade. It's the one we're using to make money. And as you said earlier, whenever we use a long call to make money we need time on our side, because we need time for the stock to move. So we want to have a minimum of 45 days, and here we're using 132 days."

"And the short call," said Aaron," is called our *limiting* instrument because, by using it to take a credit into our account, we are lowering our cost basis and thus limiting our risk in the trade."

"Now," said Nate, "this combination of options—a long call slightly out of the money and a short call further out of the money—is called a *bull call*. It's designed to optimize a bullish trend. The whole idea is to place the long call just slightly out of the money so that it will go *in* the money as the stock rises in value: the long call then goes up in value too, and that's how we make money—riding this bullish trend until we sell the long call for a profit. Anyway, that's why it's called a *bull* call, and, because we do it by using both call options, it's called a bull *call*.

> *That's how we make money in this trade: the long call increases in value and we sell it to someone else for a profit.*

"Now we place the short call one or two strikes further out of the money than the long call," he continued, "because we *don't want* the short call strike to go in the money. If it goes in the money, then we face that whole problem of having to buy shares in order to be able to sell them *at a loss*. (Remember, our short call obligates us to sell shares at this strike price of 45, and that will happen if the market price goes higher than $45. In that case we would have to go out on the market and buy shares at the higher market price and turn around and sell them at $45—a guaranteed loss.) So we don't want that. On the other hand, if we go more than two strikes away, or more than $5 away, the credit we take in drops considerably. Then the short call doesn't bring in enough credit to be worth it. So we want the short call strike to be further out of the money than the long call strike, but we typically don't want more than a $5 spread between them."

"So in this case," said Nate, "we place the short call at the 45 strike—that's one strike further out of the money than the long call, and it's not more than $5 away. And we take in a credit of $1.75 for selling this option."

NET DEBIT AND RISK

"Now notice what this means," said Aaron. "We paid a debit of $3.70 for the long call but took in a credit of $1.75 from the short call. That means our 'net debit'—our net expense—for the trade is $1.95 ($3.70 – $1.75). That's how much we're in the hole."

"Right, it's a debit trade," said Lon.

"Good," said Nate, "and that net debit is also our *risk* in the trade. That's how much we have to lose: the difference between the debit we paid out and the credit we took in. Think about it. If the stock takes a dive, the options will both take a dive, too. But even if they both go to zero, that doesn't change our net debit at all; we've still paid out only $3.70 and taken in a credit of $1.75. So our investment is still $1.95, and that means that's all we can lose, no matter what."

"Now notice," said Aaron, "if we owned the underlying stock, our risk situation would be much different. If we paid $39.49 for our shares and the stock went to zero, we would be out the whole $39.49. So if we were long in the stock, *and* had our bull call spread with a net debit of $1.95, our risk would be $41.44 ($39.49 plus $1.95). And that's why in this bull call spread trade we don't own the underlying stock. It's not designed for that. All we're doing is combining the options themselves and managing the spread between them."

REWARD

"Now our maximum reward," said Aaron, "is based on the fact that we can never make more than the difference in the two strike prices. The difference between (1) the debit we pay out for our long call and (2) the credit we take in for our short call, will never be greater than the difference between the strike prices. It's a mathematical principle of the relationship between strikes and bid/ask amounts. So typically the maximum spread will be $5 or less, just as it is in this trade. And since our net debit in this trade is $1.95—we're already in the hole that much—the most we can make in this trade is the difference between $5 and $1.95, which equals $3.05."

"So the formula," said Aaron, "for determining our maximum reward in a bull call is: *the difference in the two strike prices minus the net debit (our net expense in the trade)*, in this case, $5 − $1.95, or $3.05."

> *Our goal is for the long call to increase in value so that we make a profit. Once we make the profit, we close the deal.*

"Now $3.05 is our maximum reward in this trade, but we don't hold out for that," cautioned Nate. "Remember, we're looking for a 20 to 25 percent return, and when we get it, we close the trade and move on to the next one."

"And here's how we figure our return," said Aaron, "and let's pick 20 percent as our target for this example. Remember that our expense, our net debit in the trade, is $1.95: the $3.70 we paid for the long call minus the $1.75 credit we took in for the short call. So right now we're in the hole $1.95. To reach our target return of 20 percent we simply have to make back this $1.95, *plus 20 percent*. In other words, we have to make about $2.35 in profit (that's 1.20 × $1.95) in order to reach our 20 percent return. And that's what will happen if the stock is bullish."

"I suppose this is the 'primary exit' for the bull call," remarked Shorty. "Our goal is for the long call to increase in value so that we make a profit. Once we make the profit, we close the deal."

"That's right," answered Nate.

HOW PROFIT IS GENERATED

"But just a second," interrupted Lon. "I don't get it. You're talking about the long call increasing in value as the stock increases, but what about the short call? It increases in value too. Look at the option chain again. The bid and ask values *both* go up as you get closer to the money and they both continue to go up the further you go *in* the money. That means the short call is going up just like the long call is going up. So we start with a net debit—a negative spread between the two of $1.95—but if both options go up in value as the stock goes up in value, how do we ever get out of that $1.95 hole, let alone make 20 percent more? I don't get it. It looks like we'll always have that $1.95 deficit."

Jan 08 Calls							(41 days to expiration) NOK@39.49							Jan 08 Puts
NAYAF	9.79	0	9.50	9.70		1.00	30.00	NAYMF	0.08	0	0.05	0.10	45.8	-.03
NAYAG	5.00	0	4.90	5.10	34.2	.87	35.00	NAYMG	0.40	0	0.35	0.40	36.9	-.14
NAYAH	1.52	0	1.50	1.60	31.3	.50	40.00	NAYMH	1.85	0	1.90	1.95	33.3	-.50
NAYAI	0.25	0	0.25	0.30	31.7	.13	45.00	NAYMI	6.10	0	5.60	5.80	37.5	-.82
Apr 08 Calls							(132 days to expiration) NOK@39.49							**Apr 08 Puts**
NAYDF	10.40	0	10.50	10.70	42.5	.90	30.00	NAYPF	0.80	0	0.65	0.75	46.0	-.12
NAYDG	6.70	0	6.50	6.70	38.6	.76	35.00	NAYPG	1.65	0	1.65	1.75	42.0	-.25
NAYDH	3.70	0	3.60	(3.70)	37.2	.56	40.00	**Long Call**					39.9	-.44
NAYDI	1.75	0	(1.75)	1.85	36.5	.35	45.00	**Short Call**					40.4	-.63
NAYDJ	0.85	0	0.80	0.90	36.9	.19	50.00	NAYPJ	10.80	0	10.80	11.00	43.7	-.75
Jul 08 Calls							(223 days to expiration) NOK@39.49							**Jul 08 Puts**
NAYGF	10.90	0	10.70	11.00	31.2	.92	30.00	NAYSF	1.10	0	1.10	1.20	43.6	-.14
NAYGG	7.10	0	7.00	7.30	32.3	.77	35.00	NAYSG	2.45	0	2.35	2.50	41.3	-.26
NAYGH	4.30	0	4.20	4.50	32.5	.58	40.00	NAYSH	4.60	0	4.50	4.60	40.4	-.41
NAYGI	2.50	0	2.35	2.50	32.1	.40	45.00	NAYSI	7.60	0	7.50	7.70	41.1	-.56
NAYGJ	1.22	0	1.20	1.30	31.7	.24	50.00	NAYSJ	12.30	0	11.30	11.50	43.2	-.67

FIGURE 36.4 Option Chain
Source: Screenshot courtesy of optionsXpress, Inc. © 2008.

"That's a great question," replied Nate, "but look at the option chain again. The answer is there, and it's in a concept you've already learned." (See Figure 36.4.)

"I'm looking, but I'm not seeing it," answered Lon.

"Me either," added Shorty.

"Well, let me ask you a question," said Nate. "You say that both options will go up in value as the stock goes up in value. Great. But the question is, do they go up *at the same rate?*"

"Oh, I get it," exclaimed Lon, suddenly seeing the point. "*The deltas are different.* The short call is further out of the money than the long call, so its delta is smaller. Right now it's only going up $0.35 as the stock goes up $1, while the long call is going up $0.56 as the stock goes up $1. So as the stock goes up in value, both options go up in value—*but the long call goes up faster.*"

"Right," agreed Shorty, "and when the long call goes in the money its delta will go up even more, creating an even bigger spread between the two."

"That's right," said Aaron. "And that's an additional reason for the short call to be placed further out of the money than the long call: it will have a lower delta, and this makes it possible for the spread between the two to grow—and this, after all, is what makes us a profit. Of course, as we've already seen, the deltas of both options will change—they're not constant—but the delta of the long call will always be higher than the delta of the short call because the short call is placed further out of the money."

"But just a minute," interrupted Shorty. "I thought the spread between the two was the *problem*. We're in the hole $1.95 and we're trying to overcome that. So what's so great about the spread getting larger? I must be missing something."

> *What we're doing here is taking advantage of the* spread *between the values of the two options. In this type of debit trade, our profit grows as the spread grows.*

"Well yes, you are," chuckled Aaron. "But that's our fault. We just haven't made it explicit yet. So let's start over. Remember what we've done here. The long call is simply an option that we've *bought*—we've paid a $3.70 debit for the right to be able to buy shares at a 40 strike price. And the short call is simply an option that we've *sold*—we've taken in a $1.75 credit for the guarantee that we will sell shares at a 45 strike price if we're assigned. We're in the hole because what we bought was more expensive than what we sold. That's the essence of a debit trade."

"But in closing this trade," said Nate, "we now do just the opposite. We take our long call—the option we bought—and *sell* it to someone else. It has now increased in value, say to $6.50. At the same time, we take our short call—the option we sold—and now *buy it back*. And, of course, it, too, has gone up in value, *but not as fast as the long call*—say, to $4.15. So now in closing this trade we are *selling* an option for $6.50 and *buying* one for $4.15, which is a *positive* spread of $2.35: we're taking *in* $2.35 more than we're paying out."

"So we started the trade," said Aaron, "with a negative spread between them of $1.95—that was our net debit, the amount we were in the hole—and we end the trade with a *positive* spread of $2.35. That's our 20 percent profit. Our net credit at the close of the trade ($2.35) is 20 percent higher than the net debit ($1.95) we had at the opening of the trade. Again, that's our profit."

"Okay," said Nate, "now with all this talk of buying and selling let's make sure you remember: since we bought to open the long call at the ask price, and sold to open the short call at the bid price, when we close the trade we will do just the opposite—we will *sell* to close the long call, at the *bid* price, and we will *buy* to close the short call, at the *ask* price. That means in determining our profit we will be comparing the *bid* price of the long call to the *ask* price of the short call. Those are the numbers we compare as we check our progress. When the difference reaches $2.35, we close the trade and move on."

"So let's summarize the bull call this way." (See Figure 36.5.)

BULL CALL

Bullish trend

Long Call ⌐ Same expiration month
Short Call └ At least 45 days out

Long Call (P)
- Buy to open at the ask price.
- Choose a strike price NTM or slightly OTM.

Short Call (L)
- Sell to open at the bid price.
- Choose a strike price 1 to 2 strikes *more* OTM than the long call strike (but no greater than $5 spread).

Debit Trade: We start out in the hole: we pay out in debit more than we take in in credit

Goal: The long call increases in value faster than the short call, and we close both for a net profit

Maximum RISK: The amount we paid for the long call (the debit) minus what we took in (the credit). This is our expense in making the trade and is called the "net debit." So debit minus credit.

Maximum REWARD: The difference in strike prices minus our expense to make the trade (the net debit). So (short call strike minus long call strike) minus the net debit

Primary Exit: 20% ROI (We make back our expense in the trade—our net debit—plus 20%; we achieve this when the difference between the bid price of the long call and the ask price ofthe short call is 20% higher than the net debit of the trade).

Sell the long call at the bid price and buy back the short call at the ask price.

FIGURE 36.5 Bull Call Summary

REVIEW

Jun 08 Calls — (3 days to expiration) — GRMN@43.48 — Jun 08 Puts

Call	Last	Chg	Bid	Ask	Vol	Δ	Strike	Put	Last	Chg	Bid	Ask	Vol	Δ
GQRFX	21.40	-1.40	20.80	21.30	302.3	.99	22.50	GQRRX	0	0	0	0.05	267.0	-.01
GQRFE	20.48	0	18.30	18.80	258.0	.99	25.00	GQRRE	0.10	0	0	0.05	227.6	-.01
GQRFF	15.30	0	13.30	13.80	180.7	.98	30.00	GQRRF	0.01	0	0	0.05	158.5	-.01
GQRFG	8.80	-1.50	8.30	8.70	89.9	.99	35.00	GQRRG	0.02	0	0	0.05	98.5	-.02
GQRFH	3.70	-1.90	3.50	3.70	59.9	.91	40.00	GQRRH	0.20	+0.10	0.15	0.02	68.0	-.11
GQRFI	0.50	-1.10	0.45	0.55	59.1	.30	45.00	GQRRI	2.00	+0.91	2.00	2.10	61.6	-.69
GQRFJ	0.05	-0.11	0.05	0.10	79.3	.05	50.00	GQRRJ	6.50	+2.10	6.50	6.80	90.9	-.92
GQRFK	0.04	-0.01	0	0.05	102.3	.02	55.00	GQRRK	8.70	-0.99	11.30	11.70		-1.00
GQRFL	0.01	-0.04	0	0.05	133.9	.01	60.00	GQRRL	15.40	0	16.30	16.70		-1.00
GQRFM	0.05	0	0	0.05	162.1	.01	65.00	GQRRM	21.20	+0.80	21.10	21.70		-1.00

Jul 08 Calls — (31 days to expiration) — GRMN@43.48 — Jul 08 Puts

Call	Last	Chg	Bid	Ask	Vol	Δ	Strike	Put	Last	Chg	Bid	Ask	Vol	Δ
GQRGE	26.00	0	18.30	19.00	101.7	.98	25.00	GQRSE	0.05	0	0	0.10	88.2	-.01
GQRGF	14.40	-9.10	13.30	13.90	64.7	.98	30.00	GQRSF	0.10	0	0	0.10	61.8	-.02
GQRGG	9.60	-1.00	8.60	9.00	54.7	.92	35.00	GQRSG	0.42	+0.17	0.40	0.45	62.8	-.10
GQRGH	5.00	-1.70	4.70	5.00	55.1	.73	40.00	GQRSH	1.44	+0.49	1.45	1.50	59.2	-.28
GQRGI	2.15	-1.05	2.15	2.20	54.5	.45	45.00	GQRSI	3.76	+2.01	3.80	3.80	58.1	-.54
GQRGJ	0.85	-0.60	0.75	0.85	54.1	.22	50.00	GQRSJ	7.40	+1.60	7.40	7.60	60.8	-.75
GQRGK	0.30	-0.20	0.25	0.35	56.3	.09	55.00	GQRSK	11.20	+0.90	11.60	12.10	61.7	-.88
GQRGL	0.16	-0.04	0.10	0.20	61.7	.05	60.00	GQRSL	14.90	0	16.50	16.90	70.2	-.92
GQRGM	0.05	-0.05	0.05	0.15	68.8	.03	65.00	GQRSM	19.90	0	21.40	21.90	80.5	-.94

Oct 08 Calls — (122 days to expiration) — GRMN@43.48 — Oct 08 Puts

Call	Last	Chg	Bid	Ask	Vol	Δ	Strike	Put	Last	Chg	Bid	Ask	Vol	Δ
GQRJE	29.74	0	18.40	19.20	54.0	.97	25.00	GQRVE	0.32	0	0.30	0.45	65.0	-.05
GQRJF	16.00	0	14.00	14.30	49.9	.93	30.00	GQRVF	0.90	+0.13	0.95	1.05	62.7	-.11
GQRJG	11.00	-0.70	10.30	10.90	56.8	.80	35.00	GQRVG	2.20	+0.40	2.10	2.25	60.8	-.21
GQRJH	7.80	-1.20	7.20	7.50	54.9	.67	40.00	GQRVH	3.80	+0.50	3.90	4.20	59.8	-.33
GQRJI	5.00	-1.10	4.90	5.10	55.0	.53	45.00	GQRVI	6.66	+0.76	6.50	6.80	59.3	-.46
GQRJJ	3.28	-0.78	3.20	3.40	54.8	.40	50.00	GQRVJ	9.96	+0.56	9.90	10.10	60.1	-.58
GQRJK	2.20	-0.65	2.10	2.25	55.3	.29	55.00	GQRVK	13.70	+1.50	13.60	13.90	60.1	-.68
GQRJL	1.45	-0.45	1.35	1.45	55.4	.21	60.00	GQRVL	17.90	+1.70	17.80	18.20	61.8	-.76
GQRJM	1.00	-0.20	0.85	0.95	55.6	.14	65.00	GQRVM	21.60	0	22.00	22.70	61.6	-.82

Source: Screenshot courtesy of optionsXpress, Inc. © 2008.
Review

Suppose you wanted to structure a bull call on this stock.

1. Which expiration month would you choose? Why?
2. Where would you place the long call? Why?
3. Where would you place the short call? Why?

4. What is the maximum risk for this trade?

5. What is the maximum reward for this trade?

6. What is the primary exit for this trade?

7. What's the actual dollar amount you need to achieve in that case?

Jul 08 Calls								Jul 08 Puts				
		(30 days to expiration) WFMI@26.33										
FMQGE	2.48	0	1.93	1.98	38.2	.70	25.00	FMQSE	0.78	+0.23	0.71	0.73	43.3 -.31
FMQGQ	1.25	-0.40	1.32	1.36	37.7	.57	26.00	FMQSQ	1.21	+0.36	1.11	1.15	43.1 -.43
FMQGP	0.87	-0.29	0.85	0.89	37.4	.44	27.00	FMQSP	1.63	+0.31	1.65	1.71	43.5 -.55
FMQGO	0.61	-0.13	0.53	0.56	37.5	.31	28.00	FMQSO	2.35	+0.40	2.32	2.38	44.1 -.66
FMQGC	0.30	-0.16	0.33	0.35	38.4	.21	29.00	FMQSC	2.87	+0.27	3.10	3.20	46.3 -.74
FMQGF	0.17	-0.12	0.20	0.21	39.0	.14	30.00	FMQSF	3.20	0	3.95	4.20	51.5 -.78
FMQGA	0.17	0	0.11	0.14	39.9	.09	31.00	FMQSA	4.35	0	4.85	5.20	56.7 -.81
FMQGB	0.10	0	0.05	0.09	40.1	.06	32.00	FMQSB	3.80	0	5.85	6.05	59.6 -.85
FMQGS	0.08	0	0.03	0.07	42.3	.04	33.00	FMQSS	0	0	6.75	7.15	65.8 -.86
FMQGT	0.05	0	0.02	0.04	43.2	.03	34.00	FMQST	5.45	0	7.75	8.15	71.7 -.87
FMQGG	0.04	0	0.01	0.04	46.0	.02	35.00	FMQSG	6.44	0	8.75	9.15	77.8 -.87
Aug 08 Calls			(58 days to expiration) WFMI@26.33									**Aug 08 Puts**
FMQHD	7.05	0	6.25	6.65	39.0	.97	20.00	FMQTD	0.29	+0.10	0.26	0.30	56.7 -.09
FMQHX	5.10	0	4.35	4.45	46.8	.83	22.50	FMQTX	0.57	0	0.68	0.70	53.6 -.20
FMQHTE	2.62	-0.48	2.67	2.74	46.8	.65	25.00	FMQTE	1.45	+0.18	1.47	1.50	51.6 -.36
FMQHQ	2.10	-0.40	2.13	2.19	46.5	.57	26.00	FMQTQ	2.03	+0.35	1.92	1.97	51.3 -.43
FMQHP	1.68	-0.32	1.68	1.73	46.5	.49	27.00	FMQTP	1.90	0	2.46	2.50	51.1 -.50
FMQHO	1.70	0	1.29	1.33	46.1	.41	28.00	FMQTO	3.05	+0.35	3.05	3.15	51.2 -.57
FMQHC	1.30	0	0.99	1.02	46.1	.34	29.00	FMQTC	3.60	+0.35	3.75	3.85	51.7 -.64
FMQHF	0.71	-0.19	0.75	0.77	46.1	.28	30.00	FMQTF	4.62	+0.47	4.50	4.60	52.1 -.69
FMQHA	0.70	0	0.55	0.58	46.1	.22	31.00	FMQTA	4.60	0	5.30	5.40	52.6 -.74

Source: Screenshot courtesy of optionsXpress, Inc. © 2008.
Review

Suppose you wanted to structure a bull call on this stock.

8. Which month would you choose? Why?

9. Where would you place the long call? Why?

10. Where would you place the short call? Why?

11. What is the maximum risk for this trade with a 28 strike for the short call?

12. What is the maximum reward for this trade with a 28 strike price for the short call?

13. What is the maximum risk for this trade with a 31 strike for the short call?

14. What is the maximum reward for this trade with a 31 strike price for the short call?

15. What is the primary exit for this trade?

16. What's the actual dollar amount you need to achieve in that case—with a 28 strike price?

17. What is the primary exit for this trade—the actual dollar amount you need to achieve—with a 31 strike price?

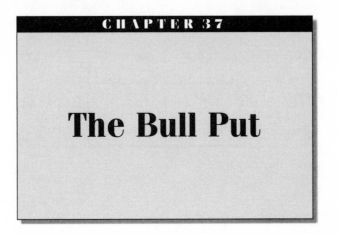

The Bull Put

"**O**kay, so we've looked at a trade for a bullish trend based on *call* options," said Nate, "and it was a debit trade. Now we're going to look at a bullish trade based on *put* options, using a *credit* strategy. And remember that we won't own any stock; we'll work only with the option instruments themselves." (See Figure 37.1.)

"The trade we're going to talk about is called the *bull put*," said Aaron. "It's called a *bull* put because it optimizes a bullish (though also a stagnant) trend, and it's called a bull *put* because it uses the put options to do so.

"In this trade," he continued, "the short put option is our primary instrument because it's the one we're using to make money in the trade; we use it to take in a credit. So you can already see why this is a credit trade: the main way we make money is with the credit we take in for this short put."

"Now recall what we learned about short puts," said Nate. "They're risky. If our strike price goes in the money—and remember, with puts that means the stock price goes lower than the strike price—we will be assigned, and we will have to buy shares at higher than the market price."

The main way we make money is with the credit we take in for this short put.

"And we don't want to do that normally," interjected Aaron, "so we do three things to limit our risk. The first thing we do is place our short

Long Call	Short Call
Right to Buy	May have to Sell
Long Put	Short Put
Right to Sell	May have to Buy

FIGURE 37.1 The Bull Put

put strike out of the money. We want to finish out of the money, so we obviously want to start out of the money. The second thing we do is place this trade with a short time frame—30 days or fewer. This gives the stock less time to drop below our strike price and put us in the money."

"And the third thing we do to limit our risk," said Nate, "is to open a long put at the same time. Adding the long put allows us to make money if the stock does turn bearish and puts us in the money. Remember, in buying the long put, we're buying the right to sell shares at a certain price. If we place the strike in the right place, it will protect us from the risk of the short put.

"To see all this," continued Nate, "let's look at the option chain in Figure 37.2."

"We open both a short put and a long put in the same expiration month—with no more than 30 days of time value. Notice that in this case that's exactly what we have."

Jul 08 Calls		(30 days to expiration)				RIMM@143.14					Jul 08 Puts	
RULGD	25.71	+1.71	25.40	25.70	64.0	.85	120.00	RULSD	2.29	-0.05	2.20	2.20	64.3	-.15
RULGE	21.45	+1.05	21.45	21.60	62.5	.80	125.00	RULSE	3.15	-0.15	3.10	3.20	62.4	-.20
RULGV	17.75	+0.75	17.65	17.75	60.4	.74	130.00	RULSV	4.30	-0.30	4.30	4.25	60.3	-.26
RULGW	14.25		**Long Put**				135.00	RULSW	5.90	-0.30	5.80	(5.90)	58.6	-.33
RULGH	11.08		**Short Put**				140.00	RULSH	7.75	-0.48	(7.75)	7.85	57.2	-.41
RULGI	8.60	+0.45	8.50	8.00	55.8	.58	145.00	RULSI	10.30	-0.38	10.10	10.20	55.7	-.50
RULGJ	6.30	+0.20	6.30	6.40	54.6	.42	150.00	RULSJ	13.10	-0.60	12.90	13.00	54.6	-.58
RULGQ	4.60	+0.20	4.55	4.60	53.4	.34	155.00	RULSQ	16.00	-0.90	16.10	16.25	53.4	-.66
RULGR	3.20	+0.05	3.15	3.25	52.4	.26	160.00	RULSR	19.90	-0.65	19.75	19.90	52.7	-.74
RULGM	2.30	+0.21	2.18	2.23	51.9	.20	165.00	RULSM	24.65	0	23.75	24.00	52.7	-.80

FIGURE 37.2 Applying the Bull Put
Source: Screenshot courtesy of optionsXpress, Inc. © 2008.

"Right," added Aaron, "and we place the short put out of the money. The stock is selling at \$143.14, and our strike is 140. By selling this put we take in a credit of \$7.75. Now if the stock stays above our 140 strike, we won't be assigned and we won't be forced to buy shares. That's what we want here: to just keep the credit without having to buy shares. That's why we placed our strike out of the money, and why we picked such a short time frame."

> *Even if the stock surprises us and goes down, we are still able to sell at a reasonably high price. That's how we reduce our risk.*

"It's also why we added a long put," said Nate. "Think about the obligation we have with the short put. Suppose, for example, that the stock goes bearish on us and drops below our 140 strike price after all. Imagine it goes all the way down to \$100. In that case, our short put will work against us: we're committed to buying shares at \$140 when the market price is only \$100. That hurts, but that's where our long put comes in. For notice: we bought our put (opened our long put) at a 135 strike price, and that means we have the right to *sell* shares at \$135. So now we have this situation: we still have to buy shares at \$140 (our short put commits us to do that), but we can turn around and sell those shares at \$135—a lot higher than the market price of \$100. So having this long put turns a \$40 deficit into a \$5 deficit. That's much more manageable."

"So do you see," asked Aaron, "how the long put limits our risk? Even if the stock surprises us and goes down, we're still able to sell at a reasonably high price when assigned. That's how we reduce our risk."

"Got it," said Lon. "And we place the long put—the limiting instrument—at a strike price that is further out of the money than the short put because if we didn't it would cost more than we take in with the short put. Look at the chain again. If we placed both puts at the same strike, say 140, we'd be taking in a \$7.75 credit but paying out a \$7.85 debit. We'd be losing money on the trade from the start."

"And we don't place it too far from the short put strike," added Shorty, "because the further away it is, the less protection it provides. For example, if we placed our long put even further out of the money—say, at a strike of 130—our guaranteed sale price would be \$5 less. That's \$5 less in protection. So we want the long put strike to be further out of the money than the short put strike, but not by too much."

"That's right," said Nate. "Just as with the call trades, we place the limiting instrument further out of the money than the primary instrument, but generally we don't want more than a \$5 spread."

NET CREDIT AND REWARD

"Now let's look at our trade," said Aaron. "We paid a debit of $5.90 for the long put but took in a credit of $7.75 from the short put. That means our 'net' credit—our starting position for the trade—is plus $1.85. It's $7.75 (the credit we took in) minus $5.90 (the debit we paid), which equals $1.85. So the formula for this is simply: *credit minus debit*. This is called our *net credit*."

"That net credit on the trade of $1.85 is our maximum reward," said Nate. "All we're trying to do here is make money in the short term without too much risk. We've opened a short put to take in a credit, and we've opened a long put just to protect ourselves in case we get surprised. But, of course, we've taken in more than we've paid out, and that difference is our profit. All we want now is for the time to run out and for both options to expire worthless. Then we simply keep our net credit of $1.85 and we don't have to do anything with any shares of stock. Pretty slick. And that's our primary exit: time runs out and both options expire worthless."

> *All we're trying to do here is make money in the short term without too much risk.*

"And this means," added Aaron, "that this trade works in a stagnant trend as well as in a bullish trend. All we need is for the stock price to stay higher than our strike price; whether it's flat or rising doesn't matter as long as it doesn't go *down* and drop below our strike price. Either way we keep the net credit we start out with, without getting assigned and having to buy shares."

"Got it," said Shorty. "So because we profit on this trade due to the net credit we *build into* the trade, that net credit is our reward. We figure it by simple subtraction: *the credit (what we take in) minus the debit (what we pay out)*."

RISK

"That's right. And we figure our risk," added Aaron, "by first noticing that we can't lose any more than the difference between the two strike prices. In the worst case, we're committed to buying shares at $140 (that's what our short put commits us to do), but we have the right to *sell* shares at $135 (that's what our long put buys for us). So the worst that can happen is that we buy shares for $140 and sell them for $135—a loss of $5. But remember, we've already taken in a net credit of $1.85, so our loss is reduced by that much. In other words, we have a loss of $5 but we have a gain of $1.85, so our real loss—our net loss—is $3.15 ($5 – $1.85). So that's our total risk: $3.15."

"So," said Lon, "we figure our risk in this trade by simple subtraction again: *the difference between the strike prices (the maximum we can lose) minus the net credit (what we've already taken in)*."

"That's right," said Nate, "so let's summarize our bull put this way." (See Figure 37.3.)

BULL PUT

Stagnant to bullish trend

Short Put ⎤ Same expiration month
Long Put ⎦ 30 days or fewer

Short Put (P)
- Sell to open at the ask price.
- Choose a strike price OTM.

Long Put (L)
- Buy to open at the bid price.
- Choose a strike price *further* OTM than the short put strike (but no greater than $5 spread).

Credit Trade: We take in in our credit more than we pay out in our debit.

Net Credit: The difference between what we take in for the short put (our credit) and what we pay out for the long put (our debit). So: credit minus debit.

Maximum REWARD: The net credit.

Maximum RISK: the difference between the strike prices (the maximum we can lose) minus the net credit (what we've already taken in).

Primary Exit: Both options expire worthless. We keep our net credit without having to do anything with actual shares of stock.

FIGURE 37.3 Bull Put Summary

REVIEW

Jul 08 Calls			(30 days to expiration)			BA@74.34					Jul 08 Puts
BAGM	10.10	0	9.70	10.00	37.9	.90	65.00	BASM	0.43	+0.03	0.40	0.45	38.5 -.10
BAGN	5.90	+0.50	5.50	5.70	33.8	.75	70.00	BASN	1.12	-0.03	1.10	1.20	33.9 -.25
BAGO	2.55	-0.05	2.50	2.55	32.1	.49	75.00	BASO	2.93	-0.17	2.95	3.10	31.7 -.51
BAGP	0.83	-0.07	0.80	0.85	30.7	.22	80.00	BASP	6.10	-0.25	6.20	6.50	30.6 -.78
BAGQ	0.22	0	0.20	0.25	30.9	.08	85.00	BASQ	10.70	-0.30	10.50	10.90	29.3 -.93
BAGR	0.10	0	0.05	0.10	33.2	.03	90.00	BASR	14.10	0	15.40	15.80	34.1 -.97
BAGS	0.05	0	0	0.05	35.5	.01	95.00	BASS	21.50	0	20.40	20.80	42.5 -.97
BAGT	0.05	0	0	0.05	41.9	.01	100.00	BAST	14.60	0	25.40	25.80	50.5 -.97

Aug 08 Calls			(58 days to expiration)			BA@74.34					Aug 08 Puts
BAHJ	27.00	0	24.40	24.80	49.8	.98	50.00	BATJ	0.10	0	0	0.10	45.0 -.01
BAHK	21.20	0	19.50	20.10	47.4	.95	55.00	BATK	0.17	0	0.10	0.20	41.8 -.03
BAHL	14.50	0	14.70	15.20	39.6	.93	60.00	BATL	0.50	0	0.30	0.40	37.9 -.07
BAHM	10.58	0	10.20	10.50	34.4	.86	65.00	BATM	0.95	-0.03	0.90	0.95	36.1 -.15
BAHN	6.50	-0.10	6.30	6.60	32.3	.71	70.00	BATN	2.20	+0.06	2.05	2.15	34.4 -.30
BAHO	3.80	+0.20	3.40	3.60	31.0	.51	75.00	BATO	4.00	-0.25	4.10	4.30	33.3 -.49
BAHP	1.70	0	1.60	1.70	30.3	.30	80.00	BATP	7.20	-0.10	7.20	7.50	33.1 -.68
BAHQ	0.70	+0.03	0.60	0.70	29.7	.15	85.00	BATQ	11.50	+0.20	11.10	11.50	33.2 -.82
BAHR	0.25	0	0.20	0.30	29.9	.07	90.00	BATR	15.70	0	15.50	16.10	33.9 -.91
BAHS	0.15	0	0.05	0.15	30.8	.03	95.00	BATS	20.70	0	20.30	21.00	37.5 -.94
BAHT	0.05	0	0	0.10	32.9	.02	100.00	BATT	17.98	0	25.20	25.90	40.8 -.96

Source: Screenshot courtesy of optionsXpress, Inc. © 2008.
Review

Suppose you wanted to structure a bull call on this stock.

1. Which expiration month would you choose? Why?
2. Where would you place the short put? Why?
3. Where would you place the long put? Why?
4. What is the net credit for this trade?
5. What is the maximum risk for this trade?
6. What is the maximum reward for this trade?
7. What is the primary exit for this trade?

Suppose you wanted to structure a bull put on this stock.

8. Which expiration month would you choose? Why?
9. Where would you place the short put? Why?

Jul 08 Calls						(30 days to expiration)		AAPL@181.20					Jul 08 Puts	
APVGL	23.95	-0.25	23.65	23.90	47.5	.84	160.00	APVSL	2.31	+0.16	2.25	2.27	47.1	-.16
APVGM	19.90	-0.05	19.65	19.75	45.8	.78	165.00	APVSM	3.23	+0.19	3.15	3.20	45.6	-.22
APVGN	16.00	-0.25	15.95	16.00	44.6	.72	170.00	APVSN	4.48	+0.23	4.40	4.50	44.4	-.28
APVGO	12.60	-0.30	12.60	12.70	43.7	.64	175.00	APVSO	6.00	+0.05	6.05	6.15	43.4	-.36
APVGP	9.75	-0.15	9.70	9.75	42.7	.55	180.00	APVSP	8.25	+0.36	8.15	8.20	42.5	-.45
APVGQ	7.25	-0.15	7.25	7.35	42.1	.64	185.00	APVSQ	10.80	+0.40	10.70	10.75	41.8	-.54
APVGR	5.45	+0.15	5.30	5.35	41.4	.38	190.00	APVSR	13.75	+0.25	13.75	13.80	41.3	-.63
APVGS	3.75	-0.05	3.75	3.80	40.9	.29	195.00	APVSS	17.15	-0.10	17.20	17.30	41.0	-.71
APVGT	2.65	+0.04	2.60	2.65	40.7	.22	200.00	APVST	21.00	+0.20	21.05	21.15	40.8	-.78
Oct 08 Calls						(121 days to expiration)		AAPL@181.20					Oct 08 Puts	
APVJL	31.75	-0.10	31.65	31.85	47.4	.73	160.00	APWL	9.35	+.0.35	9.10	9.20	46.4	-.27
APVJM	28.81	0	28.45	28.60	46.9	.69	165.00	APWM	10.80	-0.05	10.80	10.95	46.0	-.30
APVJN	25.55	-0.15	25.40	25.55	46.4	.65	170.00	APWN	12.90	+0.30	12.75	12.90	45.6	-.34
APVJO	22.75	+0.05	22.55	22.75	45.9	.61	175.00	APWO	15.20	0	14.90	15.05	45.2	-.39
APVJP	19.90	-0.40	20.00	20.15	45.5	.57	180.00	APWP	17.40	+0.15	17.25	17.40	44.7	-.43
APVJQ	17.70	-0.15	17.60	17.75	45.1	.53	185.00	APWQ	20.10	+0.35	19.85	20.00	44.3	-.47
APVJR	15.50	-0.05	15.40	15.55	44.7	.49	190.00	APWR	22.85	+0.30	22.65	22.80	44.0	-.51
APVJS	13.65	0	13.45	13.60	44.4	.45	195.00	APWS	25.94	+0.49	25.70	25.80	43.7	-.55
APVJT	11.80	-0.05	11.65	11.80	44.0	.41	200.00	APWT	29.00	-0.15	28.90	29.05	43.5	-.60

Source: Screenshot courtesy of optionsXpress, Inc. © 2008.
Review

10. Where would you place the long put? Why?

11. What is the net credit for this trade?

12. What is the maximum risk for this trade?

13. What is the maximum reward for this trade?

14. What is the primary exit for this trade?

CHAPTER 38

Bull vs. Bull

"Now notice something about the bull call and the bull put," said Nate. "Both are basically bullish trades, of course; it's just that one, the bull call, is a debit trade and the other, the bull put, is a credit trade. Everything else about them follows from this central fact: the difference between a debit and a credit trade."

"If you think about it, for example," said Aaron, "you'll know that because the bull call is a debit trade, the primary instrument has to be the one we *buy*: it'll be the long instrument. And, of course, in the case of a bull call, that means it will be the long call."

"Right," said Shorty. "We're using the long call as the primary instrument to make money. As a result, we place it only slightly out of the money so that it will go *in* the money and generate a profit. And, of course, that's why it's expensive: strike prices that are slightly out of the money are always more expensive than those that are further out."

"And that's why this is a debit trade," summarized Nate. "We are *buying* this expensive option rather than selling it. Of course, we do sell an option—in this case, we place a short call. But because the short call is used primarily to limit risk, we place it further out of the money, and therefore it is less expensive. And that's why we start out in the hole in this trade—what we're buying is more expensive than what we're selling. That's what it means for this to be a debit trade."

So if we remember that the bull call is a debit trade, we can figure practically everything else out.

"There's another thing we know because this is a debit trade," said Aaron.

"And I know what it is," Shorty jumped in. "It's that we make a profit by having the spread between the value of the long call and the value of the short call *grow*. When it grows enough to give us a 20 to 25 percent profit, we close the deal and move on."

"Right," added Lon, "and we're going to close it by selling the long call and buying back the short call. That's what we do when the spread reaches this 20 to 25 percent return. And, of course, this means that we want *time* in the trade. We need enough time for the stock to go bullish enough that it will create this profitable spread. So we want a minimum of 45 days for this trade, and often much longer."

"So if we remember that the bull call is a debit trade," said Aaron, "we can figure practically everything else out: (1) the long call will be our primary instrument; (2) it will be placed slightly out of the money; (3) the short call will be our limiting instrument and it will be placed further out of the money; (4) we make a profit by having the spread between the value of the long call and the value of the short call grow enough to give us a 20 to 25 percent return; (5) this will work only in a bullish trend; and (6) we need time value in the trade."

"Now we can do the same thing with the bull put," said Nate. "If we remember that it's a credit trade we can figure practically everything else out."

"One thing we know, for example," remarked Shorty, "is that the primary instrument will be the one we *sell*: it will be the short put we place. The credit we receive for this short put is the way we make money in this trade. Normally, we don't want to go in the money and have to buy shares, so we definitely place this short call out of the money—and not just *slightly* out of the money. We want to *stay* out of the money and simply pocket this credit at the end of the expiration period."

"Which means," added Lon, "that our limiting instrument will be the long put, and we place it further out of the money than the short put. And because it's placed further out of the money, it's less expensive. So in this case we're taking *in* more than we're paying out, and, of course, that's what it means for this to be a credit trade. Here we're not starting out in the hole, with a net debit. We're starting out with a net *credit*."

"And how do we make a profit in this credit trade?" asked Aaron.

"Our profit is simply this net credit—the credit we received minus what we paid for the long put," answered Shorty. "So all we're trying to do in this bull put is protect this profit that *we start with*. We just want both options to expire worthless and be done with it. And of course that's why this trade also works in a stagnant trend: whether the stock is rising or staying stagnant doesn't matter as long as it just stays higher than our strike price and thus stays out of the money. Either way, we keep our credit without being assigned and having to purchase shares. It's just the nature of a credit trade—how we make profit—that it will work in a stagnant trend as well as a bullish one."

> *If we remember that the bull put is a credit trade, we can figure practically everything else out.*

"And all of this means," added Lon, "that we want a short time period—30 days maximum. We don't want enough time for either a stagnant or bullish trend to go bearish on us. So the shorter the time frame, the better."

"So, see?" said Nate. "Simply by knowing that this is a credit trade, we know a lot of other things: (1) the short put will be our primary instrument; (2) we will place it out of the money; (3) the long put will be our limiting instrument and it will be placed further out of the money; (4) we make a profit by simply keeping the net credit we start with; (5) the trade will work in either a bullish or a stagnant trend; and (6) we want a short time frame."

"Here's what these two bullish trades look like if we represent them both on one option chain," said Aaron. (See Figure 38.1.)

"So each trade has its pros and cons," said Nate. "The bull call can take more time and it requires a strong bullish move to create the necessary spread, but it can make the most of a bullish movement. The bull put will often make less, but it can work in two trends and it has a quick turnaround time. You pick the way you would rather go. The bull call might be best in

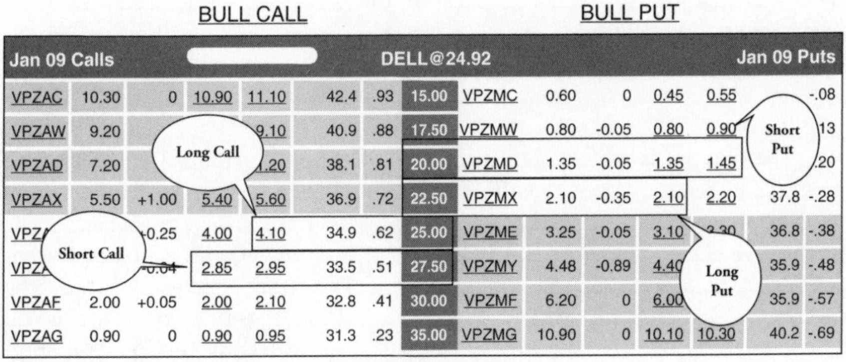

FIGURE 38.1 The Two Bullish Trades
Source: Screenshot courtesy of optionsXpress, Inc. © 2008.

Debit Trade	Credit Trade
1. Long call is primary instrument.	1. Short put is primary instrument.
2. It is placed slightly OTM.	2. It is placed OTM.
3. Short call is limiting instrument and is placed further OTM.	3. Long put is limiting instrument and is placed further OTM.
4. Profit mechanism: spread between the two options grows, turning starting net debit into 20 to 25 percent return.	4. Profit mechanism: start out with a net credit and keep it.
5. Bullish trend only.	5. Stagnant to bullish trends.
6. Needs time value.	6. Needs *short* time frame.

a strong bullish trend, but it *requires* a strong bullish trend to create the necessary spread for a profit. The bull put, however, is more flexible; all it requires is that something *not* happen—that the stock not go bearish—and it is closed more quickly. You just go with what you're most comfortable with in a particular situation."

"Now, obviously," said Aaron, "you want to paper trade both of these spread strategies a lot before you ever trade with real money. These things take getting used to, and the only way to get used to them is to practice them. So practice . . . and have fun. Deal?"

"Deal."

REVIEW

The bull call is a _____ trade. That means the
_____ is the _____ instrument and is
placed _____ or slightly _____.
The _____ is the _____
instrument and is placed _____ further _____.
This trade makes profit as the _____ between _____
grows. This trade is for a _____ trend and it
needs _____.

The bull put is a _____ trade. That means the
_____ is the _____ instrument and
is placed _____. The _____
is the _____ instrument, and is placed further
_____. This trade makes profit by the
_____ we _____ with. This trade is for
_____ to _____ trends and needs a short
_____.

Understanding Bearish Spread Trades

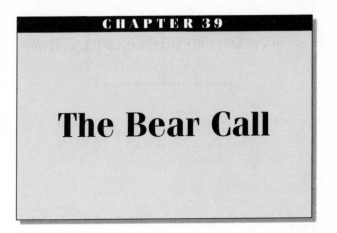

CHAPTER 39

The Bear Call

"Now, we talked earlier about a debit strategy in using the call instruments," said Nate. "In the 'bull call,' we paid more for our long call than we took in for our short call and thus started out with a net debit—we started out in the hole."

"And," continued Aaron, "in that trade we used the long call as our primary instrument—as the main way to make profit. We did this by placing the long call strike near the money so that it would grow faster in value as the stock grew in value. And we used the short call as the limiting instrument—as the main way to reduce risk in the trade."

"And notice," added Nate, "that this short call reduced our risk in two ways. For one thing, by merely selling this call we brought a credit into the trade and thus reduced our cost basis—the total amount of our investment. But in addition, we also placed the short call strike further out of the money than the long call, which meant that it would have a lower delta—and would therefore grow in value more slowly than the long call. This was what allowed the spread between the values of the two options to grow, and thus was the basis for making a profit. And keep in mind that this strategy was designed for a bullish trend; it works only when the stock price is increasing."

Long Call	Short Call
Right to Buy	May have to Sell

Long Put	Short Put
Right to Sell	May have to Buy

FIGURE 39.1   The Bear Call

"But now we're going to see how to use these same call instruments in a *credit* trade," said Aaron, "in a way that will take advantage of a stagnant or bearish trend. We call it a *bear call*—because it's designed for a bearish-type trend and because it uses the call instruments." (See Figure 39.1.)

"Now in this trade," said Aaron, "we're looking to optimize a bearish trend by taking in a credit. We're not looking for a big hit here; we just want a high probability of making a profit. So in this trade, the short call is our primary instrument: taking in a credit from the short call is the way we make money in this trade."

"Now remember," added Nate, "the worst thing that can happen to us in a short call is for the strike we choose to go in the money—for the market price of the stock to move higher than our strike price. In that case, we'll get assigned and we'll have to buy shares—and remember that we don't already own this stock—at this high market price in order to be able to turn around and meet our obligation to sell them at the lower strike price. As you said earlier, Shorty, that's a world of hurt. We can't let ourselves get in that situation. We took in a credit, it is true, but that won't be enough by any means to offset the loss we could suffer."

"So we do three things to limit our risk," explained Aaron. "First, we choose an out-of-the-money strike price for the short call. It's important to finish out of the money, so we have to start out of the money. We pick a strike that is far enough out of the money to give us good safety in the trade.

"Second," he continued, "we give ourselves a short time frame. Again, we don't want to give the trade time to turn on us and go in the money. This isn't that critical when we're doing a covered call—adding a short call to stock we already own. In that case, as you discovered on your own and as we saw in talking about covered calls, it's not the worst thing in the world to have to sell our shares. We already own them, and we will have paid a lower price for them than the strike we will be selling them at if we get assigned. That's why we can look at expiration periods anywhere from 3 to 12 months: the longer time frames give us larger credit amounts."

> *Taking in a credit from the short call is the way we make money in this trade.*

"But in the case of this bear call we're talking about, we're assuming, again, that we *don't* own the underlying stock. And in this situation a short time frame is critical, as I just mentioned. So in this case, we want 30 days or fewer for our expiration period."

"And third," said Nate, "is our long call. Remember that the long call gives us the right to *buy* stock at a certain price. That's crucial in limiting our risk. To see this, think of an extreme example. Let's suppose Plum stock is selling at $37 and we place a short call for 100 shares at an out-of-the-money strike of 40 with a 25-day expiration period. Seems safe enough, right? But let's suppose the stock goes bullish—the market price goes through the roof and the stock ends up at $60. Our short call still obligates us to *sell* 100 shares for $40. And that means, as I said above, that we first have to go out on the market and buy shares—at $60—so that we can turn around and *sell* them for $40. It's an automatic $20 loss."

> *We're not looking for a big hit here; we just want a high* probability *of making a profit.*

"So here's how the long call helps us," said Aaron. "In this same example, suppose we placed a *long* call at a strike price of 42.50 in that same 25-day expiration period. That means, no matter what happens to the market price, we have the right to buy shares at $42.50. So even if the stock *does* go to $60, we can still buy shares at $42.50. True, we will have to turn around and sell them for $40, but notice that we have turned a huge loss into a loss that is at least manageable."

"So because the long call limits our risk in this way," said Nate, "it is the *limiting* instrument in the bear call. Does that make sense?"

"Absolutely," replied Shorty and Lon.

"Okay," said Aaron, "so let's bring up a sample option chain again so we can see what's going on in a bear call." (See Figure 39.2.)

Jul 08 Calls						(30 days to expiration)	AAPL@179.94					Jul 08 Puts	
APVGK	26.90	-1.35	26.85	27.00	48.6	.87	155.00	APVSK	1.67	+0.16	1.62	1.66	47.8 -.12
APVGL	23.00	-1.20	22.55	22.80	47.1	.83	160.00	APVSL	2.34	+0.19	2.34	2.38	46.3 -.17
APVGM	18.90	-1.05	18.60	18.70	45.4	.77	165.00	APVSM	3.30	+0.26	3.30	3.40	44.9 -.23
APVGN	15.00	-1.25	14.95	15.05	44.2	.70	170.00	APVSN	4.70	+0.45	4.70	4.75	43.9 -.30
APVGO	11.80	-1.10	11.75	11.80	43.3	.62	175.00	APVSO	6.40	+0.45	6.45	6.50	43.0 -.38
APVGP	9.05	-0.85	9.00	9.05	42.5	.53	180.00	APVSP	8.65	+0.76	8.65	8.75	42.1 -.47
APVGQ	6.80	-0.60	6.65	6.75	41.9	.44	185.00		Short Call				41.7 -.56
APVGR	4.95	-0.35	4.85	4.90	41.5	.35	190.00		Long Call				41.2 -.65
APVGS	3.50	-0.30	3.40	3.45	41.0	.27	195.00	APVSS	18.10	+0.85	18.10	18.15	40.8 -.73
APVGT	2.35	-0.26	2.36	2.39	40.9	.21	200.00	APVST	21.80	+1.00	22.05	22.15	40.9 -.79

FIGURE 39.2 Applying the Bear Call
Source: Screenshot courtesy of optionsXpress, Inc. © 2008.

"So here's what we do," said Nate. "We open a short call and a long call in the same expiration month—the *current* month. We want 30 days or fewer. We open the short call—again by selling at the bid price—out of the money."

"In this case, the stock price is $179.94," added Aaron, "and we choose a short call strike price of 185, which is enough out of the money to give us some safety. And the bid price for this strike is $6.65. That's the credit we receive for this short call."

"At the same time," said Nate, "we open the long call—by buying at the ask price—but we do it at a strike that is one or two strikes *further* out of the money than the short call. We keep the spread between the two no greater than $5, but we do make sure there is a spread by having them one or two strikes apart. In this case the only strike price that meets these conditions is 190. That means we pay the ask price of $4.90."

"Let's be clear," suggested Aaron, "about why we place our long call one or two strikes further out of the money than our short call. It's really for two reasons. First, remember that this is a credit trade. The way we make profit is by getting more for our short call than we pay for our long call. That gives us a net credit, and that's our profit. Look at the chain again. If we placed our long call at the same strike as the short call—185—we would be paying out $6.75 in the trade and only taking in $6.65. That would be a net debit, not a net credit. Pretty bad idea for a credit trade where we expect a bearish trend and where all we're trying to do is *start out* with a net credit and simply keep it."

"See, this relationship almost *always* holds," added Nate. "For any given strike, the ask price will be higher than the bid price (sellers generally ask more than buyers are bidding). So if I place my long call at the same strike as my short call, I will almost always be paying out more than I'm taking in because I'm placing the long call at the ask price and the short call at the bid price. So it's rare to win at the same strike price in a credit trade."

"But why not go *more than* two strike prices further out of the money, or more than a $5 spread?" asked Shorty. "What's the problem with that?"

"Well, that brings me to the second point," replied Aaron. "Remember that we're placing this long call for protection. It's the limiting instrument, the one we use to limit our risk in the trade. So let's say we place the short call at a strike of 185 and the long call at a strike of 200. And let's say the market price of the stock surprises us and goes bullish to $195. In that case, having the right to buy shares at $200 is no help to us at all. We'll still have to buy shares at the $195 market price and turn around and sell them at the price of $185 that we agreed to in our short call. That 200 strike price is so far away that it can't help us unless the stock goes *extremely* bullish and goes over $200—and it would be foolish to count on that. So this relationship always holds: *the further away our long call is, the less likely it is to help us.* Our protection then is less and so our risk is greater."

> The further away our long call is, the less likely it is to help us. Our protection then is less and so our risk is greater.

NET CREDIT AND REWARD

"Okay, let's think about our reward potential in this trade," said Nate. "We paid a debit of $4.90 to buy the long call, but we took in a credit of $6.65 on the short call. Our reward potential is the difference between them: $6.65 – $4.90, which equals $1.75. That's the net credit we start with in the trade. The formula is simple: *the credit (the amount we took in) minus the debit (the amount we paid out—our expense).* That's our net credit, and our net credit is our reward potential."

RISK

"Once we know this," said Aaron, "it's easy to figure out our risk in the trade. For example, we know that mathematically we can't lose more than the difference between the two strikes, which is $5. The difference between the bid and ask amounts for the two call instruments will never be greater than that. But we took in a net credit of $1.75, and we get to keep that no matter what happens. So the maximum we can lose is $5 minus that $1.75, which equals $3.25."

"Right," added Nate. "The formula for our risk in a bear call is simply: *the difference in the strikes, minus the net credit (the net amount we start the trade with).* That tells us the worst situation we can end up with."

"So in light of all this, how do we want this deal to end?" asked Shorty.

"We want our expiration period to end without ever going in the money," answered Nate. "If neither of our calls goes in the money, the options just expire at the end of the 30 days and we simply keep the $1.75 in profit. That's the ideal outcome for a bear call."

"So let's summarize the bear call trade this way," said Aaron. (See Figure 39.3.)

BEAR CALL

Stagnant to bearish trend

Long Call ——————┐   Same expiration month
Short Call ————————┘   *Current* month (30 days or fewer)

Short Call (P)
- Sell to open at the bid price.
- Choose a strike price OTM.

Long Call (L)
- Buy to open at the ask price.
- Choose a strike price 1 to 2 strikes *more* OTM than short call strike (but no greater than $5 spread).

Credit Trade: We take in in our credit more than we pay out in our debit.

Net Credit: The difference between what we take in for the short call (our credit) and what we pay out for the long call (our debit).

Maximum REWARD: The net credit.

Maximum RISK: The difference in strike prices minus the net credit. so (long call strike minus short call strike) minus the net credit.

Primary Exit: Both options expire worthless.

FIGURE 39.3   Bear Call Summary

REVIEW

Jul 08 Calls						(30 days to expiration)		NYX@58.07						Jul 08 Puts
NYXGI	0	0	13.10	13.55	54.2	.96	45.00	NYXSI	0.11	0	0.08	0.14	49.4	-.03
NYXGJ	9.10	-1.85	8.45	8.70	44.6	.89	50.00	NYXSJ	0.45	+0.14	0.45	0.47	45.8	-.12
NYXGK	4.75	-0.65	4.60	4.75	42.9	.70	55.00	NYXSK	1.50	+0.40	1.48	1.54	42.8	-.30
NYXGL	2.01	-0.39	1.95	2.03	41.0	.42	60.00	NYXSL	3.86	+0.66	3.75	3.85	40.8	-.58
NYXGM	0.72	-0.13	0.65	0.69	40.5	.19	65.00	NYXSM	7.41	+1.31	7.40	7.60	40.7	-.81
NYXGN	0.22	-0.04	0.17	0.22	40.7	.07	70.00	NYXSN	12.22	+1.57	11.60	12.20	34.9	-.96
NYXGO	0.09	0	0.07	0.09	44.5	.03	75.00	NYXSO	17.40	+1.99	16.65	17.05	41.2	-.98
NYXGP	0.05	0	0.05	0.06	50.9	.02	80.00	NYXSP	21.34	0	21.35	22.70	64.1	-.95
Sep 08 Calls						(93 days to expiration)		NYX@58.07						Sep 08 Puts
NYXIH	18.15	0	18.05	18.75	40.3	.97	40.00	NYXUH	0.44	0	0.35	0.42	50.6	-.05
NYXII	15.50	0	14.00	14.45	48.4	.88	45.00	NYXUI	0.92	+0.15	0.90	0.94	48.3	-.12
NYXIJ	9.80	-1.85	10.05	10.30	45.4	.78	50.00	NYXUJ	1.60	0	1.90	1.95	46.3	-.22
NYXIK	6.85	-0.55	6.70	6.90	43.4	.65	55.00	NYXUK	3.45	+0.45	3.55	3.65	44.8	-.35
NYXIL	4.25	-0.50	4.15	4.30	42.0	.49	60.00	NYXUL	6.00	+0.90	5.95	6.10	43.5	-.51
NYXIM	2.40	-0.86	2.35	2.44	40.5	.34	65.00	NYXUM	9.25	+1.33	9.10	9.30	42.4	-.65
NYXIN	1.25	-0.14	1.22	1.27	39.3	.21	70.00	NYXUN	12.95	+0.95	12.95	13.10	41.8	-.77
NYXIO	0.58	-0.12	0.54	0.59	37.8	.11	75.00	NYXUO	17.05	+1.40	17.00	17.45	39.8	-.87
NYXIP	0.30	-0.03	0.25	0.30	37.8	.06	80.00	NYXUP	23.14	0	21.60	22.30	41.7	-.92

Source: Screenshot courtesy of optionsXpress, Inc. © 2008.
Review

Suppose you wanted to structure a bear call on this stock.

1. Which month would you use? Why?
2. Where would you place the short call? Why?
3. Where would you place the long call? Why?
4. What is the maximum reward for this trade?
5. What is the maximum risk for this trade?
6. What is the primary exit for this trade? How much would you make?

Suppose you wanted to structure a bear call on the stock on page 286.

7. Which month would you choose? Why?
8. Where would you place the short call? Why?

Jul 08 Calls				(30 days to expiration)		RTN@57.71						Jul 08 Puts	
RTNGX	0	0	5.20	5.50	19.0	.96	52.50	RTNSX	0.25	0	0.25	0.30	28.4	-.11
RTNGK	3.78	-0.32	3.10	3.40	21.9	.79	55.00	RTNSK	0.55	-0.05	0.70	0.75	27.3	-.25
RTNGY	2.00	-0.16	1.65	1.70	22.7	.55	57.50	RTNSY	1.45	-0.15	1.60	1.70	26.9	-.46
RTNGL	0.88	-0.12	0.65	0.75	22.7	.30	60.00	RTNSL	2.75	+0.16	3.10	3.30	27.9	-.66
RTNGZ	0.30	-.10	0.25	0.30	23.9	.14	62.50	RTNSZ	4.49	0	5.20	5.40	31.7	-.76
RTNGM	0.15	+0.04	0.10	0.20	27.2	.08	65.00	RTNSM	7.70	0	7.50	7.80	37.2	-.85
RTNGU	0.15	0	0.05	0.10	29.4	.04	67.50	RTNSU	4.60	0	9.90	10.20	42.1	-.89
Aug 08 Calls				(58 days to expiration)		RTN@57.71						Aug 08 Puts	
RTNHJ	8.80	0	7.80	8.10	21.1	.96	50.00	RTNTJ	0.38	0	0.30	0.40	30.0	-.10
RTNHX	6.20	0	5.70	5.90	23.9	.86	52.50	RTNTX	0.73	0	0.65	0.75	28.7	-.18
RTNHK	4.30	-0.30	3.80	4.00	23.9	.72	55.00	RTNTK	1.19	+0.16	1.25	1.35	27.5	-.30
RTNHY	2.75	0	2.35	2.50	24.1	.55	57.50	RTNTY	1.93	0	2.30	2.35	27.3	-.45
RTNHL	1.50	-0.20	1.30	1.40	23.8	.37	60.00	RTNTL	3.54	+0.22	3.60	3.80	26.7	-.61
RTNHZ	0.70	-0.25	0.65	0.75	24.0	.23	62.50	RTNTZ	5.10	+0.27	5.50	5.70	28.2	-.73
RTNHM	0.40	-0.10	0.30	0.40	24.4	.13	65.00	RTNTM	7.43	0	7.60	7.90	30.1	-.81
RTNHU	0.20	0	0.15	0.25	25.8	.08	67.50	RTNTU	9.19	0	10.00	10.30	34.4	-.85

Source: Screenshot courtesy of optionsXpress, Inc. © 2008.
Review

9. Where would you place the long call? Why?

10. What is the maximum reward for this trade?

11. What is the maximum risk for this trade?

12. What is the primary exit for this trade? How much would you make?

CHAPTER 40

The Bear Put

"Okay," said Aaron, "earlier we saw the bull put. That's a trade we make in a stagnant or bullish trend. But we can structure another trade with puts to take advantage of a *bearish* trend. It's called a *bear put:* here, we're using put instruments to optimize a bearish trend. And again, remember that we won't own the underlying stock; we'll work only with the put instruments themselves." (See Figure 40.1.)

"In this trade," Nate continued, "the long put option is our primary instrument because it's the one we're using to make money in the trade; we want it to increase in value so we can sell it to someone else for a profit. Now recall that whenever we use a long put, we need time on our side because we need time for the stock to move down. So we want to have a *minimum* of 45 days. The short put, however, is our limiting instrument; we use it to take a credit into our account, which lowers our cost basis and thus limits our risk in the trade."

"So obviously, this is a debit trade," observed Shorty.

"Right," answered Aaron. "We're going to pay more for our long put than we take in for our short put, so we're going to start out in the hole—with a net debit. Let's look at the sample option chain to help us see what happens in a bear put." (See Figure 40.2.)

Long Call	Short Call
Right to Buy	May have to Sell
Long Put	Short Put
Right to Sell	May have to Buy

FIGURE 40.1 The Bear Put

"So here's what we do," said Nate. "We open a long put and a short put in the same expiration month—again, at least 45 days out. We open the long put—again by buying at the ask price—at or near the money.

"So the stock price is $26.83," he continued, "and we choose a long put strike price, in this case 122 days out, of 25, which is the nearest out-of-the-money strike available to us. And the ask price for this strike is $2.25. That's the debit we pay for this long put, and gives us the right to sell shares for $25."

"Now remember," said Aaron, jumping in, "we expect a bearish move and we want the 25 strike to go in the money—we *want* the market price of the stock to go below that. That's why we place the strike as near the money as we can. When the strike price goes in the money the long put will increase in value and we'll be able to sell it for a profit."

"And yet we start it out of the money, at least slightly," added Aaron, "to make sure we take advantage of the accelerated delta change that occurs just before a strike goes in the money. So out of the money but as close to the money as possible."

"Got it," said Lon.

Oct 08 Calls					(122 days to expiration)	SAY @ 26.83					Oct 08 Puts	
SAYJC	0	0	11.80	12.10	44.6	.99	15.00	SAYVC	0.48	0	0.05	0.20	59.5 -.03
SAYJW	6.80	0	9.50	9.80	51.0	.95	17.50	SAYVW	0.90	0	0.25	0.40	57.5 -.07
SAYJD	10.25	0	7.40	7.60	50.6	.88	20.00	SAYVD	0.70	0	0.60	0.75	54.9 -.14
SAYJX	8.25		Short Put				22.50	SAYVX	1.20	0	1.20	1.35	53.0 -.23
SAYJE	4.50		Long Put				25.00	SAYVE	2.15	0	2.10	2.25	51.6 -.34
SAYJF	2.05	0	4.70	2.00	18.1	.11	30.00	SAYVF	5.10	0	4.90	5.10	50.6 -.58
SAYJG	0.75	-0.40	0.70	0.80	46.8	.21	35.00	SAYVG	8.90	0	8.70	9.00	50.4 -.77
SAYJH	0.45	0	0.20	0.35	46.1	.09	40.00	SAYVH	13.30	-2.30	13.20	13.50	52.1 -.87

FIGURE 40.2 Applying the Bear Put
Source: Screenshot courtesy of optionsXpress, Inc. © 2008.

"Me, too," agreed Shorty.

"At the same time," said Nate, "we open the short put—by selling at the bid price—but we do it at a strike that is one or two strikes further out of the money than the long put. We typically keep the spread between the two no greater than $5, but we do make sure there is a spread by having them one or two strikes apart. In this case we've placed the short put at the 22.50 strike."

"Now we place the short put one or two strikes more out of the money than the long put," said Aaron, "for two reasons. First, we *don't want* the short put strike to go in the money. If it goes in the money, then we face that whole problem of having to buy shares—and buy them at higher than the market price. That's what the short put commits us to do and we normally don't want that. Second, because it is further out of the money, the delta for the short put is lower than the delta for the long put. That means the value of the long put will increase faster than the value of the short put. *Both* will increase in value as the stock goes down, but the long put will increase faster—and this creates the spread that we need for a profit. It's exactly the same principle we saw in regard to the bull call. In a debit trade, we always need the primary instrument to move faster than the limiting instrument, and that's why the limiting instrument must be placed further out of the money. It gives us a lower delta."

"At the same time," said Nate, "if we go too far out of the money, the credit we take in drops considerably. Notice, for example, that the 20 strike only brings in a credit of $0.60 and the 17.50 strike a credit of only $0.25. We want to make sure the credit we bring in is enough to be worth it. So we want the short put strike to be further out of the money than the long put strike, but not too far. And we generally don't want more than a $5 spread between them."

> *Both options will increase in value as the stock goes down, but the long put will increase faster—and this creates the spread that we need for a profit.*

NET DEBIT AND RISK

"So let's see the structure of this bear put we've been talking about," said Nate. "The stock price is $26.83, the strike of the long put is 25, and the strike of the short put is 22.50. That gives us a $2.50 spread. Now we paid

$2.25 for our long put; that's our debit. But we took in a credit of $1.20 for the short put. So, just as we said, we have a net debit in this trade—a net expense—of $1.05 ($2.25 – $1.20). Balancing the debit we paid out and the credit we took in, we're $1.05 in the hole."

"Right, it's a debit trade," said Lon, "just like the bull call."

"Good," said Aaron, "and that net debit is also our risk in the trade. That's how much we have to lose: the difference between the debit we paid out and the credit we took in. Think about it. If the stock goes bullish on us and takes off, the options will both take a dive. But even if they both go to zero, that doesn't change our net debit at all; we've still paid out only $2.25 and taken in a credit of $1.20. So our investment is still $1.05, and that means that's all we can lose, no matter what."

"So that's the basic way of figuring our risk in a bear put: it's the same as our net debit. The formula is simple: *debit (what we paid out) minus the credit (what we took in)*."

"Now, in terms of risk," said Nate, "let's suppose the stock goes bearish on us instead and dives all the way to zero. Well, think about it. It's true that we're obligated to buy shares in that case at $22.50 if we're assigned; that's what our short put strike price commits us to. But notice what the long put strike does for us: it allows us to *sell* our shares for $25, *regardless* of what other people are selling their shares for. Even zero. So, we may be forced to buy shares at $22.50, but we're still able to *sell* those shares for $25. So we actually make money."

REWARD

"Now our maximum reward," said Aaron, "is based on the fact that, mathematically, we can never make more than the $2.50 difference in the two strike prices. The difference between (1) the debit we paid out for our long put and (2) the credit we took in for our short put will never be greater than the difference between the strike prices. So the maximum can't be more than the $2.50. So we start with that $2.50 and notice that we've already spent $1.05 to make the trade in the first place. Remember, that's our net debit, our investment: the debit of $2.25 we paid out for the long put minus the credit of $1.20 we took in for the short put. So we're already in the hole $1.05. So the maximum we can make in the trade is the $2.50 spread minus what we've already spent: $1.05. The difference is $1.45 ($2.50 – $1.05 = $1.45). So that's the maximum we can make in the trade: $1.45."

"So the formula," said Aaron, "for determining our maximum reward in a bear put is: *the difference in the two strike prices minus the net debit (our net expense in the trade)*, which in this case, comes to $1.45."

"Of course, as we keep telling you," reminded Aaron, "we're never trying to make the maximum on these debit trades. We just want to make our 20 to 25 percent return, close the deal, and move on to the next trade. Let's say we want 20 percent. In that case, we simply want to make 20 percent more than the hole we started out in. That is, we make back our net debit, *plus* 20 percent. That would be $1.2 \times \$1.05$, or $1.26. When we make that $1.26, we close the deal."

"Now remember the logic we learned for making profit in a bull call," said Aaron. "The same principle applies here. Recall that the long put here is simply an option that we've *bought*—we've paid a $2.25 debit for the right to be able to sell shares for $25. And the short put is simply an option that we've *sold*—we've taken in a $1.20 credit for the guarantee that we will buy shares at $22.50 if we get assigned. We're in the hole because what we bought is more expensive than what we sold. Again, that's the essence of a debit trade. It's just that this time we're doing it with puts instead of calls."

> *We're never trying to make the maximum on these debit trades. We just want to make our 20 to 25 percent return, close the deal, and move on to the next trade.*

"So in closing this trade," said Nate, "we simply reverse our buy and sell, just as we did with the calls in the bull call. We take our long put—the option we bought—and *sell* it to someone else. It has now increased in value, say to a $3.20 bid. At the same time, we take our short put—the option we sold—and now *buy it back*. That's how we cancel it. And, of course, it too has gone up in value, *but not as fast as the long put*—say, to a $2 ask. So now in closing this trade we are selling an option for $3.20 and buying one for $2, which is a positive spread of $1.20: we're taking *in* $1.20 more than we're paying out.

"Now, the principle of buying back the short put," he continued, "is the same principle that we saw with the short call in the bull call trade. Remember that you *sold* this put, and you sold it so that you could take in a credit. But this means that you entered a contract which gave you an obligation to buy shares of the stock if you were assigned. That's what your short put means. So part of closing this trade is to buy back this contract—to buy

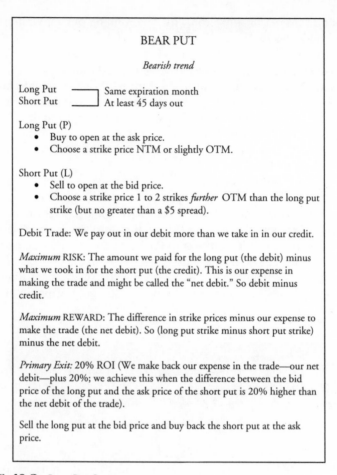

FIGURE 40.3 Bear Put Summary

back your short put—which not only closes the trade, but also releases you from this obligation to buy shares."

"Now remember," cautioned Aaron, "in case Nate went too fast for you: because we bought to open the long put at the ask price, and sold to open the short put at the bid price, when we close the trade we will do just the opposite. We will *sell* to close the long put—at the *bid* price—and we will *buy* to close the short put—at the *ask* price. That means, in determining our profit we will be comparing the bid price of the long put to the ask price of the short put. Those are the numbers we compare as we check our progress. When the difference reaches $1.26 we close the trade and move on."

"So let's summarize the bear put trade this way." (See Figure 40.3.)

REVIEW

Jul 08 Calls — (3 days to expiration) — SYK@64.31 — Jul 08 Puts

Call	Last	Chg	Bid	Ask	Vol	Δ	Strike	Put	Last	Chg	Bid	Ask	Vol	Δ
SYKFJ	15.10	0	14.10	14.50		1.00	50.00	SYKRJ	0.35	0	0	0.05	106.7	-.01
SYKFK	9.30	0	9.10	9.50		1.00	55.00	SYKRK	0.02	0	0	0.05	70.1	-.02
SYKFL	4.30	+0.60	4.10	4.50		1.00	60.00	SYKRL	0.10	0	0	0.05	34.9	-.03
SYKFM	0.40	+0.10	0.25	0.35	21.3	.32	65.00	SYKRM	0.90	-0.65	0.95	1.10	23.3	-.66
SYKFN	0.05	0	0	0.05	40.7	.02	70.00	SYKRN	5.90	0	5.50	5.90	40.8	-.98
SYKFO	0.05	0	0	0.05	67.5	.02	75.00	SYKRO	9.80	0	10.50	10.90	68.0	-.98
SYKFP	0.05	0	0	0.05	91.3	.01	80.00	SYKRP	20.20	0	15.50	15.90	92.4	-.99
SYKFQ	0.05	0	0	0.05	112.9	.01	85.00	SYKRQ	22.40	0	20.50	20.90	114.7	-.99

Jul 08 Calls — (31 days to expiration) — SYK@64.31 — Jul 08 Puts

Call	Last	Chg	Bid	Ask	Vol	Δ	Strike	Put	Last	Chg	Bid	Ask	Vol	Δ
SYKGJ	14.30	0	14.20	14.80	46.6	.97	50.00	SYKSJ	0	0	0	0.10	41.6	-.02
SYKGK	0	0	9.40	9.90	38.0	.93	55.00	SYKSK	0.25	0	0.10	0.20	34.0	-.05
SYKGL	4.30	0	4.90	5.20	29.5	.80	60.00	SYKSL	0.80	0	0.60	0.70	29.8	-.20
SYKGM	1.90	-0.10	1.70	1.85	26.9	.47	65.00	SYKSM	2.25	-0.25	2.30	2.45	27.2	-.53
SYKGN	0.40	+0.15	0.30	0.40	25.6	.15	70.00	SYKSN	5.70	0	5.80	6.10	26.3	-.85
SYKGO	0.05	0	0	0.10	26.1	.03	75.00	SYKSO	10.12	0	10.30	10.90	25.4	-.98
SYKGP	0	0	0	0.05	32.1	01	80.00	SYKSP	0	0	15.30	15.90	35.2	-.98

Sep 08 Calls — (94 days to expiration) — SYK@64.31 — Sep 08 Puts

Call	Last	Chg	Bid	Ask	Vol	Δ	Strike	Put	Last	Chg	Bid	Ask	Vol	Δ
SYKIJ	14.90	0	14.60	15.20	34.7	.94	50.00	SYKUJ	0.30	0	0.15	0.25	31.1	-.04
SYKIK	8.80	0	10.10	10.40	29.7	.87	55.00	SYKUK	0.60	0	0.55	0.65	28.9	-.12
SYKIL	6.10	0	6.10	6.40	27.4	.73	60.00	SYKUL	1.65	0	1.55	1.70	27.4	-.27
SYKIM	3.20	+0.40	3.10	3.30	25.7	.51	65.00	SYKUM	4.10	0	3.50	3.70	26.0	-.49
SYKIN	1.30	+0.05	1.25	1.40	24.5	.28	70.00	SYKUN	6.60	0	6.60	6.80	24.9	-.71
SYKIO	0.45	0	0.35	0.45	23.0	.11	75.00	SYKUO	10.30	0	10.40	11.00	23.0	-.89
SYKIP	0.25	0	0.05	0.20	23.3	.04	80.00	SYKUP	19.90	0	15.30	15.90	28.4	-.92
SYKIQ	0.45	0	0	0.10	24.9	.02	85.00	SYKUQ	0	0	20.20	20.90	33.7	-.93

Review

Suppose you wanted to structure a bear put on this stock.

1. Which month would you choose? Why?

2. Where would you place the long put? Why?

3. Where would you place the short put? Why?

4. What is the maximum risk for this trade?

5. What is the maximum reward for this trade?

6. What is the primary exit for this trade—the actual dollar amount you need to achieve?

Jul 08 Calls							(31 days to expiration)	MSFT@28.80						Jul 08 Puts	
MQFGD	9.00	0	8.80	8.90	54.7	.99	20.00	MQFSD	0.02	0	0	0.02	52.1	-.01
MSQGX	6.50	0	6.35	6.55	54.5	.95	22.50	MSQSX	0.04	0	0.02	0.04	42.8	-.02
MSQGD	5.09	0	4.90	5.10	47.0	.92	24.00	MSQSD	0.08	0	0.07	0.08	39.3	-.05
MSQGE	4.05	0	3.95	4.15	42.1	.89	25.00	MSQSE	0.14	0	0.12	0.14	36.9	-.09
MSQGR	3.20	0	3.05	3.25	38.5	.83	26.00	MSQSR	0.22	0	0.22	0.23	34.6	-.14
MSQGY	1.92	0	1.85	1.88	31.8	.71	27.50	MSQSY	0.49	0	0.50	0.52	31.6	-.29
MSQGB	0.99	0	0.95	0.97	30.3	.49	29.00	MSQSB	1.05	0	1.10	1.11	30.1	-.51
MSQGF	0.58	0	0.55	0.57	29.8	.35	30.00	MSQSF	1.64	0	1.69	1.70	29.4	-.66
MSQGC	0.32	0	0.31	0.32	30.1	.22	31.00	MSQSC	2.36	0	2.45	2.48	30.2	-.78
MSQGZ	0.15	0	0.12	0.14	31.1	.11	32.50	MSQSZ	3.65	0	3.55	3.80	22.7	-.96
MSQGL	0.07	0	0.05	0.07	33.1	.05	34.00	MSQSL	6.70	0	5.00	5.25		-1.00
MSQGG	0.03	0	0.02	0.04	33.4	.03	35.00	MSQSG	7.75	0	5.95	6.25		-1.00
MSQGM	0.02	0	0.01	0.03	35.3	.02	36.00	MSQSM	7.60	0	6.95	7.25		-1.00
MSQGU	0.03	0	0	0.03	39.2	.01	37.50	MSQSU	9.40	0	8.45	8.75		-1.00
Oct 08 Calls							(122 days to expiration)	MSFT@28.80						Oct 08 Puts	
MQFJD	9.15	0	8.95	9.25	42.2	.95	20.00	MQFVD	0.14	0	0.11	0.13	39.3	-.04
MSQJD	5.40	0	5.35	5.60	35.3	.85	24.00	MSQVD	0.45	0	0.46	0.47	34.0	-.15
MSQJE	4.70	0	4.50	4.60	31.7	.82	25.00	MSQVE	0.60	0	0.62	0.63	32.6	-.19
MSQJR	3.87	0	3.75	3.80	30.6	.76	26.00	MSQVR	0.83	0	0.83	0.85	31.4	-.25
MSQJS	3.10	0	3.05	3.10	29.9	.69	27.00	MSQVS	1.09	0	1.11	1.13	30.4	-.31
MSQJT	2.48	0	2.41	2.43	28.8	.61	28.00	MSQVT	1.46	0	1.47	1.49	29.6	-.39
MSQJB	1.90	0	1.85	1.88	28.0	.53	29.00	MSQVB	1.88	0	1.91	1.94	28.8	-.47
MSQJF	1.43	0	1.39	1.41	27.4	.45	30.00	MSQVF	2.40	0	2.45	2.47	28.4	-.55
MSQJC	1.05	0	1.02	1.03	26.9	.36	31.00	MSQVC	3.00	0	3.05	3.10	27.8	-.63
MSQJO	0.75	0	0.72	0.74	26.4	.29	32.00	MSQVO	3.85	0	3.75	3.85	27.9	-.70
MSQJP	0.54	0	0.50	0.52	26.2	.22	33.00	MSQVP	4.55	0	4.55	4.65	28.4	-.76
MSQJL	0.39	0	0.34	0.36	.6.0	.16	34.00	MSQVL	6.20	0	5.25	5.50	27.2	-.82
MSQJG	0.25	0	0.24	0.25	26.1	.12	35.00	MSQVG	6.00	0	6.10	6.40	27.2	-.82

Review

Suppose you wanted to structure a bear put on this stock.

7. Which month would you choose? Why?

8. Where would you place the long put? Why?
   If you chose a 25 strike for the short put:

9. What is the maximum risk for this trade?

10. What is the maximum reward for this trade?

11. What is the primary exit for this trade—the actual dollar amount you need to achieve?

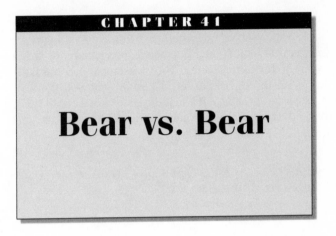

CHAPTER 41

Bear vs. Bear

"Now let's compare these bearish trades just as we compared the bullish ones," said Aaron. "To begin with, of course, both are basically bearish trades; but one, the bear call, is a credit trade, and the other, the bear put, is a debit trade. Just as with the bullish trades, everything about these bearish trades follows from the difference between a debit and a credit strategy."

"We know, for example," said Nate, "that because the bear call is a credit trade, the primary instrument has to be the one we *sell*: it'll be the short instrument. And, of course, in the case of a bear call, that means it will be the short call."

"Right," said Lon, "the credit we receive for this short call is the way we make money in this trade. And since we don't want to go in the money on this short call, we definitely place it out of the money—and not just *slightly* out of the money either. We want to *stay* out of the money and simply pocket this credit at the end of the expiration period."

"All this means," added Shorty, "is that our limiting instrument will be the long call, and we place it further out of the money than the short call. And because it's placed further out of the money, it's less expensive. So, in this case, we're taking in more than we're paying out: and, of course, that's what it means for this to be a credit trade. We're starting out with a *net credit*."

"And how do we make a profit in this credit trade?" asked Nate.

"Our profit is simply this net credit—the credit we received minus what we paid for the long call," answered Shorty. "So all we're trying to do in this bear call is protect this profit that we start with. We just want both options to expire worthless and be finished. And, of course, that's why this trade also works in a stagnant trend: whether the stock is falling or staying stagnant doesn't matter as long as it just stays lower than our strike price and thus stays out of the money. Either way, we keep our credit without having to buy shares on the open market just so we can sell them, at a loss, at the strike price we agreed to. It's just the nature of a credit trade—how we make profit—that it will work in a stagnant trend as well as a bearish one."

> *If we remember that the bear call is a credit trade, we can figure practically everything else out.*

"And all of this means," added Lon, "that we want a short time period—we always want the options to expire in the current month. We don't want enough time for either a stagnant or bearish trend to go bullish on us. So the shorter the time frame, the better."

"So, see?" asked Nate. "Simply by knowing that this is a credit trade we know a lot of other things: (1) the short call will be our primary instrument; (2) we'll place it out of the money; (3) the long call will be our limiting instrument and it will be placed further out of the money; (4) we make a profit by simply keeping the net credit we start with; (5) the trade will work in either a bearish or a stagnant trend; and (6) we want a short time frame."

"Now we can do the same thing with the bear put," said Aaron. "If we remember that it is a debit trade we can figure practically everything else out."

"Right," said Lon. "We're using the long put as the primary instrument to make money. As a result, we place it only slightly out of the money so that it will go *in* the money and generate a profit as the stock price falls. And, of course, that's why it's expensive: strike prices that are slightly out of the money are always more expensive than those that are further out."

"And that's why this is a debit trade," summarized Nate. "We are buying this expensive option rather than selling it. Of course, we do sell an option—in this case, we place a short put. But because the short put is used primarily to limit risk, we place it further out of the money and therefore it's less expensive. And that's why we start out in the hole in this trade—what we're buying is more expensive than what we're selling. That's what it means for this to be a debit trade."

> *So if we remember that the bear put is a debit trade, we can figure practically everything else out.*

"Because we know this is a debit trade," said Aaron, "we also know how we make a profit: it's by having the spread between the value of the long put and the value of the short put *grow*. When it grows enough to give us a 20 to 25 percent profit, we close the deal and move on."

"Right," added Shorty, "and we're going to close it by selling the long put and buying back the short put. That's what we do when the spread reaches this 20 to 25 percent return. And, of course, this means that we want *time* in the trade. We need enough time for the stock to go bearish enough that it will create this profitable spread. So we want a minimum of 45 days for this trade, and often much longer."

"So if we remember that the bear put is a debit trade," said Aaron, "we can figure practically everything else out: (1) the long put will be our primary instrument; (2) it will be placed slightly out of the money; (3) the short put will be our limiting instrument and it will be placed further out of the money; (4) we make a profit by having the spread between the value of the long put and the value of the short put grow enough to give us a 20 to 25 percent return; (5) this will work only in a bearish trend; and (6) we need time value in the trade."

"Here's what these two bearish trades look like if we represent them both on one option chain," said Aaron. (See Figure 41.1.)

"So just as with the bullish spread trades, each bear trade has its pluses and minuses," said Nate. "The bear put can take more time and it requires a strong bearish move to create the necessary spread, but it does make the most of a bearish movement. The bear call will often make less, but it works in two trends and it has a quick turnaround time. You just choose which direction you prefer. The bear put might

BEAR CALL   BEAR PUT

Jan 09 Calls							DELL@24.92					Jan 09 Puts	
VPZAC	10.30	0	10.90	11.10	42.4	.93	15.00	VPZMC	0.50		Short Put	44.9	-.08
VPZAW	9.2		0.90	9.10	40.9	.88	17.50	VPZMW	0.80	-0.05	.90	41.9	-.13
VPZAD	7	Short Call	7.00	7.20	38.1	.81	20.00	VPZMD	1.35	-0.05	1.35 1.45	39.8	-.20
VPZAX	5.50	+1.00	5.40	5.60	36.9	.72	22.50	VPZMX	2.10	-0.35	2.10 2.20	37.8	-.28
VPZAE	4.05	+0.25	4.00	4.10	34.9	.62	25.00	VPZME	3.25	-0.05	3.10 3.30	36.8	-.38
VPZAY	2.81		2.85	2.95	33.5	.51	27.50	VPZMY	4.48	-0.	Long Put 00	35.9	-.48
VPZAF	2.00	Long Call	2.00	2.10	32.8	.41	30.00	VPZMF	6.20		00	35.9	-.57
VPZAG	0.90	0	0.90	0.95	31.3	.23	35.00	VPZMG	10.90	0	10.10 10.30	40.2	-.69

FIGURE 41.1 The Two Bearish Trades
Source: Screenshot courtesy of optionsXpress, Inc. © 2008.

Credit Trade

1. Short call is primary instrument.
2. It is placed OTM.
3. Long call is limiting instrument and is placed further OTM.
4. Profit mechanism: start out with a net credit and keep it.
5. Stagnant to bearish trends.
6. Needs *short* time frame.

Debit Trade

1. Long put is primary instrument.
2. It is placed slightly OTM.
3. Short put is limiting instrument and is placed further OTM.
4. Profit mechanism: spread between the two options grows, turning starting net debit into 20 25 percent return.
5. Bearish trend only.
6. Needs time value.

be best in a strong bearish trend, but it *requires* a strong bearish trend to create the necessary spread for a profit. The bear call, however, is more flexible; all it requires is that something *not* happen—that the stock not go bullish—and it is closed more quickly. You just go with what you're most comfortable with at a given time, all things considered."

"And obviously," said Aaron, "you have to paper trade these strategies just like you paper trade the bullish ones. There's nothing like practice to familiarize you with how they work. So practice, practice, practice . . . and the good news is, it's always fun to practice."

"Yeah, a lot more fun that losing real money," said Shorty.

"That's right. So get good before using any of that stuff. Let's start by completing this review."

REVIEW

The bear put is a _____ trade. That means the _____ is the _____ instrument and it is placed slightly _____. The _____ is the _____ instrument and it is placed _____ the money. The bear put makes profit as the _____ between _____ grows. This is effective for a _____ trend and needs _____.

The bear call is a _____ trade. That means the _____ is the _____ instrument and it is placed _____. The _____ is the limiting _____ and it is placed further _____ the money. The bear call makes profit because of the _____

we _____ with. This is effective for _____
to _____ trends and needs a
short _____.

"I've got a problem." It was Lon, sitting forward in his chair in full frown mode.

Getting Started

CHAPTER 42

Lifting the Fog

"What's the problem?"

"Well, how do I remember all these trades? How do I organize them in my mind? Right now they're just a jumble of terms—*bull puts, bear calls, bear puts, bull calls.* I can't keep them straight. I can see the pieces, but I can't see the whole picture. I can't make sense of it all. It's like I'm in a thick fog: I know the world makes sense, but that doesn't help me much if I can't *see* it."

"I feel the same way," said Shorty. "I can't see the thread that would help me remember what a bull put is. Or a bear call. Or any of them. Right now, it seems like I'll have to look up the definition every time someone uses one of those terms. I hate that. I'd like to understand what's going on so that I can remember what the terms mean intuitively, or at least be able to figure them out."

"I know what you mean," answered Nate. "When I learned all this, I learned it through constant exposure and brute force. It was hard. But I think we can make it easier for you. Let me begin by asking you some questions, okay?"

"Sure."

"First, what trend do we normally associate with a *call* instrument?"

"Well, I would say a bullish trend," answered Lon. "I know we can use a short call to optimize other trends, but calls are often thought of in terms of long calls, and long calls optimize bullish trends."

"Good. So it seems logical to put the terms *bull* and *call* together, doesn't it? It makes sense that we're going to use calls to optimize a bullish movement, right?"

"Right."

"So, what about a put instrument? What trend do we normally associate with puts?"

"I would say a bearish trend. Of course, short puts can be used to make the most of other trends, but normally puts are thought of in terms of long puts, and long puts optimize bearish trends."

"That's right. So it seems logical to put the terms *bear* and *put* together. That's intuitive. It makes sense that we're going to use puts to optimize a bearish movement. Right?"

"Right. I see that."

"So," added Aaron, "these terms seem logical on their face: *bull call* and *bear put*. And notice what they have in common: both are debit trades. Both start out in the hole—with a net debit—and rely on movement in the market to make money. The bull call relies on a bullish trend, and the bear put relies on a bearish trend. And both make sense when you hear them. *Bull* goes with *call*, and *bear* goes with *put*."

> *If you remember that they're debit trades, you can figure out everything else about them.*

"So you're saying," observed Lon, "that one way to remember the bull call and the bear put is (1) to notice that they make sense, and (2) to remember that if they make sense they're debit trades. Is that right?"

"Yes, that's right. And if you remember that they're debit trades, you can figure out everything else about them. So it's a huge clue."

"But," said Nate, "that brings us to the bull put and the bear call. From the way we just talked, both of these sound contradictory, don't they? Using puts to optimize a bullish trend? And using calls to optimize a bearish trend? Both sound odd, even, as I just said, contradictory on the surface. And notice what they have in common: both are *credit* trades. Both start out with a net credit and we simply want to protect that net credit by having both options expire worthless in a short time frame."

"So in this case," said Shorty, "you're saying that one way to remember the bear call and the bull put is (1) to notice that they don't make obvious sense—they sound contradictory—and (2) to remember that if they sound contradictory on the surface they're credit trades. And knowing that they're credit trades allows us to figure everything else out about them, right?"

"Right," said Aaron. "The terms that sound logical are debit trades, and the terms that sound contradictory are credit trades. Just by knowing this, you can remember that the bull call and bear put are debit trades, and that the bull put and bear call are credit trades. Everything else simply follows from this."

"And to demonstrate this, let me ask you a question," said Nate. "What is the primary instrument in a debit trade—the instrument we use to make money?"

"Well, it's the long instrument, the one we buy," answered Shorty.

"How do you know that?"

"Well, just because it's a debit trade . . . which means we start out in the hole. The option we're buying has to be more expensive than the option we're selling if we're in the hole."

"And obviously that means that the limiting instrument is the short option," said Lon.

"Right. So which one gets placed further out of the money? The long option or the short option?"

"The short option. That has to be, because the less expensive option has to be further out of the money than the more expensive option. That's the way the option chain works."

"Okay, good," said Nate. "So now what about a credit trade? What's the primary instrument—the one used for making money—in that case?"

"It's the short instrument."

"How do you know that?"

"Just because it's a credit trade . . . which means that we start out ahead, with a net credit. The option we're selling has to be more expensive than the option we're buying if we start out ahead."

> *If you know just a couple of elements, you can figure everything else out easily.*

"And, of course, that means that the limiting instrument is the long option."

"So in a credit trade, which option gets placed further out of the money?"

"The long option. That has to be, again, because the less expensive option has to be further out of the money than the more expensive one. That's the way the option chain works."

FIGURE 42.1 Trends and Trades

"See, you've got it," said Aaron. "If you know just a couple of elements, you can figure everything else out easily. That's good. So let's put all this in a chart, like the one in Figure 42.1."

"Once you know the trend and the type of trade, it's easy to fill in the rest. Just remember that the credit trades sound a bit counterintuitive and the debit trades sound logical. The rest is easy."

RISK AND REWARD IN THE DEBIT SPREAD TRADES

"It will also be easy," said Nate, "to remember how to calculate the risk and reward for the debit trades when you realize that you calculate both of them exactly the same way. Whether it's a bull call or a bear put, you calculate everything the same way just because they're both debit strategies."

"Right," added Aaron. "Just remember that you always start by calculating the net debit first. You're buying an option and selling an option, and the one you're buying is more expensive than the one you're selling. So the first thing you do is calculate that difference; that's the net debit in the trade, and that net debit is your risk. It's the most you can lose. Simple."

"Yes," said Nate, "and then to calculate your maximum reward, you simply start with the difference between the two strike prices you've chosen, and then subtract the net debit from that. That tells you the maximum you can *make* on the deal. Again, it's simple, and you do it the same way for both debit trades, the bull call and the bear put."

RISK AND REWARD IN THE CREDIT SPREAD TRADES

"Let me handle the credit trades, okay?" asked Shorty. "They're even easier."

"Sure. Go for it."

"All right. Well, we're still buying one option and selling another, but in these credit trades—the bear call and the bull put—the option we're selling is more expensive than the one we're buying. That gives us a net credit to start with, and that's the first thing we need to calculate."

"Right," added Lon, "and that net credit tells us our maximum reward in the trade. The net credit we start out with *constitutes* the maximum we can make."

"Yes, and once we know that net credit, we also use it to determine our risk. We do that by subtracting it from the difference in the two strike prices. So the difference in strike prices minus the net credit tells us our maximum risk."

"So just as with the debit trades," said Aaron, "we calculate these two credit trades in exactly the same way. For both the bear call and the bull put, we start by calculating the net credit and figure everything else out from there."

"Good," said Nate, "and we can represent this all in a simple table. Let me draw it out for you." (See Figure 42.2.)

"When I was first learning," said Aaron, "and once I got past the 'brute force' stage, I discovered it was easiest for me to remember that in credit trades the net credit always constitutes the reward. I could remember that much, and that was enough because I found that I could figure everything else out from there. For example, if the net credit is the reward, then I automatically know that I'll figure the risk by using the difference in the strike prices . . . and then it dawns on me that I'm supposed to subtract the net credit from that. Voila! I have the risk."

	DEBIT *(Bull call, bear put)*	CREDIT *(Bear call, bull put)*
Risk	Net debit	Difference in strikes minus net credit
Reward	Difference in strikes minus net debit	Net credit

FIGURE 42.2 Remembering Risk and Reward

"And then we figure the debit trades from there," added Nate. "I remember that the 'net' stuff applies to the *risk* in debit trades, not the reward. It's the opposite of the credit trades. I also know that we're talking debit trades here, so it's the net *debit* I'm concerned with. And that tells me the risk because the net debit *is* the risk. Then I remember that I figure the reward by using the difference in the strike prices, and again it dawns on me that I'm supposed to subtract the net debit (it's a debit trade after all) from that. Like magic, I have the reward."

> *All you need is one part of the table that is most intuitive and obvious to you, and you can figure everything else out from there.*

"Now it might seem difficult," said Aaron, "hearing it laid out like that, but it's not. Both of you can do it. You might have a starting place that makes more sense to you, and that's fine. All you need is one part of the table that is most intuitive and obvious to you, and you can figure everything else out from there. It doesn't matter where you start. So trust me; you can do it."

"And here's your chance," added Nate. "Completing this chart will be part of your review."

REVIEW

"First fill in the following chart."

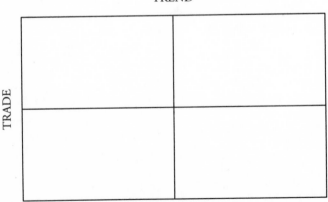

TREND

TRADE

"Now fill in this one."

TRADE		
	DEBIT *(Bull Call, Bear Put)*	CREDIT *(Bear Call, Bull Put)*
RISK		
REWARD		Net credit

Review

CHAPTER 43

The Launch

Nate closed his notebook/binder/notes/whatever with a satisfying thump. "That's it," he announced. "We've gone through everything I had hoped to teach you."

Lon glanced at Shorty, who was suddenly grinning from ear to ear. "I'm exhausted," Lon said, "but Shorty looks pretty pleased with himself over there."

"Well, I am!" Shorty laughed. "Not long ago Lon and I were just making stuff up, and now we know how to spread trade like experts."

Nate laughed but Aaron was quick to object. "Okay, okay, you do have a good foundation, but you're not exactly experts. After all, you haven't actually made any trades yet, and besides, there are a lot more trades we haven't taught you at all."

"Don't rain on my parade, Aaron." Shorty wagged a finger at him. "We know the option instruments and how they work, strike prices, option chains, the technical indicators, a basic idea of the option industry—*and a lot more*. Plus, we can do, what, five spread trades on our own? I feel fabulous. For the first time, I really feel like I can reach financial independence."

Even Lon had to nod at that. "That's right," he said. "I'm mostly thinking about what I don't know, but even so, I feel more confident about handling my money now than I ever have before."

"That's because now you know how to do it without fear of losing your shirt," Nate pointed out. "I can't emphasize enough how important this whole concept of spread trading is. The average investor in the stock market is ruled by fear, always wondering, 'Did I buy at the right time? Did I sell too soon? Did I pick the right companies?' They're miserable because they can't control the market; all they can do is risk their hard-earned money on guesses.

> *But when we spread trade, we can actually control how things turn out.*

"But when we spread trade, we can actually control how things turn out. We just structure a deal so that it has a risk we can live with and a reward we can live with, and then we're okay no matter what the market does. Investing without fear is the great dream of everyone who's ever played the stock market, and voila! It was possible all along."

"I never get over it," said Aaron. "Like Nate said earlier, it's the best deal on the planet, and virtually no one knows about it. Only a percentage of investors trade options, and an even smaller percentage trade options using spread concepts. It's unbelievable to me."

"Well, add us to the list," said Shorty. "This is what we're going to be doing from now on."

"Good for you. And you're off to an impressive start. All you really need now is to prepare and to practice."

FOUR ELEMENTS OF PREPARATION

"You need to do these four things," he continued.

"First, you should constantly review all of the elements of trading options that you've learned. The best way to do this is to review all the Review notes you've made. Take this one, for instance." (See Figure 43.1) Nate wrote on the whiteboard.

"You should be able to fill in the blanks pretty quickly . . . and doing so is the very practice that will help you keep the ideas fresh."

"Or take this one," said Aaron, also writing on the board. "You should be able to fill this in quickly, too." (See Figure 43.2.)

"And this one." (See Figure 43.3.)

"Well, you get the idea. Go over your Review notes frequently—until all this is second nature to you. The Review notes will keep you fresh."

"Second," said Aaron, "carefully choose the stocks you will put your money into. Remember what we look for."

"Right," said Shorty. "We look for at least 10 percent growth rates in sales, earnings per share, and equity. We also look for a return on invested capital of at least 10 percent per year."

INSTRUMENT	WHAT IT DOES FOR US	TREND	RISK
Long Call	Leverages a bullish trend	Bullish	
		Stagnant to slightly bearish	Unlimited (if naked), or have to sell shares
Short Put			Have to buy shares

FIGURE 43.1 Option Instruments: Basic Characteristics

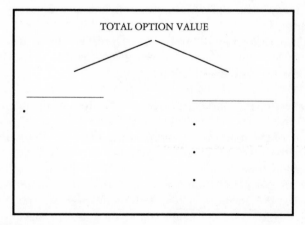

FIGURE 43.2 Option Value

TREND

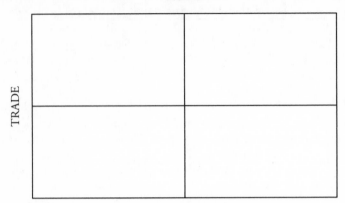

FIGURE 43.3 Trends and Trades

"Yes," added Lon, "and we also want a debt-to-equity ratio of 1.0 or less. And we also want the stock to be selling at or below the intrinsic value of the company. We generally want to steer clear of companies whose shares are overpriced—at least compared to other companies in the same industry. Better to work with strong companies that are underpriced, or at least fairly priced."

"Exactly. Those kinds of companies form the backbone of everything we do in the market. Also, you will only trade a handful of companies at a time, but you should have 15 to 20 like this that you're watching."

"Okay, third," said Nate, "is to get proficient at watching your stocks *and* the market."

"Right," Lon interrupted, "and we watch our stocks by watching their trends and by looking at the technical signals: the RSI, the EMA, and the MACD. I guess we should look at those daily."

"Right."

"And we watch the market," said Shorty, "by following three major indicators: the Dow Jones, the S&P 500, and the Nasdaq. And we pay attention to the 'mood' of the market by looking at the VIX and the total put-to-call ratio. I guess these are all things we should do regularly, if not daily. None of them take any time."

"That's all correct. I would only add that you should also create a calendar for the earnings dates of the stocks you're in. You can get these easily from *OptionsAnimal* and you *have* to pay attention to them."

"Finally," said Aaron, "make sure you chart the way we showed you and then that you paper trade at length. Remember, you can trade with $10,000 or $1 million. Just do it, and have fun.

"And remember," he continued, "once you get comfortable with the individual instruments, then build your paper trades around the *idea* of the collar trade. If you're placing a covered call, think explicitly about when you would add a protective put. If you're placing only a protective put, think explicitly about why you're not in a covered call as well. Always think in terms of the collar. That's the philosophy of the way we trade. So train yourself to always take that approach."

"And then include the other spread strategies in your paper trading as well," added Nate. "Get familiar with what happens in bull calls, bear puts, bear calls, and bull puts. The best way to do that is to paper trade and see what happens as stock trends fluctuate."

"Right," added Aaron, "and make sure you paper trade *a lot*. You should be successful in 7 out of every 10 trades before you even think about using real money. That may seem daunting, but it's not. Believe me, you'll be able to do it if you learn and if you apply what you learn."

ATTITUDE

"Now in addition to all this," said Aaron, "I want to emphasize a critical attitude you must have in spread trading. It's an attitude you've already heard us emphasize, and it's the very foundation of spread trading: *never try to make as much money as you can on any one deal*. It's far better to make a lot of 20 to 25 percent deals than to hold out for one blockbuster—a blockbuster that can just as easily turn into a disaster."

"That's right." Nate sat forward, his voice low and serious. "Gambling is a fool's game; it's a bad way to trade and a bad way to live. *And* there's no need for it. So don't be stupid. Stay away from 'hope,' from greed, from anything that will keep you from making steady, responsible trades that will add up over a little time to something magnificent . . . and all without fear."

"Which is why," added Aaron, "we always talk about the 'exits' for a trade. See, many people want to enter a trade and just 'see how it goes,' and make their minds up along the way about what to do. There's no surer sign of being ruled by 'hope' or greed than this. And believe me, it's bad. Whether we admit it or not, it means we're swinging for the fences . . . and *that* means we're very likely to strike out."

"It's a risky way to deal with money. Ridiculously risky." Nate was still sitting forward in his chair. "So no, we always enter a trade with the decision already made about how and when we will exit it. We set the terms conservatively, and we stick to them. That's something you *have* to begin in your paper trading. If you don't, you'll be practicing how to fail, and we want you practicing how to succeed. So always identify your exit before entering a trade, including your paper trades."

We know we have information that can make life better—less stressful, less fearful, more successful.

"Okay, have we emphasized that enough?" asked Aaron.

"I think so. It seems clear to me."

"Me, too."

"All right, then if you don't do what we say, and you lose money (either pretend or real), you have only yourselves to blame. Agreed?"

"Agreed."

Lon paused for a moment. "Nate, Aaron, speaking for both of us, we can't thank you enough. It's been more than I expected. By far."

"Yeah, I'm kind of worried about how we can pay you back," added Shorty. "What would you like? My car? My house?"

"Nah, don't worry about it," answered Nate. "It's actually been fun for us to teach two novices. Normally, we're teaching people who have more experience, and we usually have to *un*teach them a lot of things. Old habits are hard to break, you know. So it's actually been refreshing to spend this time with you two.

"One more thing before we finish our time together," he continued. "We've taught you some important things, and we think you've learned them well. But we didn't do this just for fun." He looked at Aaron, who nodded. "We really came here to help. We know we have information that can make life better—less stressful, less fearful, more successful. We like to be able to share that knowledge with people who can use it wisely."

"It may sound corny, but it's true," Aaron agreed, smiling a little self-consciously. "Most people don't associate option traders with philanthropy, but here we are. Spread trading can remove so much financial fear from your lives, like it has from ours. We hate to see people try to gain financial security by following methods that are themselves completely *insecure*. Especially when we know there's a better way."

WHAT WE WISH

"When we heard about what you two were doing," Nate continued, "when we decided to come here, Aaron and I talked about four things we wished you to get out of our time together. Before we leave, we'd like to tell you what those things are, and what motivated us to come to you.

"The first wish we have for you is that you face the future with confidence. If you know how to make money in the market there's no reason for you to be fearful about what the future holds—to avoid thinking about it,

or to pin all your hopes on the possibility that someone else will take care
of you in your old age."

"Right," said Aaron. "When you know how to spread trade, none of
that is necessary. You don't need to fear and you don't need to depend on
others. You can be confident and self-reliant. That's significant in this day
and age, and it's a hope we have for you."

> *This change feels almost like a gift. It's liberating.*

"The second wish," said Nate, "is that you understand the genuine opportunity that the stock market offers. It's not a gambling den, as some
picture it (and as some unfortunately use it), where you either hit it big or
lose your shirt, based simply on whether your timing is good or not. No,
when we understand spread trading, we see the market very differently."

"In fact," said Aaron, "our outlook undergoes something of a paradigm
shift. We see the market as an opportunity to make money *without gambling at all*. I think that shift in perspective is important. It means we can
trade without greed, and we can trade without fear. To me, this change
feels almost like a gift. It's liberating. It's certainly transformed how I live.

"And the third wish," he continued, "is that you understand the need
for mental and emotional discipline in trading. It's what you have to have
if you're going to operate with the correct attitude—if you're going to com-
pile small success into huge gains over time."

"That's so important," Nate said emphatically. "Without this discipline
you won't be able to trade this way; you'll find yourself emotionally way up
at times and emotionally way down at other times. Trading without fear?
Not you. So that's why you need such discipline; it's why you always identify your exits *before* you enter a trade. It's what allows you to live without
greed. And that's what allows you to live without fear."

"And fourth," said Aaron, "we want you to understand that *knowledge
is power*. We've tried to share some tools with you over the last three
nights, and also some knowledge about how to use them. Well, we can't
emphasize too much how important such knowledge is."

"Think about it," said Nate. "Consider the fact that practically any nin-
compoop can take a set of screwdrivers and wrenches and take a car apart.
Name the car. It doesn't matter. With the right basic tools, anyone can dis-
mantle it. But what we want to ask is, How many nincompoops could take
those same screwdrivers and wrenches and put the car back together?"

"See," added Aaron, "it's not enough just to have the right tools ... to
have them lying around. We also have to know how to *use* them. Well,

we've tried to help you with that. You now have the fundamentals—the tools are lying around, so to speak—*and* you know how to use them, at least in theory."

"Right," said Nate. "There's only one thing you need now: the greater knowledge, the practical knowledge, that can only come with practice. That's the next step, and you're ready for it. You need to choose stocks, watch the stocks move, watch the market move, follow all this regularly, and, based on all your information, make frequent paper trades. Just use the virtual trading site at *OptionsAnimal* as we've already shown you. That's it."

"All this will lay a great foundation for you," added Aaron. "There are a lot of nuances and additional spread strategies you can learn, but this is the starting point for them all. Do what Nate just said and you will both (1) make money safely and (2) lay the foundation for even more spread strategies. So watch the market, chart, master the option instruments, make paper trades, and all the rest—and have fun doing it!"

"Well, I certainly feel ready for that," announced Shorty. "Not to make actual spread trades yet, but definitely to dive into paper trading the way you've taught us."

"Me too," said Lon. "And Cass'll be happy I'm not using real money. She's kind of nervous about that. Don't know why, but she is."

"Well, I know why," laughed Shorty.

"All right. All right."

"The only thing I would ask," Nate said seriously once the laughter died away, "is that you begin charting call and put performance and paper trading right away. The sooner you start, the sooner you'll be good at it. That's what I'd like to see."

"That's enough for me, too," said Aaron.

"Okay, then we're on it," agreed Shorty. "We'll start immediately. Tomorrow for me."

"Me, too," added Lon. He was grinning widely, gazing upward.

"You actually seem a little *too* happy about this," said Nate, puzzled by Lon's grin and far-away look. "What are you thinking?"

"Well ... look, I hate to be so hard on my brother-in-law, but I was just thinking ... I'll never have to call myself 'Bruce' again! And I think I've finally put London, Nebraska, and that China trip behind me, too. Now I can start winning arguments around the house again."

It was true, they agreed: that *was* a lot to be happy about.

A smile fell on all, and Nate and Aaron stepped into the night.

Answers to End-of-Chapter Reviews

CHAPTER 3 ANSWERS

"I have <u>paid</u> a certain dollar amount to enter this trade. By doing so, I now have the <u>right to call out and buy 100 of Shorty's shares</u> for $40 if I want to. I also have the right to do this <u>anytime in the next six months</u>. I also have the right <u>not to call out his shares</u> if I don't want to; I can let my option expire. If I do, I <u>forfeit</u> the amount I paid to Shorty.

"Shorty, for his part, has <u>received</u> a certain dollar amount from me to enter this trade. By taking my money, he now has the obligation to <u>sell me his shares</u> for $40 if <u>I call them out</u>. Shorty has to do this if I exercise my option any time in <u>the next six months</u>. If I never exercise my option, Shorty still gets to <u>keep the $500</u> I have paid him."

CHAPTER 4 ANSWERS

"Lon has bought from me an <u>option</u> of a certain type. Because he has the right to <u>call out</u> or <u>buy my shares</u> at $40, this kind of option is called a <u>call</u>. The $40 amount we agreed to is called the <u>strike price</u>. Since Lon is buying this option, we say that he is <u>long</u>. Since I am selling this option, we say that I am <u>short</u>. Thus, from my end, this is a <u>short call</u> and from Lon's end, it is a <u>long call</u>. The $5 Lon is paying me is for him a <u>debit</u> and for me a <u>credit</u>. So we might say I am doing a <u>credit</u> trade and he is doing a <u>debit</u> trade. The whole trade might be called an option <u>contract</u>, and the date it ends is called the <u>expiration date</u>."

CHAPTER 5 ANSWERS

The chart of strike prices is based on the idea of the <u>lowest</u> strike price appearing <u>first</u> on the list. So as we read more strike prices, down the list, the strike prices get <u>higher</u>. Now, we've decided to name strike prices in terms of what is good for the person in the <u>long</u> position. Strike prices that are below the market price of the stock are called <u>in the money</u>. This is because they are worth <u>money</u> to me immediately. If I agree to a strike price that is below the market price, I can already <u>buy</u> low and sell <u>high</u> and that's what I am trying to do. In general, I want a deal that sets me <u>up</u> so that, sometime in the next six months, I can buy <u>low</u> and <u>sell</u> high. So an "in-the-money" strike price is one that is <u>lower</u> than the market price of the stock. By this same logic a strike price that is higher than the market price is <u>out of the money</u>, and a strike price that is the same as the market price is <u>at the money</u>."

CHAPTER 6 ANSWERS

"The <u>lower</u> the strike price, the better the chance that the strike price will end up <u>in the money</u> on this trade. This means Lon is willing to <u>pay more</u> for lower strike prices.

"On my end, the <u>lower</u> the strike price, the riskier the deal is for me: the <u>greater</u> the chance that Lon will end up in the money and call out my shares. So the <u>lower</u> the strike price, the <u>more</u> I will demand in a credit to make the trade.

"So it is the same for both of us: the <u>lower</u> the strike price, the <u>greater</u> the debit/credit amount will be involved in the trade.

"In call trades, there is an <u>inverse</u> relationship between <u>strike price</u> and <u>debit/credit</u> amount.

"For calls, at any given time, an in-the-money strike price is simply one that is <u>lower</u> than the market price. An out-of-the-money strike price is simply one that is <u>higher</u> than the market price. Whether a strike price is in our out of the money will <u>change</u> over time.

"For these calls, we can say that when the market price moves above the strike price, the strike price is <u>trending</u> in the money. By the same token, when the market price moves *below* the strike price, the strike price is <u>trending out of the money</u>.

"Being in the long position, Lon wants the strike price to <u>trend</u> in the money. Being in the short position, I want the strike price to <u>trend out of the money</u>."

CHAPTER 7 ANSWERS

"The longer the time frame I put around a trade, the greater the chances I will be able to buy low and sell high. So the longer the time frame, the lower my risk, and the greater the debit I will be willing to pay for it.

"For Shorty, the longer the time frame for the trade, the greater the risk in the trade: the more likely his shares will be called out by me. So the longer the time frame, the greater the credit Shorty will demand."

CHAPTER 8 ANSWERS

"If I exercise my option and call out Shorty's shares, my cost basis in this trade will be $45. It is made up of the strike price plus the debit I paid. This establishes my breakeven point. This is the point I have to get over if I'm to make any profit in the deal. My maximum potential reward is theoretically unlimited. The way I calculate my *realistic* potential reward is to add the agreed-upon strike price to the debit I paid, and subtract this total from a realistic market price. In other words: market price minus (strike price + debit).

"My maximum risk in this trade is $5. It is made up of the debit I paid to Shorty. I will lose this amount if the strike price stays out of the money, which means that the market price doesn't get higher than the strike price.

I won't call out Shorty's shares if the strike price never goes in the money (if the market price never goes higher than the strike price of $40). In that case, I realize the maximum risk; I lose my $5 debit. I will definitely call out Shorty's shares at some point if the market price goes above my breakeven point. At that point, I make a profit; I just want the market price to go as high as possible in the time I have. If I run out of time—if the expiration date is close—I will call out Shorty's shares even if the market price is not above the breakeven price, as long as it's above the *strike price*. That way I can at least reduce my losses."

"The more time I have on my side, the better my chances of the market price getting higher than the strike price, which means being in the money.

"The less time I have on my side, the better the chances of the market price staying lower than the agreed-upon strike price, which means it is out of the money. Then I realize my maximum risk."

CHAPTER 9 ANSWERS

"Let's suppose the Plum stock price moves up and goes higher than our strike price. In that case, Lon will call out my shares. So I will lose those shares but I will keep the $5 credit. So if Lon exercises his option and calls out my shares, my reward in this trade will be $5. If the stock price never moves higher than our strike price, Lon won't call out my shares. His option will expire. In that case, I will keep the credit, plus I won't lose my shares.

"So my maximum risk in this trade is to lose my shares of stock. But, even then, he pays me a total of $45 for them.

"The shorter the time frame for this trade, the greater my chances of the market price staying higher than the strike price. If that happens, I won't lose my shares.

"I ought to consider time as well as credit amount in determining the value of a trade."

CHAPTER 12 ANSWERS

"I will pay a certain dollar amount to enter this trade. By doing so, I will have the right to put my shares to you for $40 if I want to. I will also have the right to do this by whatever expiration date we agree on. I also have the right not to put my shares to you if I don't want to; I can let my option expire. If I do, I forfeit the amount I paid to you.

"You will receive a certain dollar amount, or credit from me to enter this trade. By taking my money, you will have the obligation to buy 100 of my shares at the strike price of $40 if I put them over to you. You will have to do this if I exercise my option any time in the next six months. If I never exercise my option, you still get to keep the credit."

CHAPTER 13 ANSWERS

"Again, the chart of strike prices is based on the idea of the lowest strike price appearing first on the list. So as we read more strike prices, down the list, the strike prices get higher. Now we decided to name strike prices in terms of what is good for the person who is long. In the case of puts, strike prices that are higher than the market price of the stock are called in the money. This is because they are worth money to me immediately. If the stock price moves lower than the strike price, then I am able to buy low and sell <u>high</u>, *but in reverse order:* I first <u>sell</u> to you at the <u>higher</u> strike price, and then I'm able to <u>buy</u> shares on the open market <u>at the</u> <u>lower</u> market price. So an "in-the-money" strike price, for puts, is one that is <u>higher than</u> the market price of the stock. By this same logic, a strike price that is <u>lower</u> than the market price is <u>out of the money</u>. A strike price that is the same as the market price is <u>at the money</u>.

"The <u>higher</u> the strike price, the better the chance that it will end up in the money on this put trade. This means I am willing to <u>pay more</u> for higher strike prices.

"On your end, the <u>higher</u> the strike price, the riskier the deal is: the <u>greater</u> the chance that <u>it will</u> end up in the money and I will call out your shares. So the <u>higher</u> the strike price, the <u>more</u> you will demand in a credit to make the trade.

"So it is the same for both of us when it comes to put trades: the <u>higher</u> the strike price, the <u>greater</u> the debit/credit amount will be involved <u>in the</u> trade.

"And this chart showing the relationship between strike prices and debit/credit amounts, for both calls and puts, is now called an <u>option chain</u>.

"Finally, because I am doing a debit trade—I am buying—we can say I am placing a <u>long put</u>. And since you are doing a credit trade—you are selling—we can say you are placing a <u>short put</u>."

CHAPTER 14 ANSWERS

"The longer the time frame I put around a trade, the <u>greater</u> the chances I will be able to <u>sell</u> high and <u>buy</u> low. So the longer the time frame, the <u>less</u> my risk, and the <u>greater</u> the debit I will be willing to pay for it.

"For you, the longer the time frame for the trade, the <u>greater</u> the risk in the trade: the more likely I am to <u>put my shares</u> to you <u>and force</u> <u>you to buy them</u>. So the <u>longer</u> the time frame, the <u>greater</u> the credit you will <u>demand</u>."

CHAPTER 15 ANSWERS

"Another term for my long put is a <u>protective put</u> because it <u>protects</u> the stock I own. The <u>cost basis</u> for my trade with Shorty is calculated by adding the <u>debit</u> I paid to Shorty to the price of <u>the stock</u> I already own.

"Because I am paying a <u>debit</u>, this might be called a <u>debit</u> trade.

"My maximum possible reward is calculated by considering what would happen if the market price of the stock went to <u>zero</u>. Based on that, I calculate my maximum possible reward by starting with my <u>strike price</u> and subtracting from it the <u>debit</u> I paid to Shorty.

"My potential reward is <u>capped</u> by the <u>strike price</u> Shorty and I agreed to. He is not obligated to <u>buy</u> my shares at a price <u>higher</u> than that. The reward potential for a long call is <u>theoretically unlimited</u>, but for a long put it is <u>capped</u>. The difference is that <u>with a long put the strike price</u> determines where I <u>sell</u> and with a long call the strike price determines where I buy.

"My maximum risk in this trade is <u>$1.50</u>. It is made up of <u>the debit</u> I paid to Shorty. I will lose this if the <u>strike price</u> stays <u>out of the money</u>, which means that the <u>stock</u> price doesn't get higher than the <u>strike</u> price."

CHAPTER 16 ANSWERS

"Because I am taking in a <u>credit</u> from Lon, this might be called a <u>credit</u> trade. My maximum reward is this <u>credit</u>. If the strike price stays out of the money, it will be <u>lower</u> than the market price. In that case, Lon won't <u>put his shares</u> to me and I will still get to keep the credit he has paid me. If the strike price trends in the money, it will be <u>higher</u> than the market price. In that case, Lon can <u>put his shares over</u> to me for a price of <u>$35</u>. So my risk in this trade is calculated by subtracting <u>the credit I received</u> from our <u>strike</u> price, which just means that I can end up owning <u>stock</u> I <u>like</u> at a price of <u>$33.50</u>.

CHAPTER 19 ANSWERS

1. Left-hand side
2. Right-hand side
3. $0.65
4. $0.30
5. $0.40
6. $0.60
7. $25 to $28. They are called *in the money* because they are below the stock price: If I bought the stock at any of these prices, I would be buying below the market price—which means they have monetary value for me immediately.

8. $29 to $35. They are called *in the money* because they are above the stock price: If I sold the stock at any of these prices, I would be selling above the market price—which means they have monetary value for me immediately.

9. $0.55 ($0.70 – $0.15)

10. $0.80 ($1.10 – $0.30)

CHAPTER 20 ANSWERS

1. $35, $37.50; $35 to $42.50
2. $40 to $47.50; $45 to $47.50
3a. $6
3b. $6.80
3c. $0.80
4a. $3.80
4b. $2
4c. $1.80
5a. $2
5b. I just keep the $2 credit
6a. $0.75
6b. I just keep the $0.75 credit
7a. $3.
7b. I just keep the $3 credit

CHAPTER 21 ANSWERS

1. $4,435
2. $565
3. 12.7% ($565/$4435)
4. $620
5. $480 ($11 – $6.20 = $4.80 × 100 shares = $480)
6. 77% ($480/$620)

CHAPTER 22 ANSWERS

"It's far better to make a lot of <u>20%</u> deals than to hold out for one or two <u>big</u> deals. Your goal is <u>never</u> to make as much money as you can on <u>any one</u> deal.

"If I place a short call on stock I <u>don't</u> already own, and if the <u>strike price</u> goes in the money—if the market price goes <u>higher</u> than the <u>strike price</u>—then I will have to go out on the market and <u>buy</u> shares at the <u>higher</u> market price and turn around and sell them at the <u>lower</u> strike price I agreed to. I <u>never</u> want to do that."

CHAPTER 23 ANSWERS

1. Should I be <u>long</u> in the stock?
2. What is the <u>trend</u> of this stock, and what do I <u>expect</u> the trend to be?
3. What combination of <u>option instruments</u> should I use?
4. What should the <u>strike price</u> be for each <u>instrument</u> I use in the trade?
5. What <u>time frame</u> should I use for each <u>instrument</u> I use in the trade?
6. What are my <u>exit points</u> for each trade? How do I decide when to <u>get out</u>?

CHAPTER 24 ANSWERS

"Each <u>day</u> that goes by without the stock going up enough to put the strike in the money, the <u>less</u> the chances are that it will <u>ever</u> go <u>in the money</u>. It now has one less <u>day</u> to do so—so the odds are <u>reduced</u> one day's worth.

"Most <u>time decay</u> will occur in the <u>last</u> three months, and most of that in the <u>last</u> month. So <u>time decay</u> isn't steady; it <u>accelerates</u> toward the <u>end</u>."

"For both calls and puts, the greater the time frame, the <u>greater</u> the likelihood that the option will go in the money. This means, other things equal, that <u>longer</u> time frames are <u>less</u> risky for Lon and <u>more</u> risky for Shorty.

"For both calls and puts, the <u>longer</u> the time frame, the higher the <u>bid/ask</u> amounts for strike prices."

CHAPTER 25 ANSWERS

1. January 2009
2. $5.70
3. $3.73; $1.97
4. $5.50
5. $1.27; $4.23
6. $3.80
7. $1.27; $2.53

CHAPTER 26 ANSWERS

"If we want to finish out of the money—for example, because we want to keep our shares—we need to start out of the money. That's one reason for placing our strike price high.

"Option value moves up just before going in the money. That's one reason we place our strike price at least slightly out of the money."

CHAPTER 27 ANSWERS

"We want to look at six fundamentals to examine the growth potential of a company: sales growth rate, earnings growth rate, equity growth rate, ROIC, debt-to-equity ratio, and intrinsic value. We want the growth rates to be at least 10 percent, we want the ROIC to be at least 10 percent, and we want the debt/equity ration to be 1.0 or less. P/E refers to the price-to-earnings ratio. Another term for this is multiple, which is determined by dividing the price per share by the earnings per share. We determine the intrinsic value of a company by comparing its earnings growth rate to its P/E ratio. In trading options, we obviously want a stock that is optionable. We also want the stock to trade at least one million shares per day. Finally, we want institutional ownership to be 50 percent or higher.

CHAPTER 28 ANSWERS

"We normally look at three overall indicators of market trends. They are the Dow Jones, the S&P 500, and the Nasdaq. We also determine the 'mood' or 'sentiment' of the market by looking at the <u>VIX</u> and at the total <u>put-to-call</u> ratio. In both sentiment indicators, higher numbers tell us the <u>market is</u> basically <u>bearish</u>, and lower numbers tell us the market is basically <u>bullish</u>. At the extremes, both indicate that the market may be ready to <u>change</u> its current direction."

CHAPTER 29 ANSWERS

1. Bullish
2. Bearish
3. Stagnant
4. Mid-April 2007
5. Mid-April 2007
6. The 5-day EMA was already above the 20-day EMA; it had already crossed over.
7. Late April 2007
8. Very early January
9. Early to mid-January
10. Mid-January
11. Early January; that's the first time we get buy signals from all three technical indicators.
12. About $57.50
13. About $62.50

CHAPTER 30 ANSWERS

1. $4
2. QNQUF
3. $4,000 ($4 × 10 contracts × 100 (shares per contract))
4. Any of these: place a long put, open a long put, open a long put position
5. $3.70
6. QNQUF
7. $1,850 ($3.70 x 5 contracts × 100 (shares per contract))
8. Any of these: short a put, open a short put, place a short put, open a short put position

9. Option writer

10. The Saturday following the third Friday of the month.

11. Buying; selling

12. $2; $400 ($2 × 2 × 100 (shares per contract))

13. $1.80; $360 ($1.80 × 2 × 100 (shares per contract))

14. Early assignment

15. 200

16. The strike price: $35

17. $3 ($40 market price – $35 strike price = $5, minus $2 debit he paid to open the contract, which equals a net profit of $3 per share)

18. $600 ($3 per share × 200 shares)

19. $35: the strike price

20. $360 ($1.80 per share credit × 200 shares)

21. $6.80 ($5 per share by selling + $1.80 per share from the credit)

22. $1,360 ($6.80 per share × 200 shares)

23. Worthless; credit; his shares; debit

24. Close; bid; assigned

25. Assigned; receive 200

26. Assigned; receive 200; assigned

27. Buying; to close; ask

28. Sell to close 10 contracts of Nextall calls, with a December expiration and a strike of 45 (symbol of NUFLQ), at a bid price of $10.75; owns; call; selling

29. Sell to open 5 contracts of Plum puts, with a June expiration and a strike of 32.50 (symbol PEMLZ), at a bid price of $6.50

CHAPTER 32 ANSWERS

1. $91.91

2. $3.60

3. $95.51 ($91.91 stock price + $3.60 debit)

4. $5.51 ($95.51 cost basis – $90 strike price)

5. $86.40 ($90 strike price – $3.60 debit)

6. $64.74

7. $1.75

8. $66.49 ($64.74 stock price + $1.75 debit)
9. $3.99 ($66.49 cost basis – $62.50 strike price)
10. $60.75 ($62.50 strike price – $1.75 debit)
11. $3.50
12. $68.24 ($64.74 stock price + $3.50 debit)
13. $5.74 ($68.24 cost basis – $62.50 strike price)
14. $59 ($62.50 strike price – $3.50 debit)

CHAPTER 33 ANSWERS

1. July 2008
2. 40
3. $34.57 ($38.47 stock price – $3.90 credit)
4. $34.57 ($38.47 stock price – $3.90 credit)
5. $5.43 ($40 strike price – $34.57 cost basis)
6. Option goes in the money and we are assigned: we sell our shares at $40 and keep the credit we received.

CHAPTER 34 ANSWERS

1. $14.85
2. $19.35
3. $99.50 ($104 stock price + $14.85 debit for the long put – $19.35 credit for the short call)
4. Make $3.875 ($99.50 cost basis – $103.375 long put strike)
5. $10.50 ($110 short call strike – $99.50 cost basis)
6. The short call goes in the money and we get assigned.
7. $19.30
8. $28.90
9. $179.63 ($189.23 stock price + $19.30 long put debit – $28.90 short call credit)
10. $5.37 ($179.63 cost basis – $185 long put strike)
11. $15.37 ($195 short call strike price – $179.63 cost basis)
12. Short call goes in the money and we get assigned.

CHAPTER 35 ANSWERS

There are <u>two</u> basic types of trades. One is a <u>credit</u> trade, where we buy and sell options that will give us a <u>net credit</u> to start with. That <u>net credit</u> is our <u>profit</u>, and we simply want the options to expire <u>worthless</u>. That way, we <u>simply keep</u> the <u>credit</u> without being forced to either <u>buy</u> or <u>sell</u> shares—which is what we would have to do if the options were <u>exercised</u>.

Another type of trade is a <u>debit</u> trade, where we buy and sell options that will give us a <u>net debit</u> to start with. In this case, we specifically want the value of our <u>long option</u>—the one we bought—to increase in value so that we can close our deal for a <u>20 to 25 percent</u> profit."

In both cases, we are <u>combining</u> options in order to give ourselves a chance to <u>make</u> money while <u>reducing</u> risk. Both options are critical to our trade. One is the way we make <u>money</u>; the other is the way we limit <u>risk</u>. We simply manage the <u>spread</u> between them.

CHAPTER 36 ANSWERS

1. October; it's the only expiration month with at least 45 days to expiration.
2. 45 strike; it's the nearest out-of-the-money strike price.
3. 50 strike; it's further out of the money than the long call strike, but not more than $5.
4. $1.90 ($5.10 debit for the long call – $3.20 credit for the short call)
5. $3.10 ($5 spread between the strike prices – $1.90 net debit)
6. Close both legs of the trade when we reach a 20 percent ROI, which means 20 percent higher than the net debit.
7. $2.28 (1.2 × $1.90)
8. August; it's the only expiration month with at least 45 days to expiration.
9. 27 strike; it's near the money, which increases the likelihood of the option going in the money.
10. 28, 29, 30, 31 are all possible; all are further out of the money than the long call and none creates a spread greater than $5. For learning purposes, let's look at two of these strike prices, 28 and 31.
11. $0.44 ($1.73 debit for the long call – $1.29 credit for the short call)
12. $0.56 ($1 difference between strike prices – $0.44 net debit)

13. $1.18 ($1.73 debit for the long call – $0.55 credit for the short call)

14. $2.82 ($4 spread between the strike prices – $1.18 net debit) (Notice that the risk/reward ratio of the trade with a $1 spread is $ .44/$.56, and the risk/reward ratio of the trade with a $4 spread is $1.18/$2.82.)

15. Close both legs of the trade when we reach a 20 percent ROI, which means 20 percent higher than the net debit.

16. $0.53 (1.2 × $0.44)

17. Close both legs of the trade when we reach a 20 percent ROI, which means 20 percent higher than the net debit. Thus, 1.2 × $1.18, which equals $1.42.

CHAPTER 37 ANSWERS

1. July; it's the only month with 30 or fewer days until expiration.

2. 70 strike; it's the nearest strike that is out of the money.

3. 65 strike; it's the next strike price and gives us no more than a $5 spread.

4. $0.65 ($1.10 credit for the short put − $0.45 debit for the long put)

5. $4.35 ($5 difference between the two strike prices – $0.65 net credit)

6. $0.65 (the net credit)

7. Both options expire worthless in 30 days; we keep the net credit.

8. July; we want no more than 30 days until expiration.

9. Either 180 or 175; both are out of the money. Let's go with 175.

10. 170; it's the next strike price and gives us no more than a $5 spread.

11. $1.55 ($6.05 credit for the short put − $4.50 debit for the long put)

12. $3.45 ($5 difference between the two strike prices – $1.55 net credit)

13. $1.55 (the net credit)

14. Both options expire worthless in 30 days; we keep the net credit.

CHAPTER 38 ANSWERS

The bull call is a debit trade. That means the long call is the primary instrument and is placed near the money or slightly out of the money. The short call is the limiting instrument and is placed one or two strikes further out of the money. This trade makes profit as the spread between the two options grows. This trade is for a bullish trend and it needs time value.

The bull put is a credit trade. That means the short put is the primary instrument and is placed out of the money. The long put is the limiting instrument, and is placed further out of the money. This trade makes profit by the net credit we start with. This trade is for stagnant to bullish trends and needs a short time frame.

CHAPTER 39 ANSWERS

1. July; it's the only expiration month with 30 or fewer days.
2. 60 strike; it's far enough out of the money to provide some safety, and it gives a much higher credit than the 65 strike gives.
3. 65 strike; it's further out of the money.
4. $1.26 ($1.95 credit for the short call – $0.69 debit for the long call)
5. $3.74 ($5 spread between the two strike prices – $1.26 net credit)
6. Both options expire worthless in 30 days; $1.26 per share
7. July; it's the only expiration month with 30 or fewer days.
8. 60 strike; it's far enough out of the money to provide some safety, and it gives a much higher credit than the 62.50 strike gives.
9. Either 62.50 or 65 strike; both are further out of the money than the short call strike, and neither creates a spread greater than $5. Let's go with the 65 strike for purposes of illustration.
10. $0.45 ($0.65 credit for the short call – $0.20 debit for the long call).
11. $4.55 ($5 spread between the two strike prices – $0.45 net credit)
12. Both options expire worthless in 30 days; $0.45 per share

CHAPTER 40 ANSWERS

1. September; it's the only month that gives us a minimum of 45 days.
2. 60 strike; the closest strike that's out of the money.
3. 55 strike; we want the spread to be no more than $5.
4. $1.15 ($1.70 debit for the long put – $0.55 credit for the short put)
5. $3.85 ($5 spread between the two strike prices – $1.15 net debit)
6. $1.38 (20 percent higher than the net debit—thus 1.2 × $1.15)

7. October; it's the only month that gives us a minimum of 45 days.

8. 28 strike; it is near/at the money.

9. $0.87 ($1.49 long put strike price – $0.62 credit for the short put)

10. $2.13 ($3 spread between the two strikes – $0.87 net debit)

11. $1.04 (20 percent higher than the net debit—thus 1.2 × $0.87)

CHAPTER 41 ANSWERS

The bear put is a debit trade. That means the long put is the primary instrument and it is placed slightly out of the money. The short put is the limiting instrument, and it is placed further out of the money. The bear put makes profit as the spread between the two options grows. This is effective for a bearish trend and needs time value.

The bear call is a credit trade. That means the short call is the primary instrument and it is placed out of the money. The long call is the limiting instrument and it is placed further out of the money. The bear call makes profit because of the net credit we start out with. This is effective for stagnant to bearish trends and needs a short time frame.

Index

Italicized page numbers refer to information contained in tables or figures.